Contingency Approaches to Leadership

A Symposium held at Southern Illinois University,
Carbondale, May 17–18, 1973

Edited by
JAMES G. HUNT and
LARS L. LARSON

SOUTHERN ILLINOIS UNIVERSITY PRESS
Carbondale and Edwardsville

Feffer & Simons, Inc.
London and Amsterdam

Library of Congress Cataloging in Publication Data
Main entry under title:

Contingency approaches to leadership.

Papers presented at the symposium which was sponsored by the Dept. of Administrative Sciences of the Southern Illinois University, Carbondale.
Bibliography: p.
1. Supervision   of   employees—Congresses.   2. Leadership—Congresses.
3. Management—Congresses. I. Hunt, James G., 1932–   ed. II. Larson, Lars L., 1939–   ed. III. Illinois. Southern Illinois University, Carbondale. Dept. of Administrataive Sciences.
HF5549.C723   658.3   74–17377
ISBN 0–8093–0689–1

Contents

Tables

Figures

Acknowledgments

This symposium, which was a followup to the earlier one held two years ago, required the assistance of a number of organizations and individuals whom we wish to thank. It was sponsored by the Department of Administrative Sciences with planning and arrangements handled by the Division of Continuing Education and the Leadership Symposium Committee. The committee was composed of D. N. Bateman, R. C. Bishop, R. N. Osborn, and W. M. Vicars, in addition to the two editors. The M.B.A. Association served as hosts for the symposium and provided the transportation and other assistance so important in an undertaking of this kind.

Outside support was provided from the Office of Naval Research by contract N00014-67-A-0399-006 with the Smithsonian Institution. We are grateful to Dr. John Nagay of O.N.R. for making that support possible. Dean Charles Hindersman of the College of Business and Administration, again as with the first symposium, provided much of the University support which was necessary to complement that provided by O.N.R. Other University support came from the Department of Administrative Sciences, the Division of Continuing Education, and the Office of the Vice President and Provost.

Preparation of the Farris paper was supported in part by grant NG23-005-395 from the National Aeronautics and Space Administration. Preparation of the Olmstead paper was supported in part by contract DA HC 19-70-C-0012 and project 20062107A712, Department of the Army. Preparation of the Bass and Valenzi paper was supported by contract N00014-67-A-0398-0012, Organizational Effectiveness Branch, Office of Naval Research. Bass and Valenzi are also indebted to Larry Eldridge and Dana Farrow for their many contributions to the analyses of data and scale development.

Once again Ronald Bishop Chairman of the Administrative Sciences Department, not only provided direct help as a member of the symposium committee, but perhaps even more importantly contributed to the "climate" which made an event such as this possible. And, once again, Sharon Pinkerton and Marcia Elliott came through with their usual fine help both in typing and with the myriads of other details entailed in the symposium.

Finally, Donna Hunt provided typing, proofing, and index assistance for this manuscript as she did for the one for the first symposium. Additional assistance in preparation was also provided by Doris Larson, Holly Hunt, and Douglas Hunt.

Note on Contributors

James C. Taylor is Assistant Professor of Organizational Studies, Graduate School of Management, University of California at Los Angeles.

Robert J. House is Shell Professor of Organizational Behavior, Faculty of Management Studies, University of Toronto, Ontario.

Gary Dessler is Assistant Professor of Management, Florida International University, Miami.

Robert D. Rossel is Association Professor of Sociology, Southern Illinois University at Carbondale.

Richard N. Osborn is Assistant Professor of Administrative Sciences, Southern Illinois University at Carbondale.

Martin M. Chemers is Associate Professor of Psychology, University of Utah, Salt Lake City.

Robert W. Rice is Research Fellow, University of Utah, Salt Lake City.

George F. Farris is Associate Professor of Organizational Psychology and Management, Alfred P. Sloan School of Management, Massachusetts Institute of Technology, Cambridge.

Steven Kerr is Assistant Professor of Management Sciences, The Ohio State University, Columbus.

John W. Slocum, Jr. is Professor of Organizational Behavior, The Pennsylvania State University, University Park.

Bernard M. Bass is Professor of Management and Psychology, University of Rochester.

Enzo R. Valenzi is Assistant Professor of Management and Psychology, University of Rochester.

Eric P. Prien is Professor and Coordinator of Graduate Studies, Department of Psychology, Memphis State University.

Joseph A. Olmstead is Senior Staff Scientist, Human Resources Research Organization, Division 4, Fort Benning, Georgia.

T. Owen Jacobs is Director, Division 4, Human Resources Research Organization, Fort Benning, Georgia.

Abraham K. Korman is Professor of Psychology, Baruch College, City University of New York.

Introduction

This volume summarizes the second leadership symposium, Contingency Approaches to Leadership, held at the Carbondale campus of Southern Illinois University on May 17–18, 1973. This event was a followup to the first leadership symposium, Current Developments in the Study of Leadership, held two years ago, and is believed to reflect the state of the field since that time. Perhaps one of the participants best captured the flavor of the two events when he observed that the first symposium showed where we were in the field while the second one showed where we were going.

A recurring theme running through much of the current leadership literature is concerned with situational approaches to leadership. The term *contingency approach* or *contingency model* first suggested by Fiedler with regard to his own research a decade ago has since come into such generic use, for a wide range of situational leadership approaches, as to be almost a household word among researchers in the area. It is in this generic sense that the term is used as the title of this symposium as a rubric to specify in operational terms both specific conditions under which one kind of leader behavior will be superior to another and conditions which influence the leader behavior itself. The studies included here cover the gamut from individual, to group, to total organizational perspectives, and all combine data with theory.

Like the papers in the earlier symposium, these provide a forum for both well-known scholars, widely recognized for many years, and younger scholars whose work has only recently received attention. And, as before, discussants to a large extent also follow this grouping.

The first chapter, by James C. Taylor, entitled "Technology and Supervision in the Postindustrial Era," involves technology, management ideology or climate, and both manager and peer leadership over time. Using the Michigan four-factor leadership instrument (Bowers & Seashore, 1966; Taylor, 1971a) to measure leadership of supervisors and work group peers, Taylor investigates 850 groups in eight organizations. His findings suggest that leader behavior may be influenced by interactions among management ideology, technological sophistication and time. He concludes, for example, that while there is a general tendency for more active supervisor and peer supportive and facilitative leadership to be exerted in technologically sophisticated organizations, a proactive management ideology (one which seeks ways to enhance an already progressive personnel program) makes such leadership viable in less sophisticated organizations as well. Whereas, there is evidence that a reactive ideology (one which turns to participative management as a last resort reaction to market conditions) is likely to have less supportive and facilitative leadership patterns associated with it even in organizations with highly sophisticated technology. Finally, Taylor shows that ideology and technology interact to influence the success of a planned change in leadership over time.

The second chapter, by House and Dessler, entitled "The Path-Goal Theory of Leadership: Some *Post Hoc* and A Priori Tests," utilizes a technological variable (task structure) as a moderator or contingency variable. Unlike Taylor, however, who uses leadership as his dependent variable, House at the first leadership symposium (see Fleishman & Hunt, 1973). role clarity as dependent variables. Thus, Taylor is concerned with changes in leader behavior as a function of ideological and technological considerations while House and Dessler (as are most of those working with contingency leadership approaches) are concerned with outputs as a function of leadership and the nature of the task. We should note also, that the House and Dessler paper is an extension and refinement of work reported by House at the first leadership symposium (see Fleshman & Hunt, 1973).

A third chapter, by George Farris, entitled "Leadership and Supervision in the Informal Organization," is intriguing, among other reasons, because it considers both contingency and noncontingency ("one best way") approaches to explaining leadership and innovation findings in three research and development (R & D) organizations. A framework is developed which is based on the amount and distribution of leadership influence among managers and subordinates as well as on qualitative characteristics of the leadership process. Tentative hypotheses are stated concerning which of four kinds of leadership would be best on the average as well as contingencies (supervisor and subordinate competence, importance of leadership acceptance, and time pressure) under which a particular kind of leadership would best enhance innovation in R & D groups. A particularly important point crucial to the chapter's emphasis on leadership as a superior-subordinate mutual influence process is the notion of feedback loops. Here, in addition to the traditional treatment of leadership as a causal variable, performance is implicitly and explicitly considered by Farris to influence leadership via feedback loops. This notion appears to be a particularly important one if we are to develop more sophisticated research models, especially if, as is currently fashionable, such approaches purport to be "systems models." Taken as a whole, Farris's inductively derived framework (as are those of Fiedler and House) suggests a number of important directions for leadership research.

The fourth chapter, by Chemers and Rice, entitled "A Theoretical and Empirical Examination of Fiedler's Contingency Model of Leadership Ef-

fectiveness," does a number of things. First, it provides an important historical perspective for contingency approaches in general and Fiedler's contingency model in particular. Secondly, it discusses several current issues relative
to the Fiedler model. Thirdly, it examines evidence from field studies as well
as laboratory studies by Chemers and others bearing on these issues.
Perhaps one of the most important of these issues is based on Fiedler's recent
extension of his model to cover managerial training effects. This extension,
while offering a potential breakthrough in the utilization of management
training (which has not been notably successful—see Fiedler, 1970; Hunt,
1968), has not been uncritically accepted, as is obvious from the discussant
comments.

The fifth chapter, by Bass and Valenzi, entitled "Contingent Aspects of
Effective Management Styles," suggests yet another way of considering
leadership within a contingency context. It reports preliminary results related to a contingency approach which is by far the most complex and
comprehensive of those covered in this volume. The authors suggest that
their ultimate intent is to develop a model which can form a beginning for a
formal testable theory of leadership. The model includes supervisor and
subordinate personality variables, environmental and organizational variables, and task variables culled from a thorough search of the literature.
These are hypothesized to influence both leader behavior and the relationship between such behavior and work unit effectiveness and satisfaction.
Thus, the approach is similar to Taylor's in that it specifies some leadership
behavior determinants and like the House, Fiedler, and Farris approaches in
that it specifies some contingencies under which one kind of leader behavior
is likely to be superior to another. The paper devotes a considerable amount
of time to instrument development strategies along with its discussion of
preliminary results for some aspects of the model. As should be obvious from
the description above, the undertaking is an ambitious one requiring a
carefully planned programmatic research effort. In addition to sketching
out the model, discussing instrument development, and preliminary results,
the chapter also describes the research strategy designed to test the model. It
is also interesting to note the similarities in the leader behavior dimensions
discussed in this chapter and in the earlier one by Farris. Furthermore, in
contrast to the heavy reliance on the Leader Behavior Description Questionnaire in the first syposium volume, the questionnaire is used not at all in
the studies reported in this volume (though some measures are based on
extensive adaptations of it). Can this be indicative of a trend away from the
widely used LBDQ with all its limitations (cf. House, 1973a; Korman, 1966;
Schriesheim & Kerr, 1973) and do the instruments used here have the same
limitations?

The sixth chapter in this volume is one by Olmstead entitled "Leader
Performance as Organizational Process: A Study of Organizational Compe-

tence." (This chapter and the discussant comments are presented in lieu of a paper presented by another participant at the symposium whose revision was not completed in time for inclusion in this volume.) Perhaps a quick perusal of the chapter seems initially to suggest that it may be less relevant to the leadership area than the other chapters. That this is not the case is immediately obvious from the discussant comments of Owen Jacobs. As he makes abundantly clear, the paper is an intriguing one for a number of reasons, not the least of which is its concentration on the total organization as the unit of analysis. Its emphasis on the different roles called for by the top manager and those at lower organizational levels under noncrisis versus crisis conditions generated by time pressure appears to be particularly germane within a contingency context. (Note that time pressure is also one of the variables included in Farris's approach.) Of additional importance here is the consideration of leadership as influence. If, as is almost universal, leadership is treated as influence does it have to be face-to-face influence? Or can such influence be, as suggested in earlier work (e.g., Hunt, 1971), that of the top-level administrator on those several steps removed? If so, what might be some of the organizational processes involved? These and other related questions form the heart of the Olmstead chapter.

Again, as in the volume covering the first symposium, integration of these diverse chapters has been attempted in a number of ways. First, the contingency theme itself, though broad, provides a situationally based commonality across the chapters. Secondly, the chapters were grouped in sets of two for presentation purposes with the four papers in the first two sets having a heavy microemphasis while those in the third set tend to emphasize macro factors as well. Furthermore, the chapters in the first set and some of the others also are linked by their consideration of technological or task measures as important contingency variables. In addition, as pointed out above, there is some similarity in the leadership dimensions used in at least the Farris and Bass and Valenzi chapters, though the measuring instruments are different.

Thirdly, discussant comments and summaries of the most important floor comments provide some integration as well as critiquing and raising questions. Discussant comments are based on written summaries by the discussants and generally were only lightly edited. With one exception, each discussant's comments relate to a single paper in the set and are, therefore, placed at the end of each chapter.

In contrast to the minimal editing of discussant comments, a great deal of selective editing was used to compile the summaries of floor comments to emphasize high points and provide yet another means of integration. Also, some chapters, in effect, incorporated the most salient points from the floor as an integral part of their revision, and hence require no separate discussion summaries. Consistent with this, floor comment summaries are found after the House and Dessler, and Bass and Valenzi chapters, along with an additional one at the end of the volume. As in the first symposium, the editors assume full responsibility for the selectivity exercised and for the occasional editorial comments enclosed by brackets.

As a final means of integration, Abraham Korman, based on his earlier thoughts about contingency leadership approaches (Korman, 1973a, 1973b), prepared an overview of the symposium designed to raise critical questions and to tie together common threads underlying the contingency area in general and the current papers in particular.

J. G. Hunt
L. L. Larson

Carbondale, Illinois
November, 1973

Contingency Approaches to Leadership

1

Technology and Supervision in the Postindustrial Era

JAMES C. TAYLOR

The line between contingency theories where the predicted level of a dependent variable depends on the level of another variable or variables, and a deterministic theory where the dependent variable is in fact dependent completely on the internal logic of another is a fine line indeed. For example, technological determinism has become a popular notion once again with the advent of computer controlled automation. Much has been published recently which portends to reveal the degree to which technology influences skill level, jobs, supervision and work groups, and organizational structure, and which rests on the assumption that technology evolves according to its own internally derived logic and requirements.

Whereas leadership behavior is variously seen as being caused by or dependent upon a host of variables alone or in concert, technology is at the same time being acknowledged as not leading inexorably to one or another specific organizational structure, job and work structure, or leadership pattern, but to a variety of each of these. Technology as a variable of study in contingency theory differs from leadership and supervisory behavior in that while leadership is usually thought of as resulting from, or dependent on, some prior variables, technology as a variable of interest to industrial psychology has been considered on the independent or causal side. Neither leadership nor technology, however, has escaped the recent equifinality or contingency debate.

In a paper designed to discuss the efforts of technology upon leadership behavior, having both variables embroiled in separate ends of the equifinality argument guarantees no definitive statements regarding the "one way" technology affects leadership. If, as is clear, technology interacts with other variables in affecting organizational behavior, and if many variables are held to affect leadership, then our task is to begin to sort out which of the connections and networks of variable relationships should be most fruitfully examined.

The present paper presents some evidence that technology moderates supervisory and peer leadership in several organizations without apparent need to include other independent or moderating variables. From these data it appears that leadership can be affected by sophisticated technology without regard for type of industry, dimensionality of product, or organizational size. Other data presented, however, reveal no such effect of technology in and of itself on leadership behavior, unless a particular organization stance regarding the environment is also present. In combination, these results suggest that although leadership may be directly affected by technology, that relationship is moderated by yet additional variables.

Although few studies have been undertaken to directly or specifically investigate the relationship between technolgoy and leadership behavior, a number of studies report on some aspects of it. Woodward (1958), for example, discovered that continuous process technology (a highly automated form of technology) was related to a lower span of control. While various authors have tried to interpret these findings as indications of close supervision (e.g., Dubin, 1965), Woodward herself (1965) provided evidence to the contrary.

The changing nature of supervisory activities has long been alluded to in studies of advancing technology. Some of the original work by James Bright (1958a, 1958b), for example, proposed that traditional skill requirements of dexterity and motor ability were being replaced by increased responsibility for monitoring and controlling machine process on the part of nonsupervisory employees. This conclusion has been in large measure supported by subsequent studies reported in the literature (e.g., Burack, 1969; Crossman, 1960; Friedman, 1961; Gardell, 1971; Susman, 1970).

Walker (1957), in a case study of one automated steel plant, found that the group of workers he studied over a four-year period developed a minimally supervised, autonomous style. The Tavistock Institute in London for many years studied ways of linking technical advance with multiple skilled, internally regulated work groups (Rice, 1958; Trist, Higgin, Murray & Pollock, 1963). Recently such autonomous or leaderless work groups have been successfully installed in continuous process firms in the U.S. and abroad (e.g., Englestad, 1972; Gulowsen, 1973; Ketchum, 1972; McWhinney, 1972; Prestat, 1972).

It seems apparent that even though the pattern of actual supervisory activities differs from one industry or plant to another, the trend with advanced technology is in the direction of supervisors doing less in the way of traditional management—supervising behaviors of others, attending to selection or training functions, and the like—and more in the way of acting as a facilitator, boundary controller, and communications link for the work group, or becoming more technically skilled operators themselves. This takes us back to the general observation that at more sophisticated levels of technology (automation), conventional notions of work and skills no longer apply. Workers, individually or in groups, supervise machines or processes, so that the conventional notion of supervision is no longer applicable. An indication of the evolving supervisory role in these instances may be seen in the study of supervisory job design by Davis and Valfer (1965), in which supervisors of autonomous workers spontaneously took on boundary regulating activities to keep longer range disturbances from interfering with the work of their groups.

Cooper (1972) in a recent review paper speculates that group performed activities in automated process industries may constitute only the result of a transitional stage in technological development in oil and chemical industries. If this is true, then we should not expect evidence of such leadership behavior related to sophisticated technology in other industrial settings. Although it is theoretically possible that complete automation will obviate the need for any leadership at all, it is a more realistic approach to point out that in general, technology will "advance" slowly enough to allow consideration of such matters as group or peer leadership as an alternative to more traditional supervisory forms for the next several decades.

Herbst (1962), using the Tavistock Institute research as the basis for analysis, suggests that the difference between autocratic management and autonomous work organization lies not in the amount of control exercised by the supervisor but in applying control to external factors affecting internal stability. If the technology is such that worker actions are difficult to observe, and the quality and quantity of output are easily supervised, and if the relations between the actions and output are a matter of skill, or are best known to the operators, then control will best be applied by the specification of quality and quantity of output rather than requiring and enforcing a specific activity or behavior. When technology makes it easier to evaluate results, then it is easier to supervise on the basis of results, and autocratic management of work activities is less likely. In addition, if the production demands of the group's primary task are in excess of the capabilities of any single worker, then the emergence of an organizationally meaningful work group with its own internal regulation is a realistic alternative to more traditional supervisory-group relations. How far a work group is capable of responsible autonomy and is able to adapt itself in correspondence with ongoing conditions reflects the extent to which its social structure is appropriate to the demands of the work situation. For further explication of this position see Emery and Trist (1969).

Although evidence exists in support of the case that advanced technology is related to less traditional supervision, there is no paucity of data used in support of the opposite contention. These studies range from the early

Detroit automation studies of Faunce (1958), to more recent case studies such as the steel mill studied by Chadwick-Jones (1969) in which a change to more modern technology was reported to result in closer supervision, less worker autonomy, and low group leadership. This sort of mixed result is not uncommon in the study of advanced technology and its effects on such things as skill levels, job design, and organizational structure, as well as supervision and group behavior.

In reviewing the organization and technology literature, Davis and Taylor (1973) have recently proposed the notion that technological determinism simply does not fit the facts. What this position results in is a statement of stochastic or flexible alternatives deriving from a particular technological design. In particular, Davis and Taylor (1973) assert that this flexibility or choice results from both the initial design of the technology and from its particular application.

> In the design and development of technology, we are dealing with the application of science to invent technique and its supportive artifacts (machines) to accomplish transformations of objects (materials, information, people) in support of certain objectives. The invention of technique may be engineering to an overwhelming extent, but in part it is also social system design. If, then, we look at work, we can see two sets of antecedent determinants that constrain the choices available for design of tasks and job structure. First, there are the social choices contained within the organization design undertaken to use the technology. Our present appreciation is that one rarely finds technological determinism in the pure sense of technological or scientific variables exclusively determining the design or configuration of a technical system. On the contrary, most frequently we find that technical system designs incorporate social system choices, either made intentionally or included accidentally either casually or as the result of some omission in planning. In this sense, engineers or technologists can be called social system engineers, and they are crucial to evolving new organization forms and job structure. [pp. 3–4].

Basically, the impact of this position on the present analysis of technology and leadership follows directly. The basis of this report is that whether supervision will or will not include a close monitoring of subordinate behaviors, whether it will involve task related to human oriented leadership behaviors depends in part on the original design of the technology and, for our purposes more importantly, the way in which organizational engineers and managers choose to apply that technology. Direct evidence for this position regarding technological effects on any organizational aspects is meager, yet it is beginning to accumulate. Recently, several papers have appeared which in different ways support the issue of stochastic technological effects. The first paper (Hazlehurst, Bradbury & Corlett, 1969) looks at experience with numerically controlled machines in four companies. The second (Wedderburn & Crompton, 1972) reviews several technologically differentiable plants within the same company. The third paper (Rossel, 1971) examines data from eight manufacturing organizations contained in the Yale Technology Project Files. The fourth paper (Englestad, 1972) describes an organizational redesign in a paper mill. Finally, Child and Mansfield (1972) review the evidence for technology and organizational size effects on organizational structure. In all cases, the authors speculate from the basis of logically reasonable, if not empirically indisputable, evidence that management ideology or activities powerfully moderate the relationships between technology and organizational variables.

Hazlehurst et al. (1969) compared the skill requirements of numerically controlled (NC) and conventional machine tools for eight pairs of jobs in four companies. They conclude that while NC tools reduce physical effort, demand for motor skills, and the number of decisions an operator is required to make, these new machines involve an appreciable increase in demand for perceptual skills (machine monitoring and controlling), and conceptual skills such as interpretation of drawings, instructions, and calculations. These authors also note that although the results reported above are reasonably clear in the sample they observed, the skill profiles derived reveal that the profile configurations for the NC jobs frequently have more in common with the jobs they replace than with other NC machines. The authors ascribe part of this variance in skills profiles to managerial assumptions, in the following quotation:

> Some companies regard NC machines as highly specialized, to be treated in ways related to their particular characteristics, while others regard NC as normal machine tools and subject them to the same work programming, planning and loading systems as conventional machines. Policy decisions about the number of hours per day the machines are to be worked, supervisory training, number of men per machine, whether to use setter/operators or operators, and so on, depend upon the depth of understanding by managers of the machines' fundamental characteristics, and how managers decide to use NC to deal with their own products and circumstances. All these decisions affect the job skills demanded of operators [pp. 177–178].

This conclusion is not dissimilar to one reported in a study by Wedderburn and Crompton (1972) in which three continuous process plants in the same company and location were surveyed for worker perceptions of their jobs, work group, supervision, management climate, and organizational structure. In two of the plants similar technological changes resulted in similarly titled jobs being quite different in intrinsic interest and demands as experienced by the workers. The authors report that this difference can be accounted for by planned changes in the supervisory system in one plant which acted at cross purposes with the otherwise facilitating effects of the technological change on job requirements (p. 114). These suggestions in the recent studies, that managerial discretion in decision making can intervene between technology and skill requirements, provide some evidence for at least the fact that implementation of technical systems involves psychosocial assumptions juxtaposed with technical efficiency.

Rossel's data (1971) suggest that supervisory style of four levels of management in eight manufacturing organizations is more influenced by the organization's difficulty in adapting to its environment than to its technology. This difference in effect between environmental and technical aspects, however, appears to be a matter of degree rather than kind, in light of the significant interaction effect noted in the Rossel data between technology and adaptation in their effect upon supervisory style.

Englestad (1972) reports an organizational design study in Norway, which highlights the problem of assessing technological effects on worker autonomy and supervision. This case, involving the implementation of a semiautonomous group structure in a pulp and paper mill, relates managements' insistence on maintaining a newly developed foreman role with strong internal group controls in spite of the fact that the researchers warned against its use with a technology where process control and monitoring were the primary tasks. Worker autonomy and discretion were achieved in some measure, but the company itself did not decide to eliminate the foreman role for this type of work until after four years' experience with the internal conflict it created.

Child and Mansfield (1972) note that ideology and perceived interests are likely to influence the attempts of organizational decision makers to manipulate the interactions between technology and structural aspects involving processes of bureaucratic control. A continuation of the Child and Mansfield position states that "variables which have often been regarded as independent determinants of organizational structures are . . . seen to be linked together as multiple points of reference for the process of strategic decision making" (Child, 1972, p. 15).

This position of stochastic technological effects is congruent with Fiedler's contingency theory of leadership—at least insofar as task aspects are at best partial determinants of the leader's LPC score as an indicator of degree of supervisory task orientation. Moreover, as Fiedler (1973c) himself has recently stated, "Perhaps the most important implication of this theory of leadership is that the organization for which the leader works is as responsible for his success or failure as is the leader himself [p. 234]."

In other words, to the degree that the organization defines the group tasks, it is directly defining whether a particular leadership orientation will be successful and indirectly whether that leadership orientation will (given a process of natural selection) be subsequently manifest.

According to Fiedler (1973c), and House (1973b), greater task orientation or initiating structure on the part of the leader will be expected in the case of ambiguous task settings or ones where the supervisor has little influence ("unfavorable" task settings). According to House, such facilitation reduces role ambiguity and increases the subordinate's feeling of competence. It seems reasonable to speculate that initiating structure could also reduce role conflict or overload when the task is complex and uncertain, as well as ambiguous, which is the anticipated situation in the case of sophisticated technology. Furthermore, we would expect to see an increase in perceived peer leadership especially in the task oriented factors, when the technology lends itself to more autonomous group arrangements.

The data reviewed in the present paper lend indirect support to Fiedler's thesis as described as well as providing confirmatory evidence for the general conclusions of Rossel (1971). These data, utilizing a post hoc measure of organizational adaptation (which it is felt, reflects on managerial philosophy), examine the effects of this organizational classification and work group technology on supervisory and work group leadership. The results suggest that where an organization's position in its labor and/or consumer markets is strong and it seeks (in a proactive or initiatory way) greater participative climate, then sophisticated technology is found related to higher evaluation of supervisory leadership activities. On the other hand, when the organization's position in its markets is not strong and it seeks participative management climate as a reactive or defensive maneuver, then sophisticated technology is found related to lower evaluations of supervisory leadership. This general pattern is also found for the task oriented leadership exercised by the peer or work group.

FOCUS OF STUDY

This study examined the effect of technological sophistication on supervisory and peer (work group) leadership and includes measures of that leadership over time. Data reported here were obtained from seven business organizations. These organizations include a large petroleum refinery, a small glass products company, a medium-sized plastics manufacturing plant, a large aluminum casting and extrusion plant, two cellophane plants and a fine paper mill (all three owned by the same company). These data reflect the responses of some 3,500 individuals in over 800 nonsupervisory work groups. Respondents completed the *Survey of Organizations* (Taylor & Bowers, 1972), a machine scored paper and pencil questionnaire dealing with job-related matters, developed at the Institute for Social Research, University of Michigan. These questionnaires were completed variously twice or three times in each organization over a total period of not less than one year. The overall design for which the questionnaire data were originally collected involved a planned change program toward more participative management which was expected to follow the initial survey in each organization. In two of the seven organizations the planned change program was ultimately not undertaken.

INDEPENDENT VARIABLES

Consultants from the University of Michigan introduced the planned change program. This effort began following the first questionnaire administration and prior to the second one. It involved using the by-group's results of the prior survey as a self-help diagnostic tool, and specifically developed training programs as well. Since the consultants attempted uniform diffusion of change inputs throughout the lower level ranks in each organization, this independent force is assumed constant, except in those two cases where it is known that the program was not undertaken, and in which this manipulation cannot be considered.

A useful and generally applicable system of classifying technology might involve not only an assessment of the sophistication of machines (e.g., Bright, 1958a, 1958b) and an assessment of the sophistication of the raw materials (e.g., Perrow, 1967), but the assessment of the complexity of task attributes including prescribed and discretionary activities as well (Turner & Lawrence, 1965). The best definition of technology under such a scheme is: a set of principles and techniques useful to bring about change toward desired ends. Although very broad, this definition seems to at once satisfy the general use to which the word *technology* is made, and provides for the application of a single classification scheme to many kinds of organizations.

The empirical literature dealing with the incidence and general effects of "modern technology" in plant and office is based, at least indirectly, on one or another diverse classification schemes. This is a main reason why the results of the studies reported in the literature may differ one from the other—different definitions of the situation produce different results. It is, however, not the only reason why these results vary. The results are not always comparable because of the tendency to classify definitively what might be considered in the interstices between traditional industrial techniques and automation—what may be more or less arbitrarily classified as sophisticated technology may in fact be more like old technology, for example. More extensive use of continuous scales which imply intermediate categories such as "in between," "moderate," or "medium sophisticated" technologies would be useful in this regard.

The judgments of several administrative people at each organizational site were used to obtain evaluations of the sophistication of production technology for nonsupervisory work groups within that site. Sophistication of technology was assessed using a judgmental rating form constructed to measure the qualities of standard materials input, throughput mechanizations, and output control, for each work group. This instrument utilized the structured judgments of work groups on seven separate scores by the in-plant technical administrative judges. A detailed description, including validity analysis of the instrument is presented in Taylor (1970). (The measures used in the present study are those labeled "input B," "throughput C," and "output E" in the 1970 paper [p. 37].)

Technology so measured would differ from measures of task complexity (e.g., Turner & Lawrence, 1965) in that a higher technology rating would imply a greater control or process monitoring modality, whereas most task complexity measures distinguish only the varied or complex from the repetitive. In other words, task complexity measures tend to separate those tasks with much repetition of standardized or routine actions from those emphasizing the reverse characteristics of variety or nonstandard activities. The result of this difference rests with the ability of the present measure of technological sophistication to distinguish among *craft era* jobs, requiring much manual skill or dexterity and involving much variety; *industrial era* jobs, requiring a series of repetitive operations and little variety; and *postindustrial* jobs, in which manual skill is replaced by decisional skill and responsibility coupled with the variety associated with ambiguity and complexity in process monitoring. Task complexity scales, on the other hand, tend to distinguish the repetition of the industrial era jobs from the variety of the other two classifictions taken together. If as Thompson (1967) and Touraine (1962) have implied, considerable increases in task interdependence would be found in postindustrial jobs over craft era jobs, then for the purposes of studying the peer leadership in interdependent tasks it is necessary to be able to distinguish between craft and postindustrial jobs.

Although the technological measure used in the present study provides comparability of absolute scores across organizations and differentiates among organizations as we would expect (see Table 1), it also provides the ability to reliably distinguish the sophistication of technology among work groups within a given organization. This advantage is considerable when compared with the gross measurement schemes used by Blauner, (1964), for example, in which the total organization is considered as a technological monolith. To begin with, if we compare the social system characteristics (supervisory and peer leadership in the present case) of groups within a given organization, we are able to control (as constants) variables such as location, market, labor force, as well as more ephemeral elements such as managerial philosophy. Finally, we are able to increase the number of data points if technological sophistication is considered by group rather than by organization. At the same time, group scores can be averaged in order to obtain a total organization technology score such as those presented in Table 1.

TABLE 1

Moments of the Distribution of Three Indices of
Technological Sophistication for Each Site

Sophistication of Technology Indices	Mean (E^1)	S.D. (E^2)	Skewness (E^3)	Kurtosis (E^4)
1. Refinery (N GPS = 140)[a]				
Input index	3.37	0.97	-0.15	-0.68
Throughput index	2.39	0.66	1.00	0.19
Output index	1.37	0.43	-0.76	-0.70
2. Glass products firm (N GPS = 24)				
Input index	4.01	0.75	-0.93	-0.08
Throughput index	2.11	0.76	-0.15	-1.17
Output index	1.76	0.40	0.71	-0.68
3. Plastics plant (N GPS = 41)				
Input index	3.86	0.61	0.03	-0.58
Throughput index	2.43	0.58	-0.42	0.07
Output index	1.78	0.38	1.28	0.00
4. Paper mill (N GPS = 76)				
Input index	4.04	0.71	-0.67	0.28
Throughput index	2.21	1.15	-0.36	-1.12
Output index	1.86	0.74	-0.98	0.24
5. Cellophane plant I (N GPS = 50)				
Input index	4.09	1.05	-0.55	-1.37
Throughput index	2.02	0.73	-0.89	-0.66
Output index	1.81	0.51	-0.13	-1.22
6. Cellophane plant II (N GPS = 42)				
Input index	3.58	0.51	0.77	1.69
Throughput index	2.15	0.96	-0.02	-1.38
Output index	1.64	0.53	-0.51	-0.14
7. Aluminum casting and extrusion plant (N GPS = 150)				
Input index	3.98	0.67	-0.35	-0.47
Throughput index	1.68	0.57	-0.14	-0.52
Output index	1.42	0.49	0.41	-0.46

[a]Number of groups

As described below in the analysis and results section, work groups are classified as having high or low sophistication of technology based on their being scored high or low, respectively, on all three of the component technical scales: input, throughput, and output. Table 2 presents the mean scores and standard deviations for the three technology indices for each technological category (high and low) within each organization studied. When these high and low technology categories were constructed the composition of work groups within each category for each organization was examined. The resulting composition per organization was as follows: In the refinery, the high technology category included maintenance function groups as well as groups assigned to process control, while the low technology category included engineering and quality control, as well as some other maintenance groups and janitorial groups.

In the glass products company the high technology category included industrial era fabricating technology, such as mass production cutting and grinding of plate glass, as well as the control and operation of manufacturing equipment. The low technology category included engineering and sales, craft era hand-grinding operations, as well as the loading docks. The data in Table 2 suggest that although the high technology class in the glass plant does have a reasonably sophisticated technology, the scores are neither so high as to suggest the technology levels of the continuous process plants in the sample nor so low as to suggest a traditional industrial technology for these groups.

The plastics plant high technology included most process control groups; while the low technology included test labs, engineering, equipment maintenance, and janitorial.

In the aluminum company, high technology included the continuous process casting operation and several types of mass-production tube extrusion. Low technology included some other extrusion processes and engineering, quality control and maintenance.

In the two cellophane plants the high technology groups were primarily continuous process control groups while the low technology category included maintenance, quality control, and engineering. A similar division was found for the paper mill, where groups working on continuous process machines or operations were assigned to the high technology category. The low technology category included work groups in the engineering department, maintenance, mass-production packing operations, shipping department, and some low level clerical operations. In both the cellophane plants and the paper mill, no more than 20% of the work groups classified as high technology were not directly involved with continuous process operations. Mean education was found to be significantly higher for the low technology groups in several of the organizations studied. In no organization was education found to be significantly higher for groups in the high

TABLE 2

Mean and Standard Deviation Scores for High and Low
Technology Categories within Each Organization

	Input X̄	Index s	Throughput X̄	Index s	Output X̄	Index s
1. Refinery						
High technology (n=20)	4.23	.53	2.02	.07	1.05	.10
Low technology (n=26)	2.33	.55	1.94	.13	1.04	.10
2. Glass products firm						
High technology (n=17)	4.66	.18	2.65	.21	2.08	.35
Low technology (n=7)	3.33	.48	1.19	.26	1.38	.43
3. Plastics plant						
High technology (n=8)	4.08	.46	2.84	.25	2.00	.00
Low technology (n=9)	3.74	.33	2.00	.41	1.50	.43
4. Paper mill						
High technology (n=21)	4.17	.20	3.38	.48	2.00	.00
Low technology (n=13)	3.18	.75	0.67	.43	1.31	.25
5. Cellophane plant I						
High technology (n=21)	4.84	.29	2.59	.15	2.31	.25
Low technology (n=15)	3.00	.79	1.23	.63	1.50	.00
6. Cellophane plant II						
High technology (n=11)	3.58	.34	2.97	.43	2.00	.00
Low technology (n=11)	3.40	.42	1.24	.22	1.04	.15
7. Aluminum extrusion						
High technology (n=24)	4.54	.26	2.00	.45	1.55	.30
Low technology (n=13)	3.58	.35	1.14	.14	1.19	.11

technology category. These results are not surprising since it seems quite reasonable to assume that an organization would select people with higher education to fill jobs where much discretion was required in choosing treatments for unstandardized inputs—white-collar semiprofessional, technical, and (to a lesser extent) craft maintenance, would seem to fit this model more than machine or equipment operators.

Organizational adaptation is a variable formed with the dichotomy between a management (organizational) position of contemporary strength or weakness in the consumer and/or labor markets, which is related respectively to the proactive or the reactive application of the planned change program. It is felt that this condition could reflect a managerial stance (ideology and activity) which could moderate the relationships between technology and leadership (and which could also moderate the relative success of the planned change program). Assessment of this proactive or reactive application is *post hoc* and can only be inferred. We "know" that organizations come to join with social scientists in large scale organizational studies for a variety of reasons. Unfortunately we frequently don't "know" those reasons (nor can even infer them) for some time, and sometimes don't have suspicions confirmed until after the study is finished.

The organizations used in the present analysis can be grouped into two position categories: category one, the *proactive organizations*, included those organizations (or research sites) which were seeking ways of further enhancing an already progressive manpower utilization and personnel relations program. Category two, the *reactive organizations*, included those organizations which were turning to participative management as a last resort in reacting to an unfavorable market position after finding their traditional methods had failed. Usually, however, we don't know (or perhaps haven't needed to explore fully) the motives of an organization to undertake a change program in participative management. For the purposes of the present paper, however, it seems important to attempt to identify or infer an organizational or managerial stance; which, it is speculated, may condition or moderate between technology and leadership. In the present case, the seven organizations have been assigned to the two categories, proactive and reactive, as shown below.

Proactive

1). Refinery: No labor or market problems.
                        Long history of "Human Relations," "Manager-
                        ial Grid," and other personnel relations ac-
                        tivities.

2). Glass co.:   No labor market problems.
                        Long time Scanlon Plan company.

3). Plastics plant: New technology.
                        No known market problems.
                        Subsequently undertook new organizational de-
                        sign involving autonomous work groups.

Reactive

4). Paper mill:*   Located in rural South.
                        Had experienced a close union organizational
                        drive.

*The paper mill and the two cellophane plants were owned by the same company, which was characterized as a benevolent autocracy.

5). Cellophane plant 1:   Located in rural South.
                          Had experienced a close union organizational
                          drive.
                          Cellophane market was being hurt by other pro-
                          ducts.

6). Cellophane plant 2:   Located in rural Midwest.
                          Had recently had three-month strike.
                          Planned change program was not undertaken.

7). Aluminum plant: This site was selected by company home office
                          during a time of major economic reversals in
                          this industry.
                          The planned change program never in the one
                          year of the study, reached hourly workers,
                          many of whom were laid off during that
                          period.

DEPENDENT VARIABLES

The *Survey of Organizations*, administered over time to the companies,
includes over a hundred items, some of which were used as single item
estimates of constructs or concepts; others were consolidated into mean
score index variables as measures of concepts. From this larger number of
variables, four were used in the analysis of the present study. These variables
can be categorized as falling into two classes: (a) Perceptions of supervisory
leadership in the areas of support for subordinates and work facilitation; (b)
Perceptions of work group or peer leadership in support and work facilitation.

The specific variables and questionnaire items are spelled out in more
detail below. These four measures, then, form the basis of measuring the
dependent variable—the degree and quality of supervisory and peer leadership by work group. To the degree that group means on these items increase
over time, it is postulated that the social system change attempt is successful
and resistance is low. The majority of the questionnaire items below use the
standard response alternative set which is a modification of the Likert Scale
typical of those used in many organizational survey studies.

1) To a very little extent
2) To a little extent
3) To some extent
4) To a great extent
5) To a very great extent

(a) Supervisory leadership was measured by the following two mean score indices:

Support—behavior which increases his subordinates' feeling of being worthwhile and important people. (Mean score index—three items.) In the surveys support was measured by the following questions:

How friendly and easy to approach is your supervisor?

When you talk with your supervisor, to what extent does he pay attention to what you are saying?

To what extent is your supervisor willing to listen to your problems?

Work facilitation—behavior which helps his subordinates actually get the work done by removing obstacles and roadblocks. (Mean score index—three items.) These items measured this form of behavior:

To what extent does your supervisor show you how to improve your performance?

To what extent does your supervisor provide the help you need so that you can schedule work ahead of time?

To what extent does your supervisor offer new ideas for solving job related problems?

(b) Peer (work group) leadership was measured by survey questions and indices usually identical to those used to measure the supervisor's leadership. In this case, however, the questions are worded, "To what extent are (do) persons in your work group. . . ."

Support (mean score index—three items)
— friendly and easy to approach?
— pay attention to what you're saying when you talk with them?
— willing to listen to your problems?
Work facilitation (mean score index—three items)
— help you find ways to do a better job?
— provide the help you need so that you can plan, organize, and schedule work ahead of time?
— offer each other new ideas for solving job related problems?

Justification for assuming that the operational measures described above do in fact have reasonable reliability and validity comes from many sources.

In general, it was found that individual respondent distributions for the items used as measures of dependent variables described above, including those combined into indices, have been found to be reasonably unimodal and symmetric.

The supervisory and work group leadership indices were originally described by Bowers and Seashore (1966). In that paper, the eight areas of leadership were defined and their ability to predict organizational performance was demonstrated. The internal consistency of the index measures has been subsequently examined and the results of this analysis suggested only minor modifications (Taylor, 1971a). These suggested modifications were effected in the present study. Additional analyses reported elsewhere (cf. Taylor & Bowers, 1972, Ch. 6) provide estimates of internal consistency reliability and discriminant validity for these measures.

Yunker (1972a) has compared the four supervisory indices of the original Bowers and Seashore version of the measure with the four factors measured in the Leader Behavior Description Questionnaire (LBDQ) as developed at Ohio State University (Halpin & Winer, 1957). Yunker found that the two theories do provide similar structures. Specifically the equivalence found was as follows:

F-FTQ	LBDQ
Support	Consideration
Interaction facilitation	Sensitivity
Goal emphasis	Production emphasis
Work faciliation	Initiating structure

Yunker also found that the four factors appear to predict the criteria of job satisfaction and supervisory ratings reasonably well, and further about as well as the LBDQ.

Given that consideration and initiating structure are most frequently used as representing task and human relations orientations respectively in studies reporting the Ohio State measures, it was felt that comparability and parsimony in the present study could best be served by using only the support and work facilitation indices from the Bowers and Seashore set.

GENERAL HYPOTHESES

Based on prior research on technological effects (e.g., Blauner, 1964; Trist, Higgin, Murray, & Pollock, 1963; Walker, 1957; Woodward, 1958, 1965, 1970) and an association between the present technology measures and the leadership measures (e.g., Taylor, 1971b) it was anticipated that sophisticated technology would be related to greater task oriented leadership not only by the supervisor, but by the peer or work group as well. Given also the recent findings cited above (Englestad, 1972; Hazelhurst, et al., 1969; Rossel, 1971; and Wedderburn & Crompton, 1972), we might expect to find that managerial ideology or philosophy and activity would contribute in an interactive way with the relationship between technology and leadership behavior.

If it can be expected that technology and leadership are related in the manner indicated above, prior to any change effect undertaken to modify the managerial climate and supervisor style, then an enhancing effect of the technology could be expected on the results of such change. Such an effect has been reported in Taylor (1971b) using data from the petroleum refinery included also in the present data set. In the present case, as will be recalled, the refinery has been classified as proactive in managerial or organizational adaptation. This leaves open the question of the possible moderating effects of proactive versus reactive stance on the technological relationships with the planned change effort when applied to the other four sites. (Planned change efforts were not undertaken in two sites, thus reducing the total.)

ANALYSIS AND RESULTS

The basic analysis took the form of four 2 x 2 analyses of variance in which the time one (prechange effort) data for supervisory and peer leadership in support and work facilitation were each examined in terms of high versus low technological sophistication and proactive versus reactive managerial adaptation stance. The further effects of managerial adaptation

TABLE 3

Supervisory Support in Work Groups Classified by
Technological Sophistication and Organizational Stance

		Organizational Adaptation Stance									Both Stances
		Proactive organizations				Reactive organizations					Total
		1	2	3	Total	4	5	6	7	Total	Total
High	$\overline{X}$ = 3.92		4.21	4.29	4.10	3.78	3.74	3.48	3.26	3.49	3.85
Technology	n = 19		17	8	44	21	23	11	36	91	135
Low	$\overline{X}$ = 4.14		3.35	3.64	3.95	4.02	4.03	3.80	3.90	3.91	3.93
Technology	n = 25		4	7	36	13	15	11	17	56	92
Total	$\overline{X}$ =				4.07					3.70	
Technology	n =				80					147	

Source of variation	F-Ratio	df	Significance level
Organizational stance	18.70	1	$P < .01$
Technology	1.43	1	$P > .10$
Stance and technology	18.70	1	$P < .01$

stance on the relationship between technology and the planned change effort are examined in a more discursive research postscript.

All analyses are based on group mean scores, rather than on individual level scores, for the technology measure and for the four leadership indices. These group scores were chosen for both theoretical and pragmatic reasons. In regard to the former point, since tasks in the work group are usually related to one another, it is the technology of the total group which is of interest. With respect to the latter, combining individual perceptions of supervisory and peer leadership produces more stable measures of these constructs than would individual perceptions alone.

Tables 3 to 6 present the results of the two-way analyses of variance of the group mean scores on each of the four leadership dimensions. These analyses allow comparisons to be made between the main effects of technology and the organizational stance, regarding participative management as well as the interaction effect between them.

Table 3 presents the findings for supervisory support. The main effect of organizational stance is significant, as is the interaction effect. Supervisory support is higher for the proactive sites than for the reactive ones. Further,

TABLE 4

Supervisory Work Facilitation in Work Groups Classified by
Technological Sophistication and Organizational Stance

										Both Stances
					Organizational Adaptation Stance					
	Proactive organizations				Reactive organizations					
	1	2	3	Total	4	5	6	7	Total	Total
High Technology	$\overline{X}$ = 3.45 n = 19	3.68 17	3.12 8	3.49 44	3.05 21	3.01 23	2.63 11	2.53 36	2.80 91	3.14 135
Low Technology	$\overline{X}$ = 3.20 n = 25	2.65 4	2.70 7	3.04 36	3.17 13	3.17 15	2.73 11	2.86 17	3.00 56	3.02 92
Total Technology	$\overline{X}$ = n =			3.26 80					2.89 147	

Source of variation	F-Ratio	df	Significance level
Organizational stance	23.50	1	P < .01
Technology	2.51	1	P > .10
Stance and technology	18.00	1	P < .01

the significant interaction is revealed in the enhancement of this main effect for the conditions of high technological sophistication.

Table 4, supervisory work facilitation, shows the same pattern; significant main effect for organizational stance, and a significant interaction. In situational terms, this results from greater work facilitation in the proactive organizations, which is increased in the high technology condition.

These results tend to support the findings cited earlier. That is, task oriented supervisory leadership (work facilitation) is found associated with the more complex task structure of sophisticated technology, but only in the special case of the proactive organizations. A similar effect was also found for the supervisory support index. This latter result, although not predicted, is also not at variance with effects postulated by the sociotechnical theorists who state that supervisors of high technology groups become *more* concerned with matters facilitating the work of subordinates, rather than *less* concerned as people for people. In addition, since two separate, and reasonably independent measures (cf. Taylor, 1971a) were used to assess supervisory support and work facilitation, we would not expect to obtain the sort of results found using Fiedler's LPC, in which the use of a single, bipolar scale perforce implies that as task concern increases, people concern decreases. Finally,

TABLE 5

Peer Support in Work Groups Classified by
Technological Sophistication and Organizational Stance

	Organizational Adaptation Stance									Both Stances Total
	Proactive organizations				Reactive organizations					
	1	2	3	Total	4	5	6	7	Total	Total
High Technology	$\overline{X}$ = 3.83 n = 19	3.78 17	3.97 8	3.84 44	3.78 21	4.04 23	3.65 11	3.75 36	3.81 91	3.83 135
Low Technology	$\overline{X}$ = 4.03 n = 25	3.72 4	3.70 7	3.93 36	3.93 13	4.18 15	3.90 11	3.79 17	3.95 56	3.94 92
Total Technology	$\overline{X}$ = n =			3.89 80	1				3.88 147	

Source of variation	F-Ratio	df	Significance level
Organizational stance	<1	1	−
Technology	2.80	1	$P <.10$
Stance and technology	<1	1	−

TABLE 6
*Peer Work Facilitation in Work Groups Classified by
Technological Sophistication and Organizational Stance*

| | | Organizational Adaptation Stance | | | | | | | | Both Stances |
| | Proactive organizations | | | | Reactive organizations | | | | | |
	1	2	3	Total	4	5	6	7	Total	Total
High	$\overline{X}$ = 3.47	3.38	3.22	3.39	2.90	2.99	2.71	3.11	2.98	3.19
Technology	n = 19	17	8	44	21	23	11	36	91	135
Low	$\overline{X}$ = 3.11	2.69	2.63	2.96	2.93	3.23	3.00	3.16	3.09	3.03
Technology	n = 25	4	7	36	13	15	11	17	56	92
Total	$\overline{X}$ =			3.18					3.04	
Technology	n =			80					147	

Source of variation	F-Ratio	df	Significance level
Organizational stance	5.69	1	$P < .05$
Technology	6.40	1	$P < .05$
Stance and technology	17.7	1	$P < .01$

since the condition of reactive organizational stance is characterized by an interest in human relations or participative management as a method of countering a host of organizational ills, it is not beyond speculation to consider that the reactive organizations had a lower than normal considerate or supportive supervisory climate—so low in fact as to have no overlap with the scores of the proactive organization (cf. column means in Tables 3 and 4).

Tables 5 and 6 present the findings for work groups, support and work facilitation, respectively. In Table 5, peer support is not shown to be related to organizational stance either directly or by interaction with technology. Although there appears to be a main effect of technology on peer support, this is significant only at the 10% level of confidence. This trend shows low sophistication of technology to be associated with higher peer support.

Table 6 indicates that for peer work facilitation, significant main effects for both organizational stance and technology, as well as a significant interaction between them are manifest. This result confirms the hypothesis that with more sophisticated technology, work groups exercise more task oriented leadership than do groups with less sophisticated technology—but only in the proactive organizations. The reverse tendency is observed in reactive organizations. That is, high technology groups exhibit lower peer work facilitation scores than the low technology groups in reactive organizations.

Thus peer leadership can be seen to be directly associated with technology, whereas supervisory leadership is affected by technology (so far as the data here presented are concerned) only by interaction with the organization's stance regarding participative management. This general finding that technical characteristics are related to supervisory leadership

TABLE 7

Mean Score Differences on Dependent Variables between High and Low Technology Groups, and within Groups, Over Time

Organization	Dependent Variables	Intratechnology Differences		Intertechnology Differences	
		High Tech $t_2 - t_1$	Low Tech $t_2 - t_1$	High t_1 - Low t_1	High t_2 - Low t_2
		Proactive Organizations			
1[a]	Supervisory Support	.24*[b]	-.04	-.22	.06
	Sup. Work Facilitation	.21*	.19	.25	.27*
	Peer Support	.18*	-.07	-.20	.07
	Peer Work Facil.	.28*	.08	.36*	.56**
2[a]	Sup. Support	-.20	.66	.86**	.00
	Sup. Work Facil.	-.19	.48	1.03**	.36
	Peer Support	-.16	.11	.06	.21
	Peer Work Facil.	.08	.58	.68**	.18
3	Sup. Support	-.35*	.30*	.65*	.00
	Sup. Work Facil.	.03	.45*	.42*	.00
	Peer Support	-.08	.15	.27	.04
	Peer Work Facil.	.15	.59*	.59*	.15
		Reactive Organizations			
4	Sup. Support	.30	.04	-.24	.02
	Sup. Work Facil.	.32	.31	-.12	-.11
	Peer Support	-.05	.13	-.15	-.33
	Peer Work Facil.	.22	.29	-.03	-.10
5	Sup. Support	.27	.26	-.29	-.28
	Sup. Work Facil.	.15	.28	-.16	-.29
	Peer Support	-.04	.03	-.14	-.21
	Peer Work Facil.	.33	.28	-.24	-.19

*P $<$ .05 t test
**P $<$ .01 t test
[a]Comparisons for these organizations are $t_3 - t_1$
[b]t tests for this organization are one-tailed

only in interaction with an organization's response to adaptation to its environment is a virtual confirmation of Rossel's 1971 results.

Table 7 presents mean score differences on dependent variables over time both within technological classes and between them, for the five organizations in which the planned change program was used with nonsupervisory employees. These data permit at least cursory examination of the possible effects of technology and organization stance on changes in the dependent variables as planned change efforts in the direction of participative management were undertaken. A positive score here means that for the between time comparisons the later time measure is higher than the earlier—that is, that scores on the dependent variable went up over time. For the between technology class differences, a positive score means that scores on the dependent variable are greater for the high technology groups.

The overall results tend to suggest that technology has no consistent directional effect on the results of the planned change efforts in the proactive organizations. Further, it would appear that technology has no discernible effect on the planned change efforts in the reactive organizations.

In particular, these results suggest that although facilitating effects of technology on the planned change effort may be supported by data from organization 1 (the refinery), the other two proactive sites reveal the opposite effect. That is, for organizations 2 and 3, increases in dependent variable scores over time occur in low technology groups, not in the high ones. The results for the reactive organizations are more consistent in that they show an equal increase in dependent variable scores for both high and low technology groups over time.

DISCUSSION AND CONCLUSION

We may conclude, with respect to the test of technological effects, that technological sophistication in the three industrial sites classified as proactive does have a measurable association with perceptions of participative and facilitative leadership prior to planned change efforts. Tables 3–6 reveal that high technology groups in proactive organizations are initially higher in supervisory and peer leadership (except for the case of peer support) than low technology groups before the planned change program got underway. These static relationships do not inexorably lead to statements of causality, but it seems likely that prechange levels of group leadership were caused by, rather than, caused, the advanced technology. This, of course, does not rule out a possible third variable leading to prechange levels in both technology and leadership. It is unlikely, however, that something as direct as demographic characteristics is operating on both major variables. A description of the rather detailed examination of the effects of old age, tenure, and place of respondent upbringing (urban-rural) on the evaluation of technology, and on the dependent variables in the refinery (Taylor, 1971c) revealed minimal to nonexistent influence of these chatacteristics as confounding variables.

In regard to the association between technology and the social change attempt, the results obtained are somewhat conflicting. As Table 7 revealed, groups in the high technology category began at time one with higher mean scores in both peer and supervisory leadership in all three proactive sites. Between time one and subsequent measurement in organization 1, dependent variable scores increased significantly for the high technology groups only. On the other hand, dependent variable scores increased significantly over time only for the low technology gruops in the other two proactive organizations.

Significant technological effects on leadership behaviors were not evidenced for these organizations prior to the planned change program, as Tables 3–6 revealed. Although Table 7 shows the low technology groups as consistently higher than their high technology counterparts before the change, these differences are not significant. The differences between high and low technology groups following the planned change effort are essentially the same as those preceding it. The differences over time for each technology category are also similar—the low technology category retains higher leadership scores than the high technology category over time, although those differences are not statistically significant.

In 1971 (Taylor, 1971b) I concluded that leadership patterns which marked a movement toward supervisory control of boundary conditions and toward more group leadership in internal group matters was perhaps only to be expected where technology was more sophisticated. Given the data presented here, that conclusion should be modified to read that although these leadership patterns may be most suitable in modern continuous process industries, a proactive management stance may make them viable in more traditional industrial technologies in one case; while a reactive outlook can interject traditional supervisory patterns into a modern technical system in another. Modern production technology may lend itself more directly to group leadership than industrial era assembly lines; nevertheless there are a number of technological options available to designers of leadership systems. A major element in which technical options are seen and used involves the degree to which management believes employees' potential competence in responsibility and decision making should be a part of the design equation.

Discussant Comments

BY ROBERT D. ROSSEL*

In the past it was commonly assumed that "good" leadership skills and attributes were fairly universal human qualities that could be applied with equal efficacy to a wide variety of organizational and technological situations. If an organization was encountering a problem in leadership it was quite possible to institute a "human relations" program and give supervisors the necessary skills to diagnose the psychological or motivational problems of their workers and make whatever interventions that were required to overcome the crisis and get their workers back on the road to cohesiveness, efficiency, and productivity. Now we know that it is not that simple.

The common fallacy in such thinking is that it is relatively blind to the complex mixture of organizational and technological variables that moderate the nature of good leadership. To train a supervisor in human relations when organizational and technological conditions require something closer to initiating structure is only to compound the organizational problems to which one is seeking to respond with the additional problem of inappropriate leadership. The irony of this is that, at times we unwittingly, through our ignorance of the complexities involved, completely misperceive the gestalt that is involved in interpreting the nature of the leadership problem we are trying to solve.

One of the impressive things about Taylor's paper was its suggestion that effective organizational leadership is contingent not only upon technology but upon a range of other variables including task structure, managerial ideology, organizational product area, organizational environment relations, and possibly other variables as yet unmeasured. Given these contingencies it is not easy to know the kinds of leadership training programs that are most appropriate in helping organizations overcome the particular difficulties they face. Under certain conditions of technology and managerial ideology a planned change program in participatory management may in fact have unanticipated dysfunctional consequences for the work groups and leadership activities one is trying to influence.

---

*A number of issues originally raised by Rossel were handled in Taylor's revision of his original paper. Hence, the comments here are in less depth than were his original ones. Unfortunately, he was not able to respond to Taylor's revision.

12606

In the way of critical comments regarding the Taylor paper, I would like to focus primarily on his data source and the way in which he operationalized his variables. By way of review, Taylor was interested in studying the sophistication of industrial technology and managerial ideology as they influence attempts (through a planned change program) to modify supervisory and peer leadership orientations over time. The dependent variable, leadership orientation, was measured in terms of the University of Michigan four factor index with the support and facilitation dimensions being utilized for the present study. Proactive versus reactive managerial ideology was measured through a dichotomous classification of the specific organizations studied. Essentially, it involved distinguishing the "showcase" and the "crisis" organizations in the sample.

There is a real question in my mind concerning Taylor's measure of technological sophistication. This is another dichotomous variable like managerial ideology. Departments and other units *within* specific organizations are sorted into high and low technology categories on the basis of "qualities of standard materials input, throughout mechanization, and output control, for each work group." But given the variety of organizations studied and the indiscriminate combination of staff and line units, maintenance, production, and engineering units, and, in some cases, clerical, lower managerial, and production units, it is hard to know just what the variable measures. Certainly there is the possibility that the differences attributed to technology are spurious artifacts of other unmeasured variables. To illustrate the problem, Taylor reports in some cases that maintenance units are included in high technology and in others, low. In some cases traditional mass production units are combined with process control and production units with automated or semi automated technologies as high technology. In other cases mass production units are classified as low in technological sophistication. Those of you that are familiar with Robert Blauner's study *Alienation and Freedom* (1964) no doubt recall his point that mechanization and automation as phases in technological development have radically different effects on the structure of work groups, the amount of work discretion, and the problems of supervisory and peer leadership. There is also the problem that what is perceived as relatively sophisticated technology in one organization may be perceived as quite unsophisticated in another. These difficulties cause me to question the validity of the technological classification.

I also see some difficulties in the meaning of proactive versus reactive managerial ideology. It seems to me that this variable is actually a complex combination of managerial ideology and factors involving the relation between the organization and its environment. I wonder about the nature of the crisis in each of the reactive organizations. I wonder if the crisis is a result of managerial ideology, that is, a tradition of reactive unenlightened management which has finally caught up with the organization, thus causing the crisis. Or, alternatively, is the reactive ideology a response to sudden change in the market situation of the organization, its profit position, etc., which may have effects on supervisory and peer leadership quite independent from managerial ideology? Given its lack of specification, I have a difficult time knowing just what this variable is. Certainly I would suggest the advisability of further specification of the meaning of this variable and, if the data would allow it, differentiation of the question of managerial ideology from the question of organization-environment relations.

2

The Path-Goal Theory of Leadership: Some *Post Hoc* and A Priori Tests

ROBERT J. HOUSE and GARY DESSLER

At the 1971 Southern Illinois University symposium on contemporary developments in the study of leadership, Fleishman presented a paper in which he reviewed twenty years of research on leader consideration and leader initiating structure. In that paper Fleishman (1973) reviewed the historical development of scales to measure these two dimensions of leader behavior and also reviewed the evidence concerning their relationships to subordinates' attitudes, satisfaction, and performance as well as ratings of leader performance. In the conclusion of the paper Fleishman stated that "what we need are theory and data to develop a conceptualization of situational and personality variance as these might relate to the effective operation of consideration and structure and other dimensions of leadership [p. 37]."

At the same symposium House (1973b) advanced such a theory and asserted that it served to reconcile the conflicting and confusing findings in the literature. In this theory, leader behavior is conceived of as an independent variable having its most direct effects on specific psychological states of the subordinates. Previous attempts to explain the effects of leader behavior have focused predominantly on measures of *overall* satisfaction or measures of performance. However, several intermediating variables such as attitudes, expectations of subordinates, abilities, and task characteristics can alter the relationships between leader behavior and the indirect effects of leader behavior that have been studied in previous research such as overall satisfaction and performance. It is argued here that by focusing on the psychological states of subordinates the effects of intermediating variables on less immediate outcomes can be systematically allowed for. Such a research focus should increase the likelihood of identifying the precise psychological mechanisms underlying the effects of leaders on others. Some specific psychological states of subordinates that may be affected by the leader are the subordinate's intrinsic job satisfaction, his satisfaction with extrinsic rewards, his expectancy that effort leads to effective performance, and his expectancy that performance leads to rewards. Intrinsic job satisfaction and expectancies have been found in several studies to be predictive of effort and performance and thus can be viewed as motivational variables (House & Wahba, 1972). Subordinate satisfaction with extrinsic rewards has been repeatedly found to be negatively related to job withdrawal and grievances (Lawler, 1971; Vroom, 1964). Thus these psychological states are highly relevant to the study of leadership. By viewing leadership as a process of influence on subordinates' psychological states other relevant dependent variables may be identified through future research. The central points here are a) that by conceiving of the dependent variables in leadership research as subordinate psychological states a new class of variables is opened for investigation; and b) that previously used global variables such as overall satisfaction or performance are claimed to be confounded and less meaningful.

In the following section of this chapter, a revised version of the path-goal theory of leadership will be presented. Then prior studies will be reviewed that provide tests of the theory. Finally, the results of recently conducted studies designed to test the theory will be presented.

THE THEORY

The theory originally stated by House (1973b) has been revised and extended to include environmental variables and individual difference variables. The revised statement of the theory is presented here for the first time. The theory is intended to explain the relationship between leader behavior and motivation of subordinates.

A basic proposition of the theory is that one of the strategic functions of the leader is to enhance the psychological states of subordinates that result in motivation to perform or in satisfaction with the job. From previous research on the path-goal theory of motivation it can be inferred that these strategic functions of the leader consist of 1) recognizing and/or arousing subordinates' needs for outcomes over which the leader has some control, 2) increasing personal payoffs to subordinates for work goal attainment, 3) making the path to these payoffs easier to travel by coaching and direction, 4) helping subordinates clarify expectancies, 5) reducing frustrating barriers and 6) increasing the opportunities for personal satisfaction contingent on effective performance. Because the above motivational functions of the leader are stated in terms of paths, needs and goals, the theory is referred to as the path-goal theory of leadership. At this time the dependent variables of the theory are those which have been shown in previous research on path-goal theory of motivation to have significant effects on subordinate motivation (House & Wahba, 1972). Future research on the relationships between other subordinate psychological states and motivation, performance, and satisfaction is likely to suggest other variables that can be influenced by leader behavior. At that time these variables can be incorporated into the theory as additional dependant variables.

According to the theory presented here the leader's strategic functions are complementary. That is, his strategic functions are to provide for subordinates the coaching, guidance, support and rewards necessary for effective and satisfying performance that would otherwise be lacking in the environment. (The word *performance* is used here to mean behavior directed toward attainment of organizational goals.)

Stated less formally, the motivational functions of the leader consist of increasing personal payoffs to subordinates for work goal attainment, and making the path to these payoffs easier to travel by clarifying it, reducing roadblocks and pitfalls, and increasing the opportunities for personal satisfaction en route.

The theory asserts that to the extent that the leader accomplishes these functions his behavior will increase the motivation of subordinates to perform. It should be noted that while the leader crucially effects the satisfaction of subordinates, satisfaction is assumed to be motivational for performance only when it is intrinsic to effective performance (i.e., when performance is rewarding in itself) or when satisfaction is made contingent on effective performance.

A second proposition of the theory is that the specific leader behavior that will accomplish the above motivational function of leadership is determined by the situation in which the leader operates. Two classes of situational variables are the characteristics of subordinates and the environmental pressures and demands the subordinates must cope with to accomplish work goals and satisfy their own needs. While other situational variables may also be important determinants of the effects of leader behavior they are not presently known.

With respect to characteristics of subordinates, the theory asserts that leader behavior will be viewed as acceptable to subordinates to the extent that the subordinates see such behavior as either an immediate source of satisfaction, or as instrumental to future satisfaction. For example, it would be predicted that subordinates with high needs for affiliation and social approval would see friendly, considerate leader behavior as an immediate source of satisfaction. Subordinates with high needs for achievement would be predicted to view leader behavior that clarifies path-goal relationships and provides goal oriented feedback as satisfying. Subordinates with high needs for extrinsic rewards would be predicted to see leader directiveness or coaching behavior as instrumental to their satisfaction if such behavior helped them perform in such a manner as to gain recognition, promotion, security, or pay increases.

A second characteristic of subordinates that acts as a moderator of the effects of leader behavior is the subordinates' perception of their own ability with respect to task demands. The higher the degree of perceived ability relative to task demands, the less will the subordinate view leader directiveness and coaching behavior as acceptable. Where the subordinates' perceived ability is high such behavior is likely to have little positive effect on the motivation of the subordinate and to be perceived as excessively close control.

The acceptability of the leader's behavior is thus determined in part by the characteristics of his subordinates. Leader behavior viewed as unacceptable, while possibly motivational, will usually result in dysfunctional consequences such as passive resistance, sabotage, and leader-follower conflict. An example of a circumstance in which leader behavior might be viewed as unacceptable and yet still be motivational would be one in which the leader has a high degree of punitive power over subordinates and the subordinates have no alternative but to comply with the leader's demands in order to avoid punishment.

The second aspect of the situation, namely the environment of the subordinate, consists of those factors that are not within the control of the subordinate but which are important to his need satisfaction or to his ability to perform effectively. (According to this definition, the environment of any given subordinate is determined in part by the subordinate's attribution of control and in part by what the subordinate values as important to him personally. It is yet to be determined empirically exactly what aspects of the environment have invariant moderating effects, independent of subordinates' attribution characteristics and individual values. Nevertheless, the three classsifications of environmental moderators specified below are hypothesized as having either independent moderating effects, or interacting significantly with subordinate characteristics as joint moderators of the effects of leader behavior.) Obviously, one such aspect of the environment is the subordinates' superior(s) who exercises the right to administer rewards and punishments. The theory asserts that effects of the leader's attempts to influence the psychological states of subordinates will be moderated by other parts of the subordinates' environment that are relevant to subordinate motivation. Three broad classifications of relevant environmental moderators are: 1) the subordinates' task, 2) the formal authority system of the organization, 3) the primary work group.

Assessment of the environmental conditions makes it possible to predict the kind and amount of influence that specific leader behaviors will have on the motivation of subordinates. Each of the above three environmental factors could act upon the subordinate in any of three ways. First, they may serve as stimuli that motivate and direct the subordinate to perform necessary task operations. Secondly, they may act as constraints on variance in performance. Constraints are motivational to the extent that they help the subordinate clarify expectancies that effort leads to rewards and to the extent to which they prevent the subordinate from experiencing role conflict and ambiguity. Constraints are demotivational to the extent that they restrict initiative or prevent variance in effort from being associated positively with rewards. Thirdly, environmental factors may serve as reinforcements for achieving desired performance. Thus it is possible for the subordinate to receive the necessary cues from sources other than the leader to perform his assigned task. It is also possible for the subordinate to receive the necessary rewards, independent of the leader to sustain effective performance. The effect of the leader on subordinate's motivation then will be a function of how deficient the environment is with respect to motivational stimuli, constraints, or rewards.

With respect to the environment, the theory asserts that where path-goal relationships (subordinate's expectancies that effort leads to effective performance and effective performance leads to attainment of valued rewards for him) are apparent because of the routine of the task, clear group norms, or objective system fixed controls of the formal authority systems, attempts by the leader to clarify path-goal relationships will be redundant and will be seen by subordinates as unnecessarily close control. Although such control may increase performance by preventing soldiering or malingering it will also result in decreased satisfaction.

Also with respect to the environment, the theory asserts that the more dissatisfying the task the more the subordinates will resent behavior by the leader directed at increasing productivity or enforcing compliance to organizational rules and procedures.

Finally, with respect to environmental variables, the theory asserts that leader behavior will be motivational to the extent that it helps subordinates cope with environmental uncertainties, threat from others, or sources of frustration. Such leader behavior is predicted to increase a subordinate's satisfaction with the job context and to be motivational to the extent that it increases the subordinate's perceived probability that his effort will lead to valued rewards.

The remainder of this chapter will consist of analyses of prior evidence relevant to the theory and preliminary reports of several recently conducted tests of hypotheses derived from the theory.

POST HOC INTERPRETATIONS OF PRIOR STUDIES

Six studies have been reported which compare the findings from leadership research in terms of situational differences. These studies are analogous to tests of the path-goal theory. In all six studies the authors made the comparisons for purposes other than testing the theory. However, these studies provide an inferential basis upon which to assess the validity of the theory. In addition, analyses of these studies in terms of the theory illustrates how the theory may be operationalized and how it is useful in reconciling apparently conflicting or confusing findings. The first study is that reported by Fleishman, Harris, and Burtt (1955, pp. 78–85). (This study was cited as support for the theory in the original statement of the theory [House, 1973b]. The remaining five studies have come to the attention of the authors since that time.) High leader initiating structure was found to be related to foremen ratings of proficiency but also to higher grievances; high leader consideration was found to be related to lower proficiency ratings, a tendency more pronounced in production than other departments. The specific variable that was subsequently discovered to account for the differential relations across departments was pressure for output. If it can be assumed that the tasks in the production departments were less satisfying, then it follows that under conditions of high pressure for output, leader initiating structure would be viewed as an externally imposed form of control. Such control would be more acceptable to higher managers but resented by subordinates on whom it was imposed. Leader consideration is more likely to serve as a stress reducer as tasks become dissatisfying and the pressure for output increases. Thus, the differential relationships found across types of departments can be explained in terms of the differences in task satisfaction and pressure for production. This explanation is directly deducible from the path-goal theory. Specifically, this explanation is consistent with the hypotheses that a) the more satisfying the task, the less positive the relationship between leader consideration and subordinate satisfaction and performance; and b) the hypothesis that the less satisfying the task the more negative will be the relationship between leader initiating structure and satisfaction.

Halpin (1954) and Rush (1957) both found that under noncombat conditions leader initiating structure is positively related to crew members' ratings of procedural clarity and not related to criteria of air crew performance or satisfaction. In contrast, under combat conditions leader initiating structure is positively related to both performance and satisfaction. These findings can be explained in terms of the different environments in which combat and noncombat air crews operate. Under combat conditions effective performance leads to highly valent personal outcomes, namely safety and survival. Under conditions where there is a high degree of external threat such as that experienced by combat aircrews, individuals have been shown to prefer strong (highly structured, assertive or autocratic) leaders (Mulder & Stemerding, 1963; Mulder, Ritsema, & de Jong, 1970; Sales, 1972).

There is no direct evidence as to *why* people under threat choose strong leaders. The path-goal theory would hypothesize that such leaders are preferred because they are perceived as improving the chances of adequately responding to the threat, and because such leaders reduce the dissatisfying effects of the uncertainties of the situation. Under the environmental and task conditions of the combat aircrew members described above, the path-goal theory would predict that leader initiating structure would increase the expectation that effort will lead to effective performance. Since effective performance is intrinsically valent (automatically leads to personal safety) leader initiating structure would be satisfying to subordinates. However, under noncombat conditions effective performance does not necessarily lead to valent outcomes. Since the crew members in the noncombat condition were largely in the military as a result of conscription rather than voluntarily and since the tasks they were performing were not instrinsically satisfying, the theory would predict that leader initiating structure would be viewed as an imposition of control and would be resented by crew members. Both Halpin's (1954) and Rush's (1957) findings are consistent with this interpretation. Halpin's findings (1954) are especially noteworthy since he found these results held for leaders in combat but not for *the same* leaders operating under noncombat conditions.

A study by Beer (1966) compares correlations between leader initiating structure and subordinate self-ratings under different task conditions. The sample consisted of employees in an insurance company doing both routine and nonroutine clerical work. Beer found no significant relationship between leader initiating structure and subordinate self-ratings of initiative, self-assurance, or perceived occupational level for the combined sample of routine and nonroutine employees, using the Ghiselli (1971) scale. However, when data on 44 nonroutine clerical employees were analyzed alone, significant positive correlations between leader initiating structure and subordinate initiative were found. The correlations between leader initiating structure and two other self-report measures, subordinate self-assurance and perceived occupational level, were also high for the nonroutine employees, but these correlations were not significant. The theory asserts that for subordinates whose tasks are highly structured, leader initiating structure should have a lower relationship to subordinate motivation than for subordinates whose tasks are less structured. Thus, by contrasting Beer's samples in terms of degree of task structure (nonroutine workers versus entire sample) it is possible to explain his findings in terms of the theory. Leader initiating structure was positively related to measures of subordinate motivation only for the nonroutine employees, which is exactly what the theory asserts.

A recent study by Hall and Schneider (1972) permits a similar comparison among Catholic priests in three different occupational positions: professional specialists, pastors, and assistant pastors. Work satisfaction and job autonomy were found highest among the specialists and lowest among the assistant pastors. Leader behavior characterized as supportive (participative-considerate) was correlated to respondents' feeling of work challenge .64, .38 and -.04 for assistant pastors, pastors, and specialists respectively. These findings are clearly consistent with the hypothesis of the path-goal theory that the more satisfying the task, the less positive the relationship between leader consideration and subordinate satisfaction (House, 1973b, pp. 147–148). The rationale for this hypothesis is that for dissatisfying tasks, leader consideration will tend to offset dissatisfaction associated with the task; for satisfying tasks, leader consideration will be less important.

Mott (1972) reports a substantial number of findings that can be considered inferential tests of the path-goal theory. He correlated several measures of supervisory behavior with measures of division effectiveness under various levels of task structure and task interdependence in two organizations. His measures of organizational effectiveness and task structure were shown to have high inter rater agreement, and thus convergent validity.*

The correlations between measures of leader behavior and organizational effectiveness were moderated by task structure. It was found that when task structure was medium or low virtually every measure of leader behavior was significantly related to organizational effectiveness. When task

---

*Organizational effectiveness was defined as the ability of the organization to produce, adapt, and handle temporarily unpredictable overloads of work. An overall effectiveness score was obtained for each respondent by taking the average of his responses to eight items. A division effectiveness score was obtained by taking the average individual effectiveness scores from all the respondents of the division. The individual and divisional scores were shown to correlate significantly with ratings by independent raters who were familiar with each division's performance. There was also some evidence that the individual items tended to be correlated more highly with other items in the same conceptual area (productivity, adaptability, or flexibility) than with items in different areas. Thus the measures of effectiveness showed evidence of convergent and discriminant validity.

To measure task structure a panel of judges who were well acquainted with the divisions were asked to assess the average degree of task structuring in each of forty branches within each of the twelve divisions. The technique used was Fiedler's (1967) modification of Shaw's (1963) approach, which involved ranking each branch on four dimensions of task structure: clarity of goals, multiplicity of paths to goals, verifiability of decisions, and specificity of solutions.

Of course, as indicated earlier, the effect of environmental variables such as the above task structure dimensions may be determined in part by the subject's individual characteristics. In fact, as Hackman (1969) and Pepinsky and Pepinsky (1962) have observed, tasks assigned to an individual may be subjectively redefined by him.

structure was high the relationships were lower and generally insignificant. It was also found that the more interdependent the task of the divisions, the higher the relationship between leader behavior and organizational effectiveness. The above findings hold for both instrumental leader behavior such as planning and the use of administrative and technical skills, as well as supportive leader behavior. If it can be assumed that planning activity and the use of administrative and technical skills are analogous to leader initiating structure, the findings concerning these scales are consistent with the path-goal theory. Specifically these findings are predicted by the hypothesis that the more ambiguous the task the more positive the relationship between leader initiating structure and subordinate satisfaction and expectancies (House, 1973b, p. 148).

However, the finding that under highly structured task conditions the relationship between leader supportiveness was lowest is contrary to the theory. Presumably highly structured tasks are less satisfying. For such tasks the theory would predict high positive correlations between leader supportiveness and organizational effectiveness, which is opposite of what was found by Mott. There is one possible explanation for these findings that is not in conflict with the theory. It is possible that Mott's leader behavior measures were highly interdependent. If this were the case, application of technical and administrative skills would result in clearer subordinate role perceptions and more positive expectancies while at the same time being associated with supportive leadership. As will be shown in the original data presented blow, by partialing out the correlations among leader behavior dimensions ambiguous findings become clearer and highly consistent with the theoretical predictions.

In summary, five of the six studies that are considered as *post hoc* tests of the theory are consistent with it. One study is partially consistent and also included findings that are somewhat ambiguous and possibly contradictory.

A PRIORI TESTS OF THE THEORY

Two prior studies have been conducted that are a priori tests of the theory.

House (1973b) provided support for the theory using measures of subordinate task scope and task autonomy as moderators of the relationships between leader behavior and subordinate satisfaction and performance. Here job autonomy was taken as an indicator of task ambiguity and job scope as a variable leading to task satisfaction.

House found that the more autonomous the job of the subordinates the higher the relationship between leader initiating structure and satisfaction of subordinates and the lower the relationship between leader initiating structure and performance ratings of subordinates. House also found in two samples that the lower the task scope of the subordinates, the higher the relationship between leader consideration and satisfaction and performance of subordinates. Finally, House showed that among high occupational level employees the positive relationships between leader initiating structure and satisfaction of subordinates could be attributed to a reduction of role ambiguity associated with leader initiating structure. These findings were all consistent with hypotheses derived from the theory.

House stated that while the data support the theory, the tests were somewhat weak in that the theoretical constructs concerning the task characteristics and subordinate expectancies were inferred rather than measured directly. Thus, House's earlier findings provide support for the theory based on indirect measures of the theoretical constructs.

Dessler (1973) developed measures of subordinate expectancies and task certainty (predictability of task demands) specifically to test the theory. His tests of the theory were limited to hypotheses concerned with leader initiating structure and the effect of partialling out leader consideration under various task conditions. Unfortunately, the task certainty scale Dessler intended to use as a moderator was found to have inadequate validity to test the theory directly. To deal with this difficulty Dessler classified subjects according to two criteria: their task certainty scores and their occupational level. Subjects who were both high on occupational level and low on the task certainty scale were classified as low task certainty subjects. Subjects low on occupational level and high on the task certainty scale were classified as high task certainty subjects. This procedure resulted in the elimination of subjects whose scores were incongruent with what could be expected theoretically from knowing their occupational level. Thus, Dessler's test of the theory was a stronger and more conservative test than that reported by House in that Dessler took precautions to ensure that his subjects were classified according to the theoretical moderator, task certainty, using a multimethod classification approach.

Dessler found support for the theory. Specifically, he found that the relationships between leader initiating structure and satisfaction, expectancies, and role clarity of subordinates decreased as task ambiguity decreased, holding leader consideration constant. In addition, he found that the covarying effect of leader consideration on the relationship between leader initiating structure and the dependent variables increased as task ambiguity decreased. These findings represent direct tests of the theory and provide support for it.

In addition, Dessler conducted an exploratory analysis of the interaction between leader initiating structure, task certainty, and subordinate authoritarianism as predictors of subordinates' satisfaction and expectancies. He found that for high authoritarian subordinates leader initiating structure is positively related to subordinate satisfaction, regardless of the certainty of the task. Under conditions of low task certainty leader initiating structure is positively related to satisfaction regardless of subordinate authoritarianism.

High authoritarians have been shown to place a higher valence on external structure (in this case leader initating structure) than low authoritarians, and high authoritarians view external structure as instrumental to their goal attainment more than low authoritarians do (Rokeach, 1960). Consequently, Dessler's exploratory analysis constitutes support for the proposition that leader behavior will be viewed as acceptable to the extent that the subordinate sees such behavior as a source of satisfaction or as instrumental to future satisfaction.

Meheut and Siegel (1973) conducted a study of the relationship between leader behavior and subordinate satisfaction with a management by objectives (MBO) program, eighteen months after the MBO program had been initiated. The subjects were eighty-two lower and middle managers of a federal department of the Canadian government. They found that the Fleishman (1957) leader initiating structure scale had a .06 correlation with MBO satisfaction. Using the path-goal theory as their guide, they divided the items on the initiating structure scale into role clarification items (he lets subordinates know what is expected of them; he makes his attitudes clear to the group) and autocratic items (he speaks in a manner not to be questioned, he rules with an iron hand). Role clarification and autocratic leader behavior were found to correlate .26 (p < .05) and −.21 with MBO satisfaction respectively. Further they found leader role clarification to be negatively associated with six kinds of subjects' problems with MBO while the Fleishman initiating structure scale was associated with only three kinds of problems.

They also found leader consideration to be significantly related to MBO satisfaction and negatively related to MBO problems. Meheut and Siegel's findings (1973) were all consistent with their hypotheses which were derived from the path-goal theory. Further, their findings demonstrate the importance of specifying more exactly the kind of leader behavior that leads to subordinate's role clarification and expectancies that effort leads to rewards.

The above studies suggest that the path-goal theory is promising and potentially capable of reconciling inconsistent findings concerning leader initiating structure and leader consideration. Further, the theory is asserted to be sufficiently general to permit identification of other critical dimensions of leader behavior and to reconcile conflicting evidence with respect to leader authoritarianism, general supervision, participation and hierarchical influence (House, 1973b).

Unfortunately, the House and the Dessler studies fail to demonstrate a means whereby the theory can be tested directly, without relying on the researcher's clinical knowledge of the research setting in order to make inferences about task characteristics.

SOME NEW TESTS OF THE THEORY

In an attempt to develop a more objective measure of task characteristics, additional data about the tasks of Dessler's subjects were analyzed. These analyses resulted in the development and validation of a new task moderator. The validation evidence will be presented in more detail below.

Using this new reasonably well validated measure of task structure the Dessler data were reanalyzed and an additional hypothesis was tested. The findings from these analyses were then replicated in a second sample.

The two samples, A and B, consisted of employees of medium sized electronics firms. Both samples consisted of managers, quasi-professional salaried employees, white-collar clerical employees, foremen, technicians, and low skilled blue-collar assembly workers.

Questionnaires were administered to all employees of both firms in group settings on company premises. In Company A, 206 employees completed at least some part of the questionnaire. In Company B, 96 did so. These subjects constitute the populations from which subsets or samples of subjects were drawn. The size of each subset varied depending on the particular analysis. The larger the number of items used in the analysis the smaller the sample size, because of missing data. The specific number for each analysis is indicated in the table reporting the data relevant to that analysis. For some of the analyses the small percentage of the total number of subjects is used because of the length of the questionnaire which consisted of 340 items and took approximately 90 minutes to complete. Several items used in the present analysis were located in the last half of the questionnaire. Several respondents did not complete the entire questionnaire. Since only subjects with complete data were included in this study, the useable number in several analyses was substantially lower than the number of subjects to whom the questionnaire was administered.

Respondents were asked to sign their names.

Hypotheses

Two hypotheses were tested:

Hypothesis 1. Task structure will have a negative moderating effect on the relationships between instrumental leader behavior and the following dependent variables: intrinsic and extrinsic satisfaction of subordinates, role clarity, and expectancies that effort leads to performance and performance leads to rewards. Specifically, the lower the task structure the higher will be the relationship between instrumental leader behavior and the dependent variables.

Here instrumental leadership is defined as leader behavior directed at clarifying expectations, assigning specific tasks, and specifying procedures to be followed.

This hypothesis is based on the assumption that when tasks are highly unstructured, that is, when task stimuli and instructions are complex, non-repetitive and, ambiguous, instrumental leadership will help subordinates clarify a) their perceptions concerning the contingencies they must deal with to complete the task, b) the expectancies others have of them, and c) the degree to which performance will be rewarded. When contingencies, expectations, and performance-reward relationships are clearly perceived by subjects as a consequence of instrumental leadersip it is expected that they will enjoy the intrinsic task demands more and be more satisfied with extrinsic rewards associated with their employment. In contrast, when tasks are simple and highly structured, subordinates are expected to see instrumental leadership as an imposition of control that is redundant, given existing task structure. Thus instrumental leadership is not expected to be seen as adding clarification under highly structured task conditions. Rather, instrumental leadership is expected to be seen as excessively directive and restrictive and to be resented, resulting in lower satisfaction to the subordinate and lower expectancy that his performance leads to rewards.

Hypothesis 2. Task structure will have a positive moderating effect on the relationship between supportive leader behavior and the following dependent variables: intrinsic and extrinsic satisfaction of subordinates, expectancies that effort will lead to performance and performance will lead to rewards, role clarity, and satisfaction with co-workers.

Supportive leadership is characterized as friendly and approachable, and considerate of the needs of subordinates.

This hypothesis is based on the assumption that when tasks are unstructured, i.e., more complex and varied, the challenge of the task is likely to be more intrinsically satisfying. Supportive leadership is asserted to be a source of social satisfaction for the employee which results in the reduction of frustration and stress and an increase in two-way communication between superior and subordinate. Thus, under highly structured tasks supportive leadership is hypothesized to be more positively related to satisfaction and to expectancies than under unstructured tasks. Since supportive leadership is expected to facilitate friendship relationships it is predicted to have a positive relationship to satisfaction with co-workers. This relationship is expected to be higher under high task structure because supportive leadership is assumed to reduce frustration resulting from highly structured dissatisfying tasks. If frustration and consequent dissatisfaction are not reduced, their effect would be expected to result in generally unpleasant behavior of group members toward each other.

In addition to tests of the above hypotheses, analyses were conducted concerning the relationship between participative leadership and the dependent variables. These analyses were considered exploratory since the participative leadership dimension has not been previously discussed with respect to the theory and no hypotheses concerning the relationship between participative leadership and subordinate expectancies have been stated to date. However, participative leadership may be viewed by subjects as a means of clarifying role expectations and contingencies. If this occurs, the relationship between participative leadership and the dependent variables would be expected to increase as task structure decreases. This relationship is expected to be lower under high task structure conditions because it is under these conditions that clarification of role expectations is most needed. Thus participative leadership is conceived of as a nondirective form of role clarifying behavior analogous to the more directive instrumental leadership. If this conception of participative leadership is correct task structure should bear a negative moderating effect on the relationship between participative leadership and the dependent variables.

Measures

The measures employed were of three kinds: 1) the moderator variable—the task structure scale referred to above, 2) the independent variables—subjects' perceptions of the behavior of their leaders and 3) the dependent variables—subjects' satisfaction, role clarity, and expectancies that effort leads to effective performance and performance leads to reward.

The task structure scale was developed empirically using Dessler's original subjects and additional data describing their task characteristics. The scale consisted of ten items intended to measure the degree to which the task stimuli and execution rules and procedures are simple, repetitive and unambiguous. The scale was validated against ratings of the subjects' tasks by the subjects' superiors and also against the subjects' occupational level. The scale was found to have Kuder-Richardson formula 20 reliabilities of .69 and .65 in samples A and B respectively. It correlated $-.74$ and $-.58$ in these two samples with occupational level (p. $< .001$ and $< .01$). In addition, in sample A the scale correlated .43 with ratings by the superiors of the subjects' task structure (p $< .01$). Superior ratings from sample B were not obtained. ANOVA's and Sheffé tests (Guilford, 1954) indicated that for sample A the mean score in the high occupational group was significantly lower than the mean for the medium occupational group which was significantly lower than the mean of the low occupational group. The same ordering of means held for sample B, but the low group was not significantly lower than the median occupational group.

These findings indicate that the task scale has multimethod concurrent validity and is sufficiently discriminating to classify subjects who are in the upper and lower thirds of the populations studied. (Since a significant amount of the variance in the task structure scale is related to independent criteria, namely ratings by superiors and occupational level, it is believed that the scale used here primarily reflects a complex of objective stimuli, goals, and execution instructions independent of the subordinate.) The findings also indicate that with respect to middle groups the discriminating power of the theory is somewhat marginal. The items comprising this scale are presented in Figure 1.

Three perceived leader behavior scales were factor analytically derived from sample A from a pool of 35 items using a least squares solution in the common factor model (principal factor analysis with "iteration by refactoring" Harman, 1960). Three oblique factors were identified. (Four factors were fitted, but the fourth factor was not identified. Omitting 17 of the original 35 gave a set of items each of which virtually measured one factor only.) Table 8 presents the factor loadings for the leader behavior items. These factors were labelled instrumental leadership, supportive leadership, and participative leadership. The instrumental leadership and supportive leadership factors consisted primarily of items taken from Form XII of the Ohio State Leader Behavior Description Questionnaire (Stogdill, 1963). The participative leadership factor consisted of items developed specifically for the present study plus items from the Ohio State University Consideration Scale that reflect participative leadership (Fleishman, 1957). The same items were used to constitute scales in sample B.

The instrumental leadership scale was similar to the Form XII Initiating Structure scale (Stogdill, 1963) but was different from the earlier initiating structure scales developed by Fleishman (1957) and Halpin and Winer (1957) in that it did not include items reflecting autocratic or punitive leader behavior as these scales did.

The supportive leadership scale was similar to the leader Consideration scales used by Fleishman (1957) and Stogdill (1963) but it did not include participative items as these scales did. The participative leadership scale measured the degree to which the leader allowed subordinates to influence his decisions by asking for suggestions and including subordinates in the decision making process.

Two oblique expectancy scales were derived from sample A using the same factor analytic method described above. (Three factors were fitted. The third factor, expectancy that performance leads to affiliation and acceptance of co-workers, was not used in the present study as its content does not reflect a variable directly relevant to the theory.) These scales will be referred to as E-I, the degree to which effort leads to performance, and E-II the degree to which high quality, quantity, and timely performance leads to extrinsic rewards such as increased pay, promotion, recognition or security. Table 9 presents the factor loadings for the expectancy items. As can be seen from Table 10 these scales have adequate reliabilities. Subordinates respond to these questions by indicating on a seven point Likert scale the degree to which each item is true or false as it applies to their situation. The same items were used to develop scales in sample B.

Task Structure Scale

1. Problems which arise on my job can generally be solved by using standard procedures.

Definitely not   1   2   3   4   5   Extremely true
true of my job   of my job

2. I can generally perform my job by using standardized methods

Definitely not   1   2   3   4   5   Extremely true
true of my job   of my job

3. Problems which I encounter in my job can generally be solved in a number of different ways.*

Definitely not   1   2   3   4   5   Extremely true
true of my job   of my job

4. What is the average time it takes for you to complete a typical assignment?

5__One day or less
4__Between 1 and 3 days
3__Between 3 days and 1 week
2__Between 1 and 2 weeks
1__Longer than 2 weeks

5. How repetitious are your duties?

1__Very little
2__Some
3__Quite a bit
4__Very much
5__Almost completely

6. How similar are the tasks you perform in a typical work day?

5__Almost all the same
4__Quite a few the same
3__Only a few the same
2__Very few the same
1__Almost all different

7. If you were to write a list of the exact activities you would be confronted by on an average work day, what percent of these activities do you think would be interrupted by unexpected events?

1__80-100%
2__60-80%
3__40-60%
4__20-40%
5__0-20%

*Question 3, 1 indicates high task structure, 5 indicates low task structure,
Scores on this scale must be reversed.

8. How much variety is there in the work tasks which you perform?

> 1__Very much
> 2__Quite a bit
> 3__Some
> 4__Little
> 5__Very little

9. Every job is confronted by certain routine and repetitive demands. What percent of the activities or work demands connected with your job would you consider to be of a routine nature?

> 1__0-20%
> 2__20-40%
> 3__40-60%
> 4__60-80%
> 5__80-100%

10. The tasks of some individuals are more "structured" than others: the goals are clearer, the methods to be used are more understood, and the problems are more repetitive and less unique, for example. Would you please rate what you feel is the degree of "structure" of your job by circling the best response.

| My job is highly | | | | | | My job is highly |
| Unstructured | 1 | 2 | 3 | 4 | 5 | Structured |

Fig. 1. Task structure scale.

The intrinsic satisfaction scale describes the degree to which subjects had opportunities for autonomous action, personal development, and challenging and meaningful work. The extrinsic satisfaction scale describes the degree to which subjects perceived pay, advancement, recognition, and security as adequate. The co-worker satisfaction scale describes the degree to which subjects were satisfied with their social environment. These scales are described in more detail by Rizzo, House, and Lirtzman (1970) and by House (1973b).

The role clarity scale measures the degree to which subjects see their role demands as predictable and unambiguous. The development of this scale is also described in more detail by Rizzo et al., (1970). Scale reliabilities are presented in Table 10.

Method of Analysis

Subjects in Company A were trichotomized into three approximately equal groups, according to their score in the task structure scale. Subjects in Company B were trichotomized using the cutting scores developed from Company A. Since the leader behavior scales were significantly intercorre-

TABLE 8
Factor Loadings of Leader Behavior Items
(Sample A, N=198)

Items	Factor Loadings		
Instrumental leadership items (IL)	I	II	III
He lets group member know what is expected of them	.463	-.350	-.050
He decides what shall be done and how it shall be done	.831	.231	-.068
He makes sure that his part in the group is understood	.439	-.298	.053
He schedules the work to be done	.657	.267	.096
He maintains definite standards of performance	.767	.083	.167
He asks that group members follow standard rules and regulations	.629	-.001	-.008
He explains the way my tasks should be carried out	.465	-.180	.059
Supportive leadership items (SL)			
He is friendly and approachable	-.100	-.766	.013
He does little things to make it pleasant to be a member of the group	-.025	-.969	-.232
He puts suggestions made by the group into operation	-.128	-.731	-.134
He treats all group members as his equals	-.317	-.993	.039
He gives advance notice of changes	-.064	-.662	.148
He keeps to himself	-.148	-.346	.228
He looks out for the personal welfare of group members	.127	-.650	.081
He is willing to make changes	.070	-.473	.227
He helps me overcome problems which stop me from carrying out my task	.232	-.456	.033
He helps me make working on my tasks more pleasant	.047	-.718	-.017
Participative leadership items (PL)			
When faced with a problem he consults with his subordinates	.110	.066	.771

Before making decisions he gives serious consideration to what his subordinates have to say	-.154	-.401	.618
He asks subordinates for their suggestions concerning how to carry out assignments	.125	.042	.675
Before taking action he consults with his subordinates	.008	.103	.724
He asks subordinates for suggestions on what assignments should be made	-.014	.176	.551

Responses: 5) Always 4) Often 3) Occasionally 2) Seldom 1) Never

TABLE 9
Factor Loadings of Leader Expectancy
(Sample A, N = 198)

Items	Factor Loadings	
Effort Leads to Performance (E-I)	I	II
Putting forth as much energy as possible leads to my turning out my production requirement on time	-.697	.149
Putting forth as much energy as possible leads to my producing high quality output	-.601	-.018
Doing things as well as I am capable leads to turning out my production requirement on time	-.722	-.031
Doing things as well as I am capable leads to high quality output	-.687	-.077
Putting forth as much energy as possible leads to my producing a high quality of output	-.766	.069
Doing things as well as I am capable leads to a high quantity of output	-.728	-.082
Trying as hard as I can leads to turning out my production requirement on time	-.825	.033
Giving the job all I can leads to turning out my production requirement on time	-.722	.053
Trying as hard as I can leads to high quality output	-.531	-.031
Trying as hard as I can leads to a high quantity of output	-.637	.066
Giving the job all I can leads to a high quantity of output	-.752	-.008
Giving the job all I can leads to a high quality of output	-.681	-.054

47

Performance Leads to Rewards (E-II)

Producing a high quality output increases my chances for promotion	-.053	-.579
Producing a high quantity of output increases my chances for promotion	-.147	-.614
Producing a high quality output is rewarded with higher pay here	.062	-.617
Producing a high quantity of output is rewarded with higher pay here	.068	-.651
Getting the job done on time increases my chances of promotion	.034	-.564
Getting the job done on time is rewarded with higher pay here	.079	-.680
Producing a high quality output leads to job security here.	.036	-.709
The company gives me recognition for producing high quality output	.092	-.880
Producing a high quantity of output leads to job security here	-.069	-.857
The company gives me recognition for getting my job done on time	.007	-.950
The company gives me recognition for producing a high quantity of output	.022	-.952
Getting the job done on time leads to job security here	-.070	-.842

lated, the hypotheses were tested using partial correlations. That is, the relationship between a given dimension of leader behavior and a dependent variable was computed with a zero order correlation, holding the other two dimensions constant. One tailed significance of difference tests were computed between comparable correlations within each moderated group. In addition, tests of significance of pairs of correlations were computed, and the trends of the direction of changes (low to high or high to low) in correlations associated with different levels of task structure were inspected.

Results

The first hypothesis stated that the lower the task structure the higher will be the relationship between instrumental leadership and the dependent variables. From Table 11 it can be seen that the first hypothesis is confirmed in sample A with respect to differences in the high versus low task

TABLE 10
Scale Reliabilities

	Sample A n = 129		Sample B n = 75	
1. Leader initiating structure	.72[a]	(.72)[b]	.76[a]	(.78)[b]
2. Leader consideration	.82	(.74)	.79	(.69)
3. Leader participation	.67	(.78)	.68	(.79)
4. Role clarity	.47	(.58)	.59	(.66)
5. Intrinsic satisfaction	.83	(.85)	.80	(.80)
6. Satisfaction with co-workers	.62	(.81)	.61	(.81)
7. Task structure	.69	(.65)	.65	(.55)
8. Expectancy I	.84	(.73)	.84	(.73)
9. Expectancy II	.88	(.82)	.84	(.74)
10. Extrinsic satisfaction	.85	(.75)	.81	(.67)

[a]Kuder Richardson Formula 20

[b]Internal consistency reliability, Mean correlation between items and sum of scores. This measure is more appropriate for short scales

structure group correlations concerning intrinsic satisfaction, extrinsic satisfaction, and E-II. There is also a slight trend toward increases in E-I as task structure increases, as predicted, but the differences in the correlations are very small. The hypothesis is also supported with respect to differences in the medium versus low task structure group correlations concerning role clarity. However, the difference in the high versus low task structure group, while in the predicted direction, is not significant. From Table 11 it can also be seen that the finding with respect to intrinsic satisfaction is replicated in sample B and the trend with respect to E-I found in sample A is strongly and significantly confirmed in sample B. The findings with respect to extrinsic satisfaction in sample A are replicated although the differences in correlations in sample B are not significant. The findings in sample A concerning E-II and role clarity are not replicated in sample B.

The second hypothesis stated that the lower the task structure the lower the relationship between supportive leadership and the dependent variables. The data relevant to the second hypothesis are presented in Table 12. For sample A all three hypotheses concerning subjects' satisfaction receive support, since the differences in the high versus low task structure groups are statistically significant. Also there is some support for the hypothesis with respect to E-I since the difference between the correlations

TABLE 11
Correlations between Instrumental Leadership and
Dependent Variables for Moderated Groups [a]

	Sample A		
	Task Structure		
	High	Medium	Low
Intrinsic satisfaction	-.33*	.19	.26
	(33)[b]	(33)	(33)
Extrinsic satisfaction	-.16	-.05 -------------	.32*
	(30)	(27)	(33)
Expectancy I	-.07	.11	.14
	(35)	(37)	(35)
Expectancy II	-.28*	-.35 -------------	33*
	(33)	(38)	(36)
Role clarity	.14	-.13	.37
	(35)	(38)	(36)

	Sample B		
	Task Structure		
	High	Medium	Low
Intrinsic satisfaction	-.48*	-.23 -------------	.40
	(13)[b]	(19)	(12)
Extrinsic satisfaction	-.48*	-.36	.12
	(11)	(16)	(11)
Expectancy I	-.24	.08 -------------	.59
	(13)	(19)	(11)
Expectancy II	.13	-.24	.24
	(13)	(19)	(11)
Role clarity	.33	.04	.08
	(12)	(19)	(12)

Note.—Solid line connecting two coefficients indicates significant difference in correlations at ≤.05 level of significance. Dashed line indicates difference in r at p ≤.10. Dotted line indicates difference in r at p ≤.01.

[a]Coefficients are partial correlations holding SL and PL constant.

[b]Numbers in parentheses indicate N on which correlation is based. This N varies due to missing data.

*p ≤.05.

TABLE 12
Correlations between Supportive Leadership and Dependent Variables for Moderated Groups[a]

	Sample A		
		Task Structure	
	High	Medium	Low
Intrinsic satisfaction	.52**	.40**	.11
	(33)[b]	(33)	(33)
Extrinsic satisfaction	.55**	.20	.06
	(30)	(27)	(33)
Expectany I	.11	.41**	-.08
	(35)	(37)	(35)
Expectancy II	.23	.41**	.20
	(33)	(38)	(36)
Satisfaction with co-workers	.36*	.32*	-.05
	(31)	(33)	(35)
Role clarity	.32	.39	.09
	(35)	(38)	(36)

	Sample B		
		Task Structure	
	High	Medium	Low
Intrinsic satisfaction	.36	.35	.03
	(13)	(14)	(12)
Extrinsic satisfaction	.06	.39	-.05
	(11)	(16)	(11)
Expectancy I	.21	-.07	-.60*
	(13)	(19)	(11)
Expectancy II	.28	.15	.10
	(13)	(19)	(11)
Satisfaction with co-workers	.34	-.03	-.26
	(12)	(17)	(12)
Role clarity	.69	.29	.14
	(12)	(19)	(12)

Note—Solid line connecting two coefficients indicates significant difference in correlations at $\leqslant .05$ level of significance.

[a]Coefficients are partial correlations holding IL and PL constant.

[b]Numbers in parentheses indicate N on which correlation is based. This N varies due to missing data.

*p $\leqslant .05$
**p $\leqslant .01$.

TABLE 13

*Correlations between Participative Leadership and
Dependent Variables for Moderated Groups*[a]

	Sample A		
		Task Structure	
	High	Medium	Low
Intrinsic satisfaction	.36**	.38**	.23
	(35)[b]	(35)	(35)
Extrinsic satisfaction	.32*	.31	.28*
	(32)	(24)	(35)
Expectany I	.35**	-.07	.24
	(39)	(39)	(37)
Expectancy II	.26	.22	.46**
	(35)	(40)	(38)
Role clarity	.04	.20	.32*
	(39)	(40)	(38)

	Sample B		
		Task Structure	
	High	Medium	Low
Intrinsic satisfaction	-.07	-.01	-.02
	(13)	(19)	(12)
Extrinsic satisfaction	.34	.35	.15
	(11)	(16)	(11)
Expectancy I	-.03	.31	.03
	(13)	(19)	(11)
Expectancy II	-.01	.20	.03
	(13)	(19)	(11)
Satisfaction with co-workers	-.10	.45	.17
	(12)	(17)	(12)
Role clarity	-.57* - - - - - - - - - - - - - -	.09	-.30
	(12)	(19)	(12)

Note.—Dashed line indicates difference in r at p ⩽.10.

[a]Coefficients are partial correlations holding IL and SL constant.

[b]Numbers in parenthesis indicate N on which correlation is based. This N varies due to missing data.
*p ⩽.05.
**p ⩽.01.

in the medium and low task structure group is significant, in the predicted direction. However, this support is weak due to the insignificant correlation in the high task structure group. There is no support for the hypothesis with respect to E-II. In both samples trends in the correlations with role clarity are as predicted; however, the differences are not significant. The trends of the correlations in sample B, although not significant, are consistent with those of sample A with the exception of extrinsic satisfaction which is disconfirmed.

In summary, the first hypothesis receives some support from both samples with respect to all dependent variables except E-II which is supported significantly in sample A but receives no support in sample B. The second hypothesis receives some support from both samples with respect to all variables except extrinsic satisfaction which is significantly supported in sample A but receives no support in sample B.

In addition to the above hypotheses, exploratory analyses of the relationship of participative leadership to the dependent variables were also conducted. These relationships are presented in Table 13. From Table 13 it can be seen that while there is a slight tendency for role clarity to be more positively related to participative leadership under low task structure, this trend is weak and insignificant and not replicated in sample B. Further, there is no consistent trend in the remaining relationships in either sample.

With respect to the exploratory analysis of participative leadership, the findings offer little that help to interpret prior studies or help to better understand the conditions appropriate for the use of participative leadership. It is likely that the most important moderators of participative leadership will be the subjects' personality rather than task variables. It is possible that the two will interact in a complex manner, as joint moderators of participative leadership–dependent variable relationships.

DISCUSSION AND CONCLUSION

The findings with respect to instrumental leadership and supportive leadership, when viewed collectively, provide general support for the theory and have important implications for understanding leadership. In leadership, when viewed collectively, provide general support for the theory. The implications of the findings are discussed below.

The strongest findings concerned the relationship between instrumental leadership and subordinate satisfaction (extrinsic and intrinsic). It was found in both samples that instrumental leadership is negatively correlated with satisfaction under highly structured tasks and that this relationship increases monotonically to a positive correlation as task structure decreases.

This finding has significance for leadership theory. One of the areas of confusion about prior research concerns the mixed and conflicting findings with respect to the relationships between leader initiating structure, one form of instrumental leadership, and subordinate satisfaction (House, Filley, & Kerr, 1971). The present findings demonstrate that the theory provides a supportable resolution to this area of confusion by specifying the conditions under which instrumental leader behavior will have a positive or negative relationship with subjects' satisfaction. Several of the items in all earlier versions of the initiating structure scale (Fleishman, 1957; Halpin & Winer, 1957; Stogdill, 1963) concern role clarifying behavior of the leader. The present instrumental leadership scale includes these items. It is argued here that the effects of role clarifying behavior by the leader vary with the situation as specified in the path-goal theory of leadership, and that an essential ingredient of leader initiating structure is role clarifying behavior. This assertion is supported by the findings of Meheut and Siegel (1973). If this assertion is valid, it follows from the theory that the prior contradictory findings concerning leader initiating structure can be explained by the theory. Further, the results of the research reported here support this position.

The findings concerning the relationship between instrumental leadership and subjects' E-I also provide support for the theory. These relationships also changed monotonically from negative to positive as task structure decreased. In sample A the direction of change was as predicted, while in sample B it was both as predicted and the differences in correlations were significant for the high and low task structure groups.

With respect to supportive leadership, the correlation with subjects' intrinsic satisfaction, satisfaction with co-workers, and role clarity support the theory. The correlations between supportive leadership and these variables were in the predicted direction for both samples. These findings, when viewed collectively, make psychological sense in that the dependent variables all have strong implications for subordinate acceptance of the leader and subordinate satisfaction, but are less relevant to extrinsic rewards. Thus supportive leadership appears to have its primary effect in terms of social or psychological maintenance and intrinsic satisfaction rather than affecting performance through control of contingent rewards. This effect is greater under structured task conditions.

The scales developed for the present tests of the theory illustrate some of the difficulties in carrying out effective field research on leadership. First, this study shows that leader behavior measures are not likely to be independent of each other. Consequently, it is necessary to ascertain the degree of interdependence and control for it where possible. When two measures of leader behavior are so intercorrelated that they reflect a common underlying dimension, tests of the theory with such measures would be invalid. However, when measures can be shown to have an oblique or orthogonal factor structure, and to be conceptually related to the theoretical constructs, tests of the theory using partial correlations are appropriate. These are demanding requirements that may not always be possible to meet in field research.

As will be recalled, Mott's (1972) findings can be interpreted as support for the theory with respect to his measures of instrumental leader behavior. However, with respect to supportive leader behavior, his findings were opposite to what the theory would predict. It was speculated above that this difference could be due to covariance between his various measures of leader behavior. Comparison of partial correlations and zero order correlations among the measures of leader behavior used in this study support this speculation. The zero order correlations, in each moderated group, were compared to comparable second order partials between the given leader scale and dependent variables, holding the other two leader behavior variables constant. For example, the zero order correlation between instrumental leadership and intrinsic satisfaction was compared to the partial correlation between instrumental leadership and intrinsic satisfaction, holding supportive leadership and participative leadership constant. The zero order correlations showed no meaningful systematic differences across various levels of subjects' task structure, while the partial correlations were consistant with theoretical predictions. These findings suggest that the same kind of covariance could have accounted for Mott's findings, which are inconsistent with the path-goal theory of leadership.

These findings also have important implications for future tests of the theory. They clearly imply that to be correctly tested, any significant covariance among leader behavior dimensions should be held constant. Failure to hold such covariance constant confounds the opposite effects of instrumental leadership and supportive leadership and masks specific variance associated with these leader behavior dimensions.

Discussant Comments

BY RICHARD N. OSBORN

The task of the discussant appears to be twofold in nature. First, he is obligated to play the role of the devil's advocate, no easy task with the House and Dessler chapter. Secondly, he should link the paper with other perspectives available within the literature. This second task is particularly important for the newly emerging contingency approaches to leadership.

As a devil's advocate, one may point to questionable areas in the path-goal theory, the statistical techniques utilized and the operational measurement of the predictors. The theory is rich in face validity and conceptual flexibility and appears to mesh well with the conventional wisdom of industrial psychologists. However, the exact dimensions of the subordinates' environment are not clearly defined. Different aspects of the environment could have differential affects. For example, do task routinization, the clarity of group norms, as well as the nature of formal authority and control systems all have an identical impact on the relationship between leadership and employee satisfaction? Are environmental variables significantly correlated with individual psychological states? (This point is particularly important when role clarity is a criterion.)

Several related questions also seem important. When could the reduction of uncertainty by the leader yield a condition which might be classified as routine? Who determines whether a task is satisfying or dissatisfying? For example, the perceptions of the researcher and the subject may differ substantially. Some may view apparently negatively valent jobs as positively valent.

From a purely statistical standpoint the results may not be as supportive of the theory as suggested. When the data are tricotomized by task structure an unknown proportion of the variance attributable to the task structure is applied to the interaction. Multiple linear regression analysis might be more appropriate since it can be used to detect the unique variance attributable to leadership, task structure, and the interaction between the two (see Kelly, Beggs, McNeil, Eichelberger, & Lyon, 1969). The statistical limitation might not be particularly important if the R^2s were high, the results were clearcut, and task structure were clearly unrelated to the criteria. The amount of explained variance is far from outstanding even after controlling for the opposite leadership dimension; in sample B only the pattern of results clearly conforms to the hypotheses; and the theoretical discussion might be interpreted to indicate a negative correlation between task structure and the criteria.

Testing for the difference between two nonsignificant correlations is statistically possible, but the practicing manager might view a theory built upon such comparisons and patterns of insignificant correlations with some suspicion. Overall, some of the results are consistent with the theory and some are not. In the role of the devil's advocate one must call the glass half empty rather than half full.

As with any broad theory, there are problems in operationalizing the variables. For example, task structure and role clarity both seem to deal with the degree of ambiguity associated with a particular job. Fortunately, House and Dessler's careful use of statistics in general and factor analysis in particular seems to have foreclosed such a possibility in this study. However, one must question the meaning of reliabilities on factor analytically derived dimensions (factor analysis, by definition, groups related items together).

House and Dessler's validation of the task structure measure also helps the analyst link this study with others. If task structure is significantly correlated with occupational level, the paper partially indicates differences by organizational level. One might expect to find managers and the like in the low task structure category, blue-collar workers at the other extreme, and foremen in the middle. From this viewpoint the House and Dessler results are not inconsistent with those of Hill and Hunt (1973) and Nealey and Blood (1968); nor are they inconsistent with the theoretical arguments of Katz and Kahn (1966) and Mann (1965) in that different leader behaviors and managerial skills may be needed at different managerial levels. Yet none of these efforts were built on a path-goal model.

In a more general comparison with other perspectives of leadership this paper confirms some older suspicions and helps resolve some conflicting findings. As in a number of other studies, the task (instrumental) and human relations (supportive) aspects of leadership are identifiable but highly intercorrelated. Only when controlling for the opposite leadership dimension do the differential impacts of the dimensions clearly emerge. To the extent that consideration (supportive dimension) is dominant, yet highly intercorrelated with the task dimension, early findings calling for both high task and interpersonal activity can be reconciled with contingency approaches to leadership. Also, to the degree that the participative dimension is unrelated to satisfaction criteria but highly correlated with a human relations type dimension, the Ohio State Form XII Leader Behavior Description Questionnaire might not be substantially different from House's measures or those proposed by the Michigan group (see Yunker, 1972a). The substantial difference between the results for samples A and B also partially confirms the suspicion that leadership just might not be the base for a theory of employee performance and satisfaction (cf. Graen, Dansereau & Minami, 1972).

Most contingency models implicitly assume that leadership is an important independent variable and that "other" variables moderate the relationship between it and organizational outcomes. Here, as in the House and Dessler chapter, leadership is typically limited to vertical relations concerning policy implementation (see Katz & Kahn, 1966). Other activities of the manager including his lateral relations (see Osborn, Hunt, & Pope, in press) are frequently considered beyond the scope of leadership analysis. (Mann, 1965 and Mott, 1972 are, of course, exceptions.) Further, situational variables are not always viewed with the same rigor as are the measures of leadership. Sophisticated analysts would not think of equating LPC, and LBDQ, for example, but apparently little consideration is given to possible differences in impacts stemming from different non-leadership variables such as organizational structure and technology.

House and Dessler are also not alone in coming dangerously close to skipping pell-mell through the individual, average individual, group, subsystems, and organizational levels of analysis (see Hunt, Osborn, & Larson, 1973; Jun & Storm, 1973). While they do *not* argue that as expectancies increase group or organizational performance will change, they do attempt to fit Mott's (1972) study into their conceptual framework with little concern for the differences in the criteria. With these limitations, coupled with the unexciting R^2s and the disparities between the results for samples A and B, one must ask an important question. To what extent is the path-goal model applicable at the group, subsystems, and organizational levels of analysis? Certainly one would not argue that changes in individual psychological states would automatically raise group or organizational performance. This last criticism is not unique to the path-goal model. Again it is part of a larger problem in the leadership literature.

It appears that a series of models using leadership as a central focus is beginning to emerge. Unfortunately, each model seems restricted to a limited set of criteria and applicable at only one level of analysis. For example, House and Dessler confine their hypothesis testing to individual psychological states while Fiedler seems to concentrate on group performance. We are potentially faced with an entire series of incompatible models. Do we really need or want one theory of leadership for the individual level of analysis, another for groups, yet another for subsystems, and still another for organizations on top of different theories for different criteria?

Such need not be the case if one takes a broad perspective. Most of the current models seem to give at least passing reference to four sources of influence: the environment of the system, the internal structure and processes found within the system, the nature of the groups operating within the system, and the characteristics of individuals. Taylor's chapter, for example, shows the importance of conditions within the environment of the organization, and management's strategic responses to the environment. Pugh, Hickson, Hinings, & Turner (1969), Melcher (in press) and Woodward (1965) also stress the importance of technological factors and the structural configuration of the system. In terms of the House and Dessler presentation, perhaps these might be viewed as constraints upon the leader behavior of lower level managers or variables which significantly influence expectancies and satisfaction. For the organizations in the present paper these factors might partially explain why the participative dimension was generally unrelated to the criteria (i.e., no participation was allowed). In leadership terminology, these may be "substitutes for leadership" (Kerr, Schriesheim, Murphy, & Stodgill, 1974, in press).

In the prediction of individual psychological states one could logically question the importance of the organization's structure, technology, or adaptation to its environment. But in comparing results for average individual data across disparate organizations such information might be important in predicting subsystems outcomes. It may be particularly useful if the traditional definition of leadership (vertical relations concerning policy implementation) is used.

In summary, when is leadership important? When is it appropriate to view leadership as a moderating variable rather than an independent one? Do we need different models of leadership as we move from the individual to the organizational levels of analysis? Do we even want to stay with leadership-based theories of organizational states and outcomes?

General Discussion

The general discussion following the Taylor and House and Dessler chapters concentrated on the meaning and treatment of contingency model variables. In reference to the House and Dessler presentation a question was raised concerning the meaning of task structure. In the House-Dessler review of the theory and its a priori tests, what in the present study is called task structure is at various times measured as task ambiguity (House, 1973b) and task certainty (Dessler, 1973). The point was made that the present study treats ambiguity, task structure, and certainty as one single variable when perhaps they may represent three different variables. Amplification of this point indicated that, in terms of the path-goal model, the essential ingredient of all three variables was the same. The more variability, complexity, and ambiguity an individual faces the less psychological structure the individual will have. Therefore, the more that variability, complexity, and ambiguity increase the more the leader, or the organization through its mechanism, must do to offset this effect and complement the psychological state of the worker [see Hunt, Osborn, & Larson, 1973, Ch. 8 for a broader but related notion].

Discussion also centered on the meaning of the role clarity variable in the House-Dessler paper. Specifically, the question was raised as to how it differed from task structure and why task structure was treated as a moderating variable and role clarity was treated as a dependent variable in the model. House indicated that the task structure variable was task oriented and determined in large part by technological considerations and could be viewed in terms of technology as in the Taylor presentation. The role clarity variable (Rizzo, House, & Lirtzman, 1970) is more social in nature and deals with the clarity with which one perceives expectancies or what is expected of him by others and is, therefore, treated as a dependent variable. However, role clarity, if looked at in terms of personality (in the general sense) might be considered a moderating vehicle. For example, a recent study (Evans, 1972) using an internal-external personality classification (Porter & Lawler, 1968; Pryor & Distefano, 1971; Riesman, 1950; Rotter, 1966; Weiss & Sherman, 1973) found that people who perceive the world in an external manner respond less to leader considerate behavior than do people who perceive the world in an internal manner. In this case, role clarity, according to House, did function as a moderating variable.

Discussion shifted to measurement scales and cross-sample comparisons. The point was raised that there was a tendency for variables to be measured on continuous scales rather than categorically. This use of continuous scales assumes that the phenomenon being measured falls into one category or classification and that the scale used is measuring degrees of difference within that category. However, it could well be that the change being measured may not be a within-category change but instead is a change from one category to another and therefore is not appropriately measured by the continuous scales. For example, in considering technology one might argue that a job shop process and a mass production process are separate and distinct categories and are not opposite ends of a continuum. A second example can be found in the House-Dessler chapter which reports an increase in task complexity between occupations. The question becomes one of determining if this is a matter of degree of complexity within a category or a difference in complexity between two different categories of occupations. If one were to factor, for example, the task scale, would we find several categorical factors?

House responded that in an earlier paper Dessler (1973) categorized people by occupational level and the results were similar to those reported in the House-Dessler chapter. However, he suggested that a problem arises in that it becomes difficult to generalize to other samples unless one has similar classifications. Frequently, occupational level and job title are unique to the organization, making comparisons difficult. He went on to suggest that if we could develop a classification that could be described with some degree of theoretical generality we could then go to other organizations and study the same phenomenon. However, it was suggested that until we find such a variable, we will have to rely on such tools as the task scales.

A response suggested that the search for this theoretical variable may be obscuring a wealth of information in the data mix with which we now work. This point led to an amplification of the comparisons between samples and the generalizability of current studies. House suggested that if we could find unique factors such as the recent intervention of a union into a company we could get more explanatory value out of our data, but it would be of little value unless we could look at other samples that also have had a recent intervention of the same type.

Taylor commented that he has experienced similar problems in attempting to bring together data from a number of organizations. He suggested that there is a strong tendency to deal with cases one at a time because they tend to be unique in a wide variety of ways. Taylor also pointed out that an additional problem with the organizations used in his study is that they are probably not representative of American industry. If anything, they are representative of organizations that have come to the Institute for Social Research over a period of time and have been willing to undertake study and research. However, given these limitations, attempts were made to categorize them into those that were relatively well off in terms of market position, etc. and those that were in trouble.

At this point a question pertaining to the appropriate level of analysis raised by Osborn in his formal remarks was brought out in the general discussion. It represented the first of numerous times during the symposium that the level of analysis question would be discussed. This discussion was directed toward the House and Dessler paper and asked why the path-goal model did not concentrate more on the influence of such variables as group process or environmental issues. House responded that it was a matter of personal choice for the researcher. He personally preferred to look at those things he could measure more precisely in an attempt to prove current theories. However, he pointed out that it did depend upon the situation. If, for example, one were a consultant for an organization and there were no variance in technology within the organization but there was a good deal of variance in the environment then he would not be inclined to test theories on environment.

3

Leadership and Supervision in the Informal Organization

GEORGE F. FARRIS

Most research reports are written in a hypothetical-deductive fashion. After years of careful thinking and perusal of the literature, the author develops a theoretical framework from which hypotheses are derived. He then develops operational definitions of his theoretical constructs and designs a study to test his hypotheses. I say that reports are *written* in that fashion, but I suspect that often they are not actually produced in quite so orderly a manner. Such is the case with the report I am about to present to you.

The report itself begins with a point of view about leadership. It suggests that there is much to be learned by considering leadership as a process of influence. This framework appears to lead to concepts of four supervisory styles and statements of conditions under which each may be more appropriate. Empirical research on supervision in the informal organization of scientists and engineers is then presented which yields results consistent with part of the framework.

But things did not happen that way. The true sequence of events is nearly the reverse! For several years one thrust of my research has attempted to identify factors which characterize a stimulating working environment for a scientist or engineer. Among the factors examined were the practices of the technical supervisor. Moreover, the "informal organization" seemed to be a good way to conceptualize the interactions among technical people and their supervisors which were found to stimulate technical performance. A framework was developed to describe the informal organization, leading to statements about "colleague role networks" in innovative groups and leaders in the informal organization. Further reflection resulted in a general framework which considers leadership in terms of influence. Finally, this point of view on leadership led me to suggest that our understanding of leadership could be advanced by treating three aspects of influence: its amount, its distribution, and qualitative characteristics of the influence process.

LEADERSHIP AS INFLUENCE

Most theories of leadership which define the term *leadership* equate it with some aspect of influence on task accomplishment or on other persons. For example, Hemphill and Coons (1957), tentatively defined leadership as "the behavior of an individual when he is directing the activities of a group toward a shared goal [p. 7]." Fiedler (1964) defined the leader as "the individual in the group who directs and coordinates task relevant group activities, or who, in the absence of a designated leader, automatically performs these functions in the group [p. 153]." Katz and Kahn (1966) defined leadership as "any act of influence on a matter of organizational relevance [p. 334]." Recently Jacobs (1970) considered leadership to be "an interaction between persons in which one presents information of a sort and in such a manner that the other becomes convinced that his outcomes (benefits/costs ratio) will be improved if he behaves in the manner suggested or desired [p. 323]."

Such definitions of leadership in terms of influence imply that leadership theory and research should be concerned with at least three types of questions: 1) How much influence is exerted? 2) How is influence distributed among group members? 3) What characterizes the process of distributing influence among group members?

The first type of question asks whether leadership is present at all in a given situation. In terms of the above definitions, is any individual "directing the activities of a group toward a shared goal," "directing and coordinating task-relevant group activities," influencing a matter of organizational relevance," or interacting in such a manner that another individual "becomes convinced that his outcomes (benefits/costs ratio) will be improved"?

The second type of question asks *where* leadership is present in a given situation. To what degree is each of the individuals potentially involved in a given situation actually directing activities, influencing matters of organizational relevance, or convincing others of improved outcomes? What characterizes those individuals exerting relatively great or relatively little leadership?

The first two questions deal with quantitative aspects of leadership, asking how much there is and how much given individuals exercise. The third question asks about qualities of the leadership process. In what ways do individuals direct activities, influence matters of organizational relevance, or convince others of improved outcomes?

The above types of questions are necessary to describe the leadership process. In addition, leadership theory and research may be concerned with the question of leadership effectiveness. The three types of questions then become transposed as follows. For greater effectiveness, 1) How much influence should be exerted? 2) How should influence be distributed among group members? 3) How should the process of distributing influence among group members be characterized?

It is my impression that past theory and research on leadership has concentrated on the third question, attempting to identify characteristics of the leadership process which relate to greater effectiveness. For example, the Ohio State studies (Fleishman, 1973) identified consideration and initiating structure in leadership behavior; the early Michigan studies (Likert, 1961) were concerned with employee orientation and production orientation. A similar emphasis on the leadership process is apparent in Bowers and Seashore's (1966) four factors of support, interaction facilitation, goal emphasis, and work facilitation; in Katz and Kahn's (1966) discussion of origination, interpolation, and administration; in Jacobs's (1970) exchange theory; and in House's (1973b) path-goal theory.

The second question—that of the distribution of influence among group members—has received considerably less systematic attention in leadership theory and research. Work on related problems has considered the matter, however. Tannenbaum's (1968) control graph conceptualizes the amount of influence which people at different hierarchical levels of an organization are perceived to exert on organizational activities. Bales's (1950) and Benne and Sheat's (1948) early work considered task and group maintenance roles which can be performed by any member of a group to influence its decision-making activities. The investigations of closeness of supervision in the early Michigan work (Kahn & Katz, 1960) were concerned with one aspect of the distribution of influence. The one theory of leadership which explicitly discussed the distribution of influence among group members was Bowers and Seashore's (1966). In their theory and research, they carefully distinguish between "managerial leadership" and "peer leadership," and in their research they examine the relationship of each type of leadership to the other and to their criteria of performance and satisfaction. [A recent study by Reaser (1972) also examined this question.]

Finally, we should note that Katz and Kahn (1966) recognize the importance of the distribution of influence, stating, "Perhaps the most persistent and thoroughly demonstrated difference between successful and unsuccessful leadership at all three levels has to do with the distribution or sharing of the leadership function [pp. 331–332]." Despite this assertion, however, Katz and Kahn's chapter on leadership does not cite the evidence which led to it, nor does their theory of leadership explicitly consider the way in which influence is distributed.

The characteristics of influential group members and successful leaders have been studied for many years. The early work of those following a trait approach to leadership attempted to identify characteristics of those individuals who exert relatively great leadership. Fiedler's (1967) more recent and more sophisticated theory proposes a framework for understanding how a leader's personality attributes affect group performance.

The first question—how much influence is exerted—has not to my knowledge been addressed directly in leadership theory and research. Katz and Kahn's (1966) definition of leadership as "any act of influence on a matter of organizational relevance" opens the door for consideration of whether or not leadership occurs regarding a particular matter. Their classification of leadership acts in terms of their effect on organizational structure suggests three general areas in which influence may be exerted—origination, interpolation, and use of structure—but their open systems leadership theory only begins to consider systematically the consequences of leadership or lack of it in each area. In view of Katz and Kahn's (1966) assertion that "an organization properly designed for its purpose will not function adequately without acts of leadership [p. 334]," it would be important to address research and theory more systematically to the consequences of leadership on organizational functioning.

To sum up, many leadership theories consider leadership to involve influence, implying that three aspects of influence should be considered: its amount, its distribution, and qualitative characteristics of the influence process. Despite the importance of the first two questions, most work on leadership has concentrated on the third, dealing with qualities of the leadership process and characteristics of the formal leader. Some attention in research has been paid to the distribution of influence among group members, but leadership theory could treat these phenomena more systematically. Although open systems theories imply that it is important to know whether or not leadership is exerted on particular matters of organizational relevance, leadership theory and research have yet to do justice to this question.

A LEADERSHIP FRAMEWORK

Four Supervisory Styles

If leadership involves influence on matters of organizational relevance, it can be exerted by any person, inside or outside of a formal organization. The person exerting leadership may or may not be in a managerial position. I shall use the term *supervision* to refer to the behavior of persons assigned to managerial positions in a formal organization. My use of supervision is essentially the same as Jacobs's (1970) term *superordinate behavior*.

Let us consider a supervisor and a single group member or subordinate who reports to him in an organization. (A similar analysis can be applied to leadership involving other subsets of people in an organization.) In working on a matter of organizational relevance, the supervisor may exercise relatively high or low influence himself, and through his behavior he may allow his subordinate to have relatively great or relatively little influence. (See Figure 2.) Thus, four pure styles of supervision are possible.

When both the supervisor and group member have substantial influence on the matter, the supervisory style may be said to be one of *collaboration*. Leadership regarding this particular matter of organizational relevance is shared by the supervisor and group member.

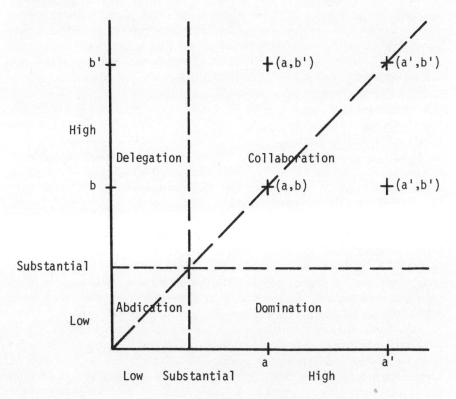

Fig. 2. Supervisory styles and influence on a matter of organizational relevance.

When the supervisor has substantial influence and the group member does not, the supervisory style may be said to be one of *domination*. Leadership regarding this matter is exercised chiefly by the supervisor.

When the supervisor does not have substantial influence on a matter of organizational relevance but the group member does, the supervisory style may be termed *delegation*. Leadership regarding this matter is exercised chiefly by the group member.

Finally, when neither the supervisor nor the group member has substantial influence on a matter of organizational relevance, the supervisory style may be called one of *abdication*. Very little leadership occurs at all regarding this matter, unless influence is exercised by someone other than the supervisor and the group member being considered.

The questions about the existence and distribution of leadership are readily answerable in terms of this framework. With supervisory styles of collaboration, domination, and delegation, influence is exerted and leadership occurs regarding the matter of organizational relevance. With a supervisory style of abdication, essentially no leadership takes place. With a style of collaboration, influence may be distributed equally between supervisor and subordinate, or one may have greater influence than the other. The important point is that both exercise substantial influence. With a style of domination, the supervisor has greater influence and with delegation, the group member is more influential. In each instance, essentially only one person exerts substantial influence.

The framework assumes that the amount of influence regarding a particular matter is not fixed. The supervisor need not gain influence at the expense of the group member. Rather, he may increase his influence without the influence of the group member being affected, and he may do this regardless of the supervisory style currently being used. In Figure 2, for example, a supervisor may increase his influence from a to a′, while the group member's influence may remain at b. The total leadership on this matter of organizational relevance would thus increase. The supervisory style would still be one of collaboration at both points (a,b) and (a′,b) in Figure 2. In each case the supervisor and the group member both exert substantial leadership on the matter of organizational relevance.

In a similar manner, the supervisory style would remain collaborative if the group member's influence increased from b to b′ in Figure 2. If both the supervisor and the group member increased their influence on the matter of organizational relevance, the total amount of leadership on the matter would increase even more. In Figure 2, more leadership is exercised at point (a′,b′) than at either point (a′,b) or (a,b′).

Close and General Supervision Reconsidered

One thrust of the early Michigan work on supervision (Kahn & Katz, 1960), contrasted close supervision with general supervision. In terms of the framework advanced here, this research contrasted high and low supervisory influence on the achievement of work goals. In the case of high supervisory influence resulting from close supervision, the supervisory style was probably one of domination. If subordinate influence was also substantial it could have been collaboration. In the case of low supervisory influence resulting from general supervision, the supervisory style could have been either abdication or delegation, depending on the amount of influence exercised by group members.

A related thrust examined relationships between group member participation and performance. In terms of the present framework, this research contrasted high and low group member influence on the achievement of work goals. In the case of high group member participation, the supervisory style could have been one of delegation and collaboration, depending on the supervisor's own influence. In the case of low group member participation, the supervisory style could have been domination or abdication, also depending on the supervisor's own influence.

Thus in both the studies of closeness of supervision and group member participation, it is not completely clear which supervisory styles were actually being compared. The results obtained in both cases could have been due to the supervisor's degree of influence, the group member's degree of influence, or some combination of the two. The framework advanced here may help to determine whether general supervision is actually delegation or abdication in a particular situation and whether participation implies delegation or collaboration. Moreover, the framework permits separation of these issues of the distribution of influence from the prior question of whether influence is exercised at all. Perhaps the most important factor for task accomplishment is not who exercises influence, but simply that it be exercised by someone.

Some Tentative Hypotheses

Two types of hypotheses may be advanced concerning the amount and distribution of leadership: "one best way" hypotheses and contingency hypotheses. The former are concerned with the question of which supervisory style is most effective on the average, while the latter are concerned with defining conditions under which each style is apt to be most effective.

At least three hypotheses regarding leadership effectiveness may be advanced. Two are concerned with the amount of leadership, while the third is concerned with its distribution.

The total influence hypothesis suggests that greater influence is associated with greater effectiveness. For all matters of organizational relevance, collaboration is probably the best supervisory style, since with collaboration, total influence is apt to be greatest. Support for this total influence hypothesis comes from consistent findings of positive relationships between total amount of influence and effectiveness of organizational units (Tannenbaum, 1968). Bowers and Seashore's (1966) complex set of findings regarding the relationships between managerial leadership, peer leadership, satisfaction, and effectiveness could perhaps also be considered to be supportive of a total influence hypothesis.

The substantial influence hypothesis suggests that only a substantial amount of influence need be exercised by some party for effective handling of a matter of organizational relevance. As with satisficing in decision making, only a minimal amount of influence has to be exerted for a matter to be dealt with adequately. Additional influence, over and above the minimally substantial amount, not only adds nothing to the execution of the matter of organizational relevance; it also is deleterious to the organization in that it drains away scarce resources which could be better applied elsewhere. Thus domination or delegation will always be superior supervisory styles. I am not aware of any research which supports this hypothesis, and the research cited above regarding total influence could be interpreted as contrary to a substantial influence hypothesis.

The egalitarian hypothesis suggests that performance and satisfaction are higher when leadership is distributed equally among all the relevant parties—for nearly all matters of organizational relevance. Only in cases of very routine tasks or very high time constraints is a more authoritarian distribution of leadership more appropriate. Thus, the best supervisory style is collaboration, with all parties having substantial and equal influence. The egalitarian hypothesis underlies such principles of democracy as "one man, one vote" and majority rule. It was supported to a degree, especially regarding satisfaction, by some studies of small group problem solving (Collins & Guetzkow, 1964; Hoffman, 1965). In Tannenbaum's (1968) studies of distribution of influence in organizations, the egalitarian hypothesis received considerably less support.

Under certain conditions it may be more appropriate for an individual to exert leadership. One of these is his competence to deal with the matter at hand. Farris and Butterfield (1972) suggested that the most parsimonious explanation of relationships between control and effectiveness of Brazilian development finance institutions was that in the more effective institutions, competence and control went hand in hand. Those individuals who were more competent had more influence in decision making. A second condition is the importance of acceptance of the outcome of the leadership. A consistent finding in studies of decision making in small groups (e.g.,

Collins & Geutzkow, 1964; Hoffman, 1965) is that individuals are more apt to accept and implement decisions which they have greater influence in making. A third condition is the presence of time pressure. For many tasks an individual acting alone can make a satisfactory decision faster than a group. Experimental studies of communications networks (Collins & Guetzkow, 1964; Glanzer and Glaser, 1959) have shown that more centralized networks, in which a single individual has much greater influence than the rest of the group, are faster than less centralized networks working on the same task.

Thus, the appropriateness of a supervisory style may be hypothesized to be contingent upon five factors: the supervisor's competence regarding the matter, the group member's competence regarding the matter, the importance of acceptance by the supervisor of the results of leadership on the matter, the importance of acceptance by the group member of the results of leadership on the matter, and the presence of time pressure. Figure 3 summarizes some of the ways in which these factors interact to determine which style is more appropriate. The first factors to be considered have to do with the competence of the supervisor and group member to deal with the matter of organizational relevance. If both are competent to exert leadership regarding it, then collaboration, domination, or delegation could be an appropriate supervisory style to employ. If the supervisor is competent but the group member is not, then domination is most appropriate. If the group member is competent but the supervisor is not, then delegation is most appropriate. If neither is competent, then abdication is the appropriate style, and the matter should be dealt with elsewhere in the organization.

If both the supervisor and the group member are competent to exert leadership regarding the matter, the importance of acceptance of the results of this leadership becomes a key determinant of the appropriate supervisory style to employ. If it is important that both the supervisor and the group member accept the results of the leadership, then collaboration is the appropriate style. If acceptance by the supervisor but not the group member is important, then collaboration or domination is appropriate. If acceptance by the group member but not the supervisor is important, then collaboration or delegation is appropriate. If acceptance by neither is important, then collaboration, domination, or delegation may be appropriate. If time pressure is high so that the matter must be dealt with quickly, then domination or delegation are preferred alternatives, since the time necessary for both parties to influence the matter may be prohibitive.

In summary, leadership as commonly defined involves acts of influence on matters of organizational relevance. A framework was advanced which considers four supervisory styles—collaboration, domination, delegation, and abdication—which describe the amount and distribution of influence. Tentative hypotheses were advanced regarding the best supervisory style

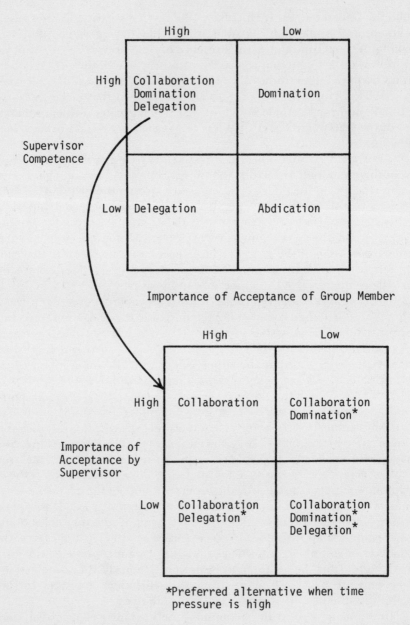

Fig. 3. Five-factor contingency hypothesis.

for leadership effectiveness and conditions under which each style may be more appropriate. A total influence hypothesis and an egalitarian hypothesis suggested a collaborative supervisory style is best on the average; a substantial influence hypothesis suggested that domination and delegation are superior to collaboration. A five-factor contingency hypothesis proposed that the appropriate supervisory style depends on supervisory and group member competence, the importance of acceptance of the results of leadership by the supervisor and group member, and the degree of time pressure present.

Now let us turn to studies of leadership and supervision in the informal organization of a research laboratory. Following a description of these studies, the findings will be related to the hypotheses just advanced.

EXPLORATORY RESEARCH ON LEADERSHIP

For the past several years I have been involved in a program of research on organizational factors which motivate performance of scientists and engineers. In all over 2,000 technical personnel from 14 university, industrial, and government organizations have participated in the research investigations. From the factors identified in the earlier work (Pelz & Andrews, 1966) it seemed likely that the technical supervisor could have important effects on the performance of the people reporting to him. Much of our recent work has focused on the role of the technical supervisor. Let me summarize highlights of three of these studies (Andrews & Farris, 1967; Farris, 1971; Farris, 1972).

Study 1: Supervisory Practices and Innovation

We began our investigation of technical supervision by pragmatically employing the concepts and research methods which were predominant in leadership theory and research at that time. Nonsupervisors were asked to describe their supervisors on 36 items asking about a variety of supervisory practices suggested by previous research and theory. Interrelationships among these items were determined, and ten measures of supervisory practices were derived with the help of a Guttman-Lingoes Smallest Space Analysis (Guttman, 1967; Lingoes, 1965). Three of these measures were concerned with task functions, three with human relations functions, two with administrative functions, and two with leadership styles of consultation and provision of freedom.

The study was conducted in a division of a NASA research center involved in research, development, and technical services. The work of the laboratory ranged from basic research on physical and chemical processes to atmospheric and deep space experiments employing rockets and satellites. Twenty-one groups participated in the study, containing a median of five members excluding the supervisor. Performance was measured by asking supervisors and senior level nonsupervisors to rank order the professionals with whose work they were familiar on *innovation*—the extent the person's work had "increased knowledge in his field through lines of research or development which were useful and new." An average of 4.4 judges assessed the work of each individual. Since interjudge agreement was reasonably good, their evaluations were combined into a single percentile score for each person. Group averages on innovation and each measure of supervisory practices were calculated after it was determined that differences between groups exceeded differences within groups on these measures. (For details, see Andrews & Farris, 1967).

Supervisory practices as seen by subordinates were then related to group innovation as judged by senior scientists. In general, we found a positive relationship between innovation and task functions, a curvilinear relationship between innovation and human relations functions with highest innovation tending to occur under supervisors moderate in human relations functions, and a negative relationship between innovation and the supervisor's administrative functions. The two measures of leadership style—provision of freedom and use of consultation—were only moderately associated with innovation. For both measures innovation was higher when supervisors scored either high or low than if they scored in the middle.

In addition to examining these simple relationships between supervisory practices and innovation, we investigated relationships involving combinations of supervisory practices, with some interesting results. First, with regard to freedom, we found something very consistent with the notion that influence and competence should go hand in hand. For supervisors low in task, human relations, and administrative functions, provision of freedom showed substantial positive relationships with innovation. For supervisors rated high in these competences, provision of freedom mattered less, and sometimes related negatively. These differences were quite pronounced; for example, for supervisors high in technical skills, provision of freedom correlated .0 with innovation; for supervisors low in technical skills, provision of freedom correlated .6 with innovation.

Consistent with this pattern, technical competence of the supervisor served as an important moderator of relationships between innovation and critical evaluation. For supervisors high in technical skills, the correlation between critical evaluation and innovation was +.5; for supervisors low in technical skills, it was −.5.

Moreover, in contrast to the notion proposed by Kahn (1956), Oaklander and Fleishman (1964), Blake and Mouton (1964) and others, we found no evidence that innovation was higher when supervisors were high in both task and human relations functions. Human relations skills had little moderating effect on the generally positive relationships between task functions and innovation, and vice versa.

Finally, consistent with the total influence hypothesis, we found that provision of freedom for subordinates was positively related to innovation when the supervisor preceded his own decision making with consultation with subordinates (correlation of +.7). Among supervisors making little use of consultation, however, provision of freedom was uncorrelated with innovation (correlation of −.1), suggesting lower total influence.

Two sets of findings in this study surprised us. First, human relations functions were unrelated to innovation, unlike relationships found between human relations skills and other criteria in previous investigations. Our failure to find a relationship may have been due to the nature of the tasks of the technical personnel (as suggested by Fiedler, 1964 and Hunt, 1967), differences in people studied (scientists vs. rank and file workers), or the use of a different criterion—innovation. Second, administrative functions were related to innovation negatively, suggesting that administration may interfere with innovation or that innovation may interfere with administration. Perhaps the results occurred because we were studying lower levels of supervision where skill mix theory (Mann, 1965) says administrative skills are less important.

On a positive side, this study demonstrates that characteristics of technical supervisors are indeed related to subordinate innovation. Two characteristics seem to be especially important: the supervisor's technical competence and the conditions under which freedom is provided to subordinates. Both of these factors were followed up in subsequent research.

A Colleague Role Model of Leadership in the Informal Organization

The findings of the study of supervisory practices and innovation suggested that it would be important to understand more fully the process through which technical supervisors utilize their technical skills to influence the problem solving of their subordinates. At the same time, other findings showing that higher performing technical personnel were in greater contact with their colleagues (Farris, 1969; Pelz & Andrews, 1966) suggested that it would also be important to understand the process through which scientists interact with one another in their technical problem solving. A search of the literature on group problem solving (especially Hoffman, 1961 and Maier, 1967) and technical communications (especially Allen & Cohen, 1969; and Pelz & Andrews, 1966) led to the development of a rough model of the technical problem solving process.

The model considers three general stages: a suggestion stage in which a person comes up with an idea, a proposal stage in which the idea is developed into a concrete scheme for action; and a solution stage, in which a decision is reached for the organization to proceed in a particular way. Throughout this process colleagues can help one another by playing colleague roles—performing activities which facilitate the problem solving of another professional. Seven colleague roles are considered, each of which is theoretically more apt to occur at one of the three stages. Providing original ideas, technical information, and organizational information are colleague roles which may help a scientist to form a suggestion. Help in thinking through a problem and critical evaluation may help the scientist to shape the suggestion into a proposal. And assuring a fair hearing and providing administrative help are colleague roles which may help to turn the proposal into a solution which is implemented in the organization. With the possible exception of the role of providing administrative help, these colleague roles are rarely specified in technical people's formal job descriptions. Hence a mapping of the colleague role relationships among members of an organization may be considered to be a description of the informal organization.

This colleague role model of the informal organization is also a process model of leadership as influence. Any person who plays a colleague role may be considered to be exerting substantial leadership. The question of the amount of leadership, raised in the beginning of this paper, may be answered by counting the number of colleagues who are useful to one another. The question of the distribution of leadership may be answered by contrasting the colleague role playing of the supervisor with that of group members. The colleague roles themselves provide a cognitive model of characteristics of the process of distributing influence.

In addition to suggesting conceptual ways to answer the questions of the amount, distribution, and process of leadership, the colleague role model implies that sociometric research methods can be used to investigate leadership and supervision. Members of an organization can be asked to name individuals who have been useful to them for the seven colleague roles. Substantial leadership can be operationally defined as occurring when an individual is named by a colleague as helpful for a colleague role. Similarly, the total amount of leadership can be measured by counting the number of times individuals are named by their colleagues for playing the various colleague roles. From this information it is possible to do several things. For example, "role networks" can be mapped showing who influences whom by doing such things as providing original ideas. Peer leadership (Bowers & Seashore, 1966) can be examined by noting the roles through which peers influence one another. Supervision can be investigated by noting the extent to which supervisors are named for playing each colleague role. Informal leaders for each role can be identified by noting members of the organization who are often named by their colleagues for playing each role.

The second and third studies of technical supervision illustrate the application of the colleague role model of the informal organization to the study of leadership as influence. The first of these investigated the principal roles through which colleagues influenced one another and identified characteristics of those colleagues who were the most influential (Farris, 1971; Swain, 1971). The second contrasted leadership in relatively more and less innovative groups (Farris, 1972).

Study 2: Characteristics of Leadership and Leaders

This study was carried out five years later in the same NASA organization as study 1. About 70% of the participants were the same. One hundred seventeen professionals including twenty supervisors participated, a 98% response rate. They were asked to name individuals who had been helpful to them for each of the seven colleague roles. As many individuals as they wished could be named for each role, and the same individual could be named for more than one role. In addition, performance was measured in a manner similar to that of study 1, and participants described several characteristics of their working environments on paper and pencil questionnaires.

Sociograms were plotted for each of the colleague roles in order to determine leadership networks for each characteristic of the influence process. One sociogram showed who named whom as useful for help in thinking about a problem. Over half of the choices were directed to peers rather than supervisors. Twenty-eight reciprocal choices were made. Thirty-five choices were made outside the division but within the research center, and an additional thirty choices were made outside the research center.

In contrast, another sociogram showed who named whom as helpful for providing administrative help and resources. Supervisors within the division received 76% of the choices for this role. Only three reciprocal choices were made. Very few choices occurred outside the division except for some by members of one branch heavily involved in providing support to other divisions within the center.

Supervisors were named often as helpful for all colleague roles. As Table 14 indicates, however, there were differences between roles in the extent to which supervisors were named as helpful to their colleagues. They received the greatest percentage of mentions for roles of a more administrative nature, reaching a high of 76% for the role of providing administrative help. They were mentioned relatively less often for more technical roles, reaching a low of 42% for the role of being helpful for original ideas.

Intercorrelations were determined among the colleague roles based on a lognormal transformation of the number of times individuals were mentioned for each role. Shared variances ranged from a high of 75% for "help

TABLE 14
*Number of Times Supervisor and Nonsupervisor
Listed as Helpful for Colleague Roles*

Role	Average number per supervisor	Average number per nonsupervisor	Percent to supervisors
Technical information	5.2	1.5	42
Help in thinking	5.4	1.2	48
Critical evaluation	5.4	0.9	55
Original ideas	3.1	0.9	42
Fair hearing	4.1	0.3	72
Administrative help	5.7	0.4	76
Division developments	6.8	1.0	59

SOURCE: Farris, 1973, with permission of *Technology Review*, edited at the Massachusetts Institute of Technology.

in thinking" and "critical evaluation" to a low of 16% for "original ideas" and "learning about developments in the organization." Factor analyses were performed on the data from the total sample using the principal components solution with varimax (orthogonal) rotation. Four factors were rotated and identified as technical, administrative, information, and ideas. When three factors were rotated, the ideas role loaded highly on the technical factor; when two factors were rotated, the information role also loaded highly on the technical factor. Quite similar results occurred when factor analyses were performed separately for nonsupervisors and supervisors.

These findings using sociometric data do not diverge greatly from findings based on Likert-type scales. Both measurement techniques have yielded technical and administrative factors to characterize aspects of the leadership process. The differences between supervisors and nonsupervisors in colleague role playing are readily explainable in terms of the formal role requirements of the supervisor to perform administrative functions and the NASA organization's emphasis on technical competence as a basis for promotion to supervisor. The analysis of the "help in thinking" and "administrative help" sociograms regarding reciprocal choices, choices of supervisors, and choices of people outside the division is consistent with these interpretations.

The "leaders" in the informal organization of the NASA organization—those persons named most often by their colleagues as helpful for each colleague role—were contrasted with the remainder of the scientists in the division. The top 15% for each factor were defined arbitrarily as informal leaders. Comparisons were made separately for the total sample and for nonsupervisors alone, for the most part with similar results. To a great extent, findings were also similar for the seven colleague roles.

In contrast to the remainder of the scientists in the division, the leaders in the informal organization differed in certain skills, motives, rewards, and characteristics of the working environment. Leaders had been and continued to be higher performers on criteria of innovation, productiveness, and especially usefulness in the organization. They saw others as having greater confidence in their abilities and they scored slightly higher on the Remote Associates Test of creative ability. The leaders in the informal organization felt more involved in their work. They tended to place greater emphasis on working with competent colleagues and less on working with congenial colleagues. They derived greater satisfaction from helping personnel to grow and develop. The leaders in the informal organization, especially the supervisors, were paid more and saw greater opportunities for advancement. The leaders talked to more people, receiving help as well as giving it. They felt more free to carry out their own ideas and more influential on their work goals. They also experienced greater time pressure.

To sum up, the leaders in the informal organization were more technically competent, more motivated by the technical aspects of their work, better rewarded, in more active contact with their colleagues, and more influential regarding their own work. Some of these characteristics were individual traits, not unlike those studies in the earlier trait approach to leadership; other characteristics of these informal leaders, however, were to a great extent a function of the particular environments in which they worked.

Study 3: Leadership In Innovative Groups

Are there differences in the informal organizations of more and less innovative groups? If so, to what extent do these differences occur in roles played by supervisors, group members, and people outside the groups? When innovation is the criterion of performance, which roles should characterize managerial leadership and peer leadership (Bowers & Seashore, 1966)?

An exploratory study of fourteen groups in the NASA laboratory investigated these questions. Groups averaged 6.2 members, excluding the supervisor. Innovation of individual group members was evaluated in the same manner as in the previous studies by an average of 7.6 judges, and group innovation scores were determined by averaging the scores of the individual members. The seven most innovative groups were compared with the seven least innovative groups in the colleague roles played by supervisors, group members, and outsiders for one another. Despite the small

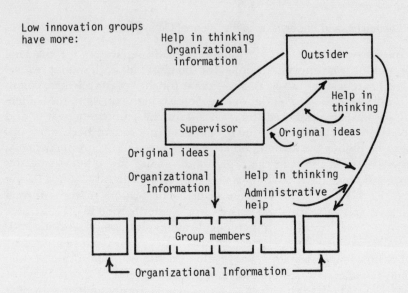

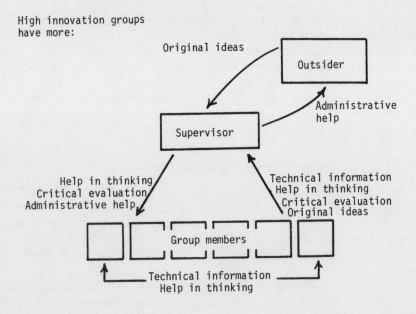

Fig. 4. Colleague roles in more and less innovative groups. (Adapted from Farris, 1973, with permission of *Technology Review*, edited at the Massachusetts Institute of Technology.)

number of groups, some consistent patterns of leadership in the informal organization emerged. See Figure 4.

In the more innovative groups the members appeared to collaborate more with one another in their technical problem solving. They named fellow group members more often as useful to them for providing technical information and help in thinking about technical problems. In the less innovative groups, on the other hand, members named one another less often as helpful, except for one colleague role: providing information about developments elsewhere in the organization.

Consistent with these differences in the peer leadership in more and less innovative groups, the more innovative groups received relatively little help from professionals outside their groups. On the other hand, members of the less innovative groups found outsiders especially useful for help in thinking about technical problems and administrative help. Apparently the more innovative groups were more cohesive.

Moreover, there were differences in managerial leadership between the more and less innovative groups. In the more innovative groups the supervisors exercised more leadership—but by playing particular colleague roles. They were especially useful to group members for critical evaluation, administrative help, and help in thinking about technical problems. In addition, group members were more helpful to these supervisors for providing technical information, help in thinking about technical problems, critical evaluation, and original ideas.

In the less innovative groups the supervisors were much less active in the informal organization. They were named more often by their groups than supervisors of more innovative groups for only two roles: original ideas and organizational information. Perhaps members of the less innovative groups were often working on their supervisors' ideas rather than their own. There were no roles at all for which members of the less innovative groups were more helpful to their supervisors than were their counterparts in more innovative groups to their supervisors.

As in the case of the group members, the supervisors of the less innovative groups collaborated more actively with outsiders than did the supervisors of the more innovative groups. Supervisors of less innovative groups were more helpful to outsiders for original ideas and help in thinking, while outsiders were more useful to them for providing help in thinking and organizational information. Supervisors of more innovative groups named more outsiders as helpful for only one role—providing original ideas, and outsiders named them more often only for administrative help.

In short, the more innovative groups appeared to operate more as teams, having greater peer and managerial leadership. The less innovative groups appeared to operate less as teams, having less peer and managerial leadership, and collaborating more with professionals outside their groups.

The supervisors of the less innovative groups were apt to exercise leadership by providing original ideas to group members and outsiders. These supervisors scored higher on the Remote Associates Test of creative ability than did the supervisors of the more innovative groups, but the performance of the two sets of supervisors was rated equally high in usefulness to the organization. Supervisors of more innovative groups were apt to exercise leadership by playing colleague roles, such as providing critical evaluation, which theoretically should help group members shape their own suggestions into proposals and solutions.

THE FRAMEWORK AND THE RESEARCH

As stated in the introduction to this paper, the leadership-as-influence framework was developed after the three research studies on leadership and supervision in the informal organization had been completed. Because these studies heavily influenced the development of the framework, several of the research findings are relevant to it. Let us turn to them now, bearing in mind that the framework was developed in part to help interpret such findings after the fact, not to predict them. A logical next step would involve research designed specifically to test hypotheses developed within the leadership-as-influence framework.

One-Best-Way Hypotheses

Three tentative "one best way" hypotheses were suggested regarding the amount and distribution of influence: the total influence hypothesis, the substantial influence hypothesis, and the egalitarian hypothesis. For different reasons the total influence hypothesis and the egalitarian hypothesis suggested that a collaborative supervisory style is best on the average. The substantial influence hypothesis suggested either domination or delegation.

The findings in the three studies seem to be most consistent with the notion that innovation is related to a collaborative supervisory style in which both the supervisor and the group members have substantial influence. In both studies of group innovation, the supervisors apparently exercised substantial leadership. Their skills were related to group innovation, and they were very active in the informal organizations of the more innovative groups, especially in playing colleague roles which involve reacting to subordinates' ideas. Group member influence also appeared to be associated with innovation. Members of the more innovative groups were frequently named as being useful for original ideas and several other technical roles.

Other findings could be interpreted to mean that domination is not associated with innovation. If being useful for original ideas can indicate domination, then the supervisors of the less innovative groups may have been dominating their technical activity. The first study indicated that a less skilled supervisor's failure to provide freedom—and perhaps to dominate through this failure—was associated with lower innovation.

If collaboration is the best supervisory style on the average, then, is this because more total influence is exercised or because leadership is distributed relatively equally? The data in the three studies do not lend themselves to a direct answer to this question, since no attempt was made to quantitatively assess the overall influence exercised by each party. Some of the findings of the studies suggest that qualitative characteristics of the distribution of influence may also have been important.

The overall pattern of results was quite consistent with Maier's (1967) theory of group problem solving. He suggested that a group is most apt to be successful when its leader performs an integrative function analogous to that of the nerve ring of the starfish. He does not dominate the discussion and produce the solution, but instead serves as an integrator by receiving information, facilitating communication among group members, relaying messages, and integrating ideas so that a single unified solution can occur. Moreover, "the idea-getting process should be separated from the idea-evaluation process because the latter inhibits the former [Maier, 1963, p. 247]."

In the more innovative groups the supervisors tended to behave very much as Maier said they should. They were named more often by their groups as useful for facilitating thinking and providing critical evaluation, two roles which can be considered integrative functions. Moreover, they received original ideas from more sources outside the group, probably relaying them to group members as appropriate. Equally important, the supervisors of the more innovative groups were seen as less useful for their own original ideas. Thus, they were probably less apt to impose their own ideas on their groups, an activity which Maier argues strongly will inhibit group innovation. Probably this situation also represented a considerable degree of separation of evaluation from the production of ideas. The supervisors of the more innovative groups were more useful for critical evaluation, but the ideas they evaluated tended to come more often from other sources—outsiders or group members.

Intriguing as these speculations are, they must be regarded as tentative due to the small number of groups in the studies. Moreover, the finding that a collaborative supervisory style seemed to work best on the average may have been due to a fortunate mix of supervisor and group member competence, the importance of acceptance to each, and time pressure. Let us now turn to the evidence for these contingency questions.

Contingency Hypothesis

The appropriateness of a supervisory style was said to depend on five factors: the supervisor's competence, the group member's competence, the importance of acceptance to the supervisor, the importance of acceptance to the group member, and the degree of time pressure present. Some of the findings in the three studies are relevant to these factors. Let us examine each in turn.

In the study of supervisory practices, direct support was found for the importance of the supervisor's competence as a moderating factor in relationships between supervisory practices and subordinate innovation. For supervisors low in skills, providing freedom was positively related to subordinate innovation; for highly skilled supervisors, providing freedom was unrelated to subordinate innovation. Moreover, for supervisors high in technical skills, critical evaluation was positively related to innovation; for supervisors low in technical skills, critical evaluation was found to be related negatively to subordinate innovation. These findings are clearly consistent with the notion that competence and leadership should go hand in hand.

No direct test was made of the moderating effect of group member competence on relationships between supervisory styles and innovation. However, more competent group members were named as leaders in the informal organization, and more informal leadership occurred in more innovative groups. Apparently "performance feedback loops" (Farris, 1969; Farris & Lim, 1969)—the causal influence of performance on the working environment—also affected the degree to which a group member exercised leadership in the informal organization. Perhaps group member competence, as evidenced in their innovation, also had a causal influence on supervisory behavior.

No data were available on the importance of acceptance to either supervisors or group members. Consistent with the idea of the moderating effect of the importance of acceptance, however, is the finding that in less innovative groups, group members were working more often on their supervisor's original ideas, which they may have been less apt to accept. No test was made of the moderating influence of time pressure on supervisory style.

In summary, the three research studies provided some evidence consistent with the contingency hypothesis although they were not designed to test it. Evidence from these studies is most consistent with the hypothesized moderating effect of the supervisor's competence.

SUMMARY AND CONCLUSION

Returning to a statement implicit in many definitions of leadership—that leadership involves influence—it was suggested that leadership theory and research should be concerned with questions of the amount and distribution of leadership as well as with qualitative characteristics of the leadership process. A framework for doing this was proposed. It suggests four supervisory styles depending on the amount and distribution of influence between a supervisor and a group member—collaboration, domination, delegation, and abdication. Tentative hypotheses were stated concerning the supervisory style which is best on the average and conditions under which a particular supervisory style would be more appropriate. "One best way" hypotheses emphasized total influence, substantial influence, and an egalitarian distribution of influence as determinants of leadership effectiveness. The moderating factors suggested in the contingency approach were the competence of the supervisor and group member, the importance of each accepting the results of leadership, and the degree of time pressure. In addition, a framework of leadership in the informal organization was advanced, describing qualitative characteristics of the leadership process in terms of roles which theoretically facilitate problem solving. This description allows investigation of the amount and distribution of influence as well as specific qualities of the leadership process.

Three research studies were described dealing with supervisory practices and innovation, characteristics of leadership and leaders, and leadership in innovative groups. These studies were related to the above framework, but not designed to test it. Overall results were consistent with the notion that collaborative leadership is best on the average, but that the appropriateness of a supervisory style depends on the competence of the supervisor, and perhaps other contingency factors as well.

This chapter should be considered as a position paper; what is needed now is a precise statement of hypotheses within the broad framework, operational definitions of constructs, and research designed specifically to test these hypotheses. In short, the next step should involve the kinds of things which happen when research is conducted in the way that it is reported.

In closing, I would like to comment on a question which may well be puzzling the reader at this point: Why return to the primitive notion of leadership as influence? Why not focus on qualities of the process of leadership in line with earlier approaches, for example, those of Ohio State, old or new Michigan, Illinois-Washington, path-goal, or exchange theory? My answer is that these lines of investigation leave me somehow feeling uneasy and incompletely satisfied, despite my great admiration for their accomplishments. Part of this uneasiness stems from my earlier research findings (Farris, 1969; Farris & Lim, 1969) suggesting that performance, which most theories assume results from leadership, in fact is an important cause of leadership. When a group member performs well, a supervisor is apt to become more considerate and to supervise less closely. Thus, I have emphasized competence as a moderating factor.

Cartwright's (1973) recent provocative observations on the case of research on the risky shift may have a message for leadership research and theory as well. An MIT master's thesis (Stoner, 1961) found that, contrary to "common sense," groups made more risky decisions than individuals. Nearly 200 studies followed, resulting in the current conclusion that groups are not invariably riskier than individuals. To a great extent it depends on the particular decision being made.

Cartwright (1973), suggested that the case was analogous to Kuhn's (1962) term *paradigm*—"the complex set of beliefs and assumptions that investigators implicitly adopted in their research on this topic [p. 230]." Cartwright's analysis suggested that despite its clear advantages, the risky shift paradigm "engendered certain self-protective processes that unnecessarily delayed progress in this line of investigation. These had to do wtih labeling, motivation, methodology, and the media of communication [p. 230]."

In a sense some of the current approaches to leadership provide paradigms, with their inherent advantages and disadvantages. As such, they may have both facilitated and inhibited progress. Some of the contingency approaches in this symposium represent dominant paradigms, while others, like the present paper, represent departures. The very existence of contingency approaches to leadership, which characterize all papers in this symposium, represents departures from "one best way" paradigms. In concluding, let me ask what paradigms are implicit in the lines of investigation represented in this volume. Would progress in our understanding of leadership best be advanced by following one or another of them, by departures, or by proceeding on both fronts simultaneously?

Discussant Comments

BY JOHN W. SLOCUM, JR.

The work presented by Farris is instructive in providing a framework to expedite our understanding of the leadership process in informal organizations. The focus of the paper is on the leadership process and its resultant effect on the productivity (measured in terms of innovation) of scientists and engineers employed at a NASA research center. Farris defines the term leadership as an influence process (similar to Hollander & Julian, 1969) and uses it as his independent variable.

The challenge of the paper lies in its ability to bring to the attention of the reader other conceptual models which might explain the results of the studies. If one considers two basic variables—technology and structure—alternative explanations to those found by Farris would appear warranted.

The type of technology involved in the NASA installations may be labelled intensive (Thompson, 1967). In an R & D organization, the nature of the tasks required and the order in which they can be applied depend on the nature of the problem to be solved. Thus, intensive technology is a custom technology. The successful employment of this type of system rests in part on the mutual interactions of various people and the resources as required by the individual problem posed. The most successful manner in which various resources are coordinated is through mutual adjustment. Mutual adjustment is necessary because of the reciprocal task interdependencies created by the system. For example, researchers at NASA installations are solving problems which have no stated solutions (or at best variable ones) and which must be solved through interaction with their peers. Thus, it was not surprising to find that in highly innovative groups, greater collaboration was reported between group members than in less innovative groups. Similarly, since the problems were ambiguous, supervisors of more innovative groups gave their subordinates greater discretion than supervisors of less innovative groups.

In 1970, Woodward proposed a control paradigm which might clarify some of the findings by Farris. As indicated below in Figure 5, the control of R & D personnel is not usually exercised by a single system. Saxberg and Slocum (1968) found that scientists have internal systems of control and dislike control to be superimposed upon them by the organization. In

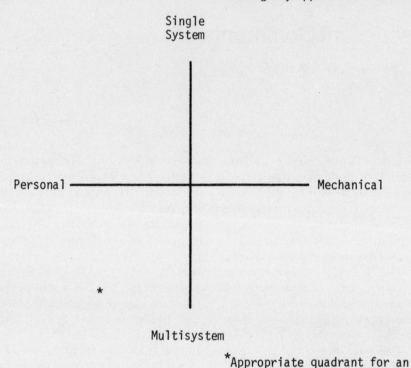

Fig. 5. Woodward's control paradigm. (Adapted from Joan Woodward, "Technology, material control and organizational behavior," in A. Negandhi [ed.], *Modern organizational theory* [Kent, Ohio: The Kent State University Press, 1973], p. 67.)

Woodward's model, the appropriate control of the R & D specialist would involve reliance on a personal value system and also be a multiple or fragmentary system. Farris indicated that supervisors of less innovative groups played roles of idea origination and organization information to a greater extent than did supervisors of more innovative groups. This is consistent with the control system in most R & D organizations and is also consistent with the values held by scientists in organizations.

Closely related to the control process, is the decision making process. If the technology is intensive and the control process both personalistic and multiple, then according to Thompson (1967) the decision making process should stress judgments rather than rely upon other tactics. According to Thompson's model represented in Figure 6 it seems clear that the preferences regarding outcomes are clear (greater innovation) but the beliefs about causes and effects are uncertain. Under these conditions, Thompson states that a judgmental decision process will be the most successful strategy. Why can't we categorize R & D personnel into that decision cell?

Cyert and March (1963) have introduced the important concept of problemistic search in connection with organizational decision making and environmental uncertainty. These researchers define problemistic search as a search stimulated by a problem and directed at finding a solution to that problem. At NASA, the problem is to increase the innovation rate of the scientists working in the laboratory. The search process is usually defined by searching for current alternatives and/or generalizing from a past solution to the present. One may label this search process as "opportunistic surveillance" (Thompson, 1967, p. 151). As the organization becomes more complex, individuals at higher levels of the organization find themselves increasingly involved in this type of search process. Opportunistic surveillance is usually found at the institutional level of the organization (Parsons, 1960).

The function of personnel at the institutional level of the organization is to interact with the environment in which the firm is operating and reduce

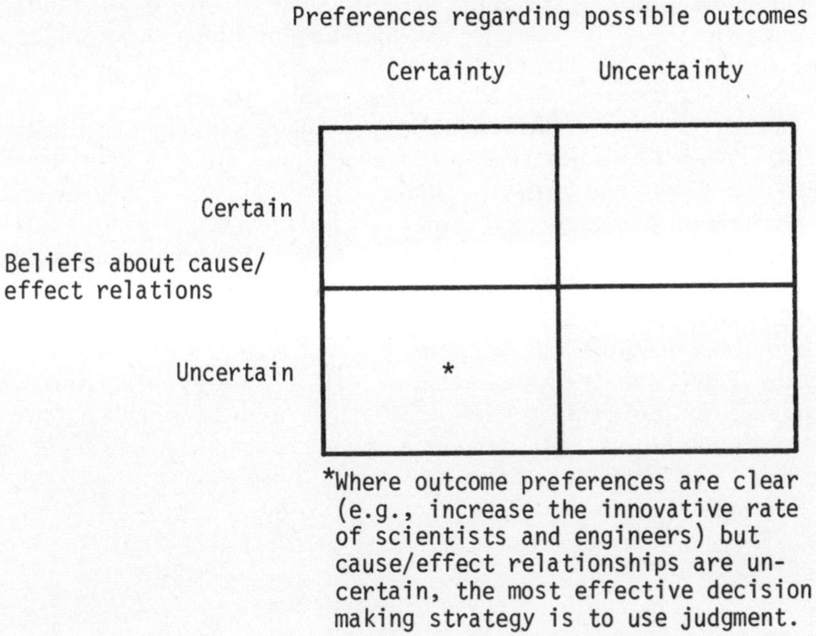

Preferences regarding possible outcomes

Certainty   Uncertainty

Certain

Beliefs about cause/
effect relations

Uncertain   *

*Where outcome preferences are clear
(e.g., increase the innovative rate
of scientists and engineers) but
cause/effect relationships are uncertain, the most effective decision
making strategy is to use judgment.

Fig. 6. Thompson's processes of decision making. (Adapted from *Organizations in Action* by J. Thompson. Copyright 1967 McGraw-Hill, Inc. Used with permission of McGraw-Hill Book Company.)

the uncertainty—market or technological—that the firm may face. Thus organizational personnel operating at this level are performing in a highly unstructured task environment. They are more likely to engage in a decision strategy of judgment because of the uncertainties about cause and effect relationships in the environment. A supervisor who gives technical assistance is attempting to reduce the uncertainty in the environment and is more likely to be in charge of highly innovative groups than supervisors who do not give this assistance. This was confirmed by the data of Farris and is also supported by House's path-goal model (1973b).

A typical R & D organization may be classified as a utilitarian organization (Etzioni, 1964). This type of organization is highly selective of its personnel and expects that they have been socialized before joining the organization. This socialization process occurs through the educational and professional training processes. As Etzioni states, the control mechanisms in these types of organizations rely mainly on self-control and colleague support. The data by Farris indicate that greater than one-half of the choices were directed at peers for problem solving assistance. This finding suggests that the control process is personal and draws heavily upon one's group. Farris found that the greater the group's innovation, the less it relied on external assistance. This finding might indicate that for highly innovative groups, the scientists' reference and membership groups were similar and contained within the laboratory.

In attempting to understand the leadership process in an organization, the researcher must clearly delineate the salient variables comprising his model. While Farris has considered the influence process, other variables, such as technology and structure, should be considered in future research. It is becoming increasingly important to treat the contingency approach in a scientific manner. The specification of causal relationships would be a starting point of departure. If the research has specified a model that would be applicable to path analysis, then it would be possible to ascertain whether the contingency variables are independent or moderating variables in his model. Farris's study indicates that influence is an important variable in studying the leadership process of informal organizations. What are the antecedents of the process? Are they technology, structure, or a host of other variables that researchers have not addressed to date?

4

A Theoretical and Empirical Examination of Fiedler's Contingency Model of Leadership Effectiveness

MARTIN M. CHEMERS and ROBERT W. RICE

Fiedler's (1967) contingency model of leadership effectiveness stands at the center of an important and growing interest in contingency theories of leadership. This chapter will review some of the major questions and controversies surrounding the contingency model, and where appropriate, will offer data recently obtained in experimental studies of leadership at the University of Utah. The chapter will begin with a brief review of historical trends in leadership research which have led up to the development of contingency theories. The remainder of the chapter will deal with Fiedler's contingency model. [Following Fiedler's pioneering work, this is generally referred to hereafter as "the contingency model."] The general form and assumptions of the theory and its strengths and weaknesses will be discussed. Data and interpretation will be presented which bear on three major questions related to the model: its basic predictive validity, its recent extension to include leadership training, and experience effects and the conceptual meaning of the LPC score.

AN HISTORICAL PERSPECTIVE

Although interaction or contingency approaches dominate current theories of leadership, such was not always the case. Contingency approaches are defined here as those theories or models which postulate that leadership effectiveness is *contingent* upon the *interaction* of certain leader attributes with specific parameters of the group task environment. It is useful to review the trends in leadership research which have led the majority of theorists to this position in order to provide some perspective on where we have been and where we might be going. Although scholars and laymen have long discussed the attributes of men who become effective leaders, scientific investigation of leadership has been a twentieth-century phenomenon.

The first phase of leadership research, the thirty or forty year period preceding World War II, was characterized by the search for "the leadership trait." The underlying premise which guided such research was that there did indeed exist a trait, state, or attribute of the leader, or perhaps a set of such traits, which could identify individuals who would become good leaders. The typical paradigm for leadership research during this early period called for 1) the identification of a group with leaders and followers (e.g., high school student body, basketball team, debating society, business enterprise, etc.), 2) the measurement of all group members on some trait, and 3) testing for a difference between characteristics of leaders and followers. The range of traits tested included everything from dominance, masculinity, and intelligence, to height, physical appearance, and fluency of speech. Two extremely thorough reviews of the trait studies by Stogdill (1948) and Mann (1959) effectively closed the door on this line of research. These authors concluded that while certain traits, such as intelligence, showed consistent relationships with leadership status, such relationships were far too weak and equivocal to be of any psychological significance. Instead, these reviewers and others (Gibb, 1947) clearly articulated the importance of considering the situation as well as the traits of the leader in any discussion of leadership. They argued that situations differ so radically in the demands they place upon persons who aspire to or occupy leadership positions that it makes little sense to expect a single trait or pattern of traits to be associated with leadership across all situations.

Because old theories, like old soldiers, do not die easily, the trait approach was not completely abandoned despite the negative results of the thirty year search for "the leadership trait." Instead, the trait approach was permuted into more sophisticated research approaches. Immediately following World War II, a burst of research energy attempted to examine constellations of leader behaviors or leadership styles. In essence, leadership styles thought of as enduring behavioral patterns were only one step removed from personality traits which were enduring orientations or propensities. Early reports (Lewin, Lippitt, & White, 1939; Lippitt & White, 1943) that democratically led groups were more satisfied, goal directed, and less aggressive than groups under autocratic or *laissez faire* leadership resulted in a surge of elation. Not only had the problem of leadership been solved, but the results reinforced truth, justice, and the "American Way." Unfortunately, the elation was short lived as later research (Cattell, Saunders & Stice, 1953; Haythorn, Couch, Haefner, Langhan, & Carter, 1956) indicated that the effects of variables like leader authoritarianism were much more complicated than originally hypothesized and depended on such factors as the match between leader and member styles, and task demands.

In the era following World War II, social scientists began to focus greater attention on the construct of behavior. Several projects in leadership research began to observe and catalogue leader behavior. The increasing sophistication of data analysis methods, such as factor analysis, and technologies such as the digital computer greatly aided the search for identifiable categories of leader behavior. The increased emphasis on behavior yielded fruitful results. Several studies (Bales & Slater, 1955; Couch & Carter, 1952; Halpin & Winer, 1957, Katz & Kahn, 1966) isolated distinct and replicable factors of leader behavior. The most impressive series of studies along this line were carried out by the Ohio State University group of researchers (Shartle & Stogdill, 1952). Through the observation, scaling, and factor analysis of leader behavior in hundreds of groups, the Leader Behavior Description Questionnaire (LBDQ) was developed (Fleishman, 1973). These researchers were able to verify that the behaviors measured by the LBDQ represented several factors of leader behavior.

The two most important factors, which together accounted for 82% of the common variance in leader behavior, were labelled *consideration* and *initiating structure*. Consideration is described as the degree to which the leader or supervisor shows concern, understanding, and warmth toward his group members, and the degree to which he is considerate of their needs and willing to explain his actions. Initiating structure refers to behaviors related to the assignment of roles and tasks within the group, defining goals, and setting and monitoring work procedures and standards.

These two factors are conceptually similar to the behavior categories of "employee centered" and "job centered" which were developed at the University of Michigan (Katz & Kahn, 1966) and to the concepts of "socio emotional" and "task" specialist identified by Bales and Slater (1955). These two general categories of leader behavior are still prominent in most theories of leadership.

The identification of leader behavior categories did not, however, immediately solve the question of leadership effectiveness. The research programs of the 1950s were not able to reliably specify what type of leader or set of leader behaviors were consistently associated with group effectiveness. Several studies did indicate that high levels of consideration behavior were associated with follower satisfaction (Fleishman & Harris 1962; Fleishman, Harris, & Burtt, 1955). However, even these findings suggested that the situational contexts in which leader behavior takes place are important moderators of the effects of various classes of leader behavior. In a thorough review of the relationship of leader orientation to follower satisfaction and group effectiveness, Korman (1966) found few consistent results.

The failure to find any leader traits, styles, or patterns of behavior that were consistently related to effective group performance suggested the need to consider situational factors. Arguments for the importance of situational aspects were buttressed by the appearance of several studies which indicated that purely situational variables such as task demands (Shaw, 1963; Stogdill, & Koehler 1952), communication networks (Leavitt, 1951), seating and spacing arrangements (Steinzor, 1950) and member characteristics (Gibb, 1947) strongly affected patterns of leadership emergence, behavior and effectiveness. A consideration of situational parameters became increasingly more popular among researchers at this time.

Taken as a whole this early research clearly demonstrated that no single trait or pattern of leader behavior characterized all effective leaders. Additional research demonstrated the strong effects of situational factors on various leadership phenomena (leader emergence, behavior, and effectiveness). These two major lines of research clearly pointed out the need for an interaction approach which recognized the importance of both situational and personal determinants of leadership phenomena. While many researchers (e.g., Gibb, 1969; Sanford, 1952; Stogdill, 1948) have declared the necessity of an interaction approach to leadership, Fiedler's (1964; 1967) contingency model of leadership effectiveness has gone considerably beyond the efforts of other researchers in operationalizing such an approach. The contingency model and its recent reformulations and extensions will be the subject of the remainder of this paper.

THE CONTINGENCY MODEL

The contingency model of leadership effectiveness is the result of a comprehensive program of research begun at the University of Illinois by Fred E. Fiedler in 1951. At the core of this research program is the "esteem for the least preferred co-worker" or LPC scale, a measure of leader orientation. An individual who fills out the LPC scale is asked to think of all the people with whom he has ever worked and to focus on the one person with whom "he had the most difficult time in getting a job done," i.e., his least preferred co-worker. The rater is then asked to describe this individual on a series of pipolar, eight point, descriptive adjective scales presented in the following format

Pleasant : : : : : : : : : Unpleasant

Intelligent : : : : : : : : Stupid

The scales are scored as a continuum with the most positive pole given a score of 8 and negative pole a score of 1. The rater's LPC score is simply the sum of all the individual scale scores. The distribution of LPC scores is symmetrical and roughly normal. For research purposes high LPC and low LPC persons are usually identified on the basis of a median split (or sometimes more extreme groupings) of the distribution of LPC scores of the particular population of interest.

Although the LPC scale has played a central role in a large body of empirical research, it has been a difficult measure to interpret. The interpretation of the LPC has varied over the years and is at times referred to as an index of task versus interpersonal orientation, motivational priorities, or cognitive complexity. (Later in this chapter, we will offer a fuller discussion of the question of the interpretation of LPC.) The most enduring and widely used interpretation of LPC is as a measure of the relative task versus interpersonal orientation of a group leader (Fiedler & Chemers, 1974a).

A low LPC score indicates that the rater has evaluated his least preferred coworker negatively on most items of the LPC scale. Thus, the low LPC rater is effectively saying that "if I cannot work with you, you are a bad or unworthy person." It appears that the low LPC person is using task accomplishment as a key parameter in the evaluation of other people. Such an attitude is thought to reflect a strong orientation toward successful task accomplishment.

On the other hand, a high LPC score indicates that the rater has evaluated his least preferred co-worker positively on many of the items on the LPC scale. Thus, the high LPC rater is effectively saying "although I cannot work with you, you are a good person in many respects." Such an attitude would seem to reflect a considerably lower emphasis on task accomplishment for the high LPC person. He would appear, then, to be orienting toward other aspects of group activity, most probably, interpersonal relationships. The reader will notice the obvious compatibility of this interpretation with our earlier discussion of the important leader behavior categories related to task versus interpersonal concerns.

If the interpretation of LPC is still equivocal, the question of its importance as a determinant of small group effectiveness is not. Prior to the formal presentation of the model in 1964, Fiedler and his associates collected data relating LPC to group performance in over 1,000 groups ranging from basketball teams, bomber and tank crews, surveying parties, and farm cooperative boards, to experimental groups composed of college students, managers, clergymen, and military personnel. Although the relationship between LPC and group productivity was usually present and often quite strong, a consistent and reliable relationship was not originally found. It was not until Fiedler attempted to relate LPC to situational variables in a contingency approach that a coherent pattern of results emerged.

The specification of which situational variables should be considered and how they should be weighted is a difficult question. Fiedler gave primary importance to the leader's potential for influence and control in the group, i.e. his prerogatives for leadership. Fiedler identified three major variables which contribute to the leader's influence and control or "situational favorableness" as it is labelled in the contingency model. In order of importance, the three major determinants to situational favorableness are 1) the interpersonal relations between the leader and his followers, especially the followers' acceptance of the leader, 2) the task structure or the degree to which the group's task is clearcut and unambiguous with verifiable goals and specified procedures for reaching the goal, and 3) the leader's formal power of position, that is, his ability to reward or punish the group members.

It is assumed that leadership will be easier to implement when the leader is accepted, when his task is clear, specified, and unambiguous, and when the leader has the power to entice or coerce his followers into action. (For a fuller discussion of the logic and theoretical significance of the situational favorableness dimension see Fiedler, 1967; Fiedler & Chemers, 1974a; or Fiedler & Chemers, 1974b.) In empirical work with the contingency model, each of the three variables is dichotomized to yield an eight-celled continuum of situational favorableness shown in Figure 7. In ordering the eight octants of the favorableness dimension leader member relations received twice the weighting of task structure which in turn was weighted twice as heavily as position power. While this weighting was based on a priori theoretical grounds, recent empirical evidence (Nebeker, personal communication) has supported the validity of this arrangement of the favorableness dimension.

Once the situation dimension has been specified, groups in past studies could be assigned to specific octants of the continuum based on their standing on the three variables, and the nature of the relationship between the leader's LPC score and group productivity could be assessed across situational contexts. Figure 7 shows such relationships for each of the octants based on the studies done by Fiedler and his associates prior to 1964 (Fiedler, 1967).

Octant I in the figure is the most favorable and octant VIII the least favorable. The ordinate indicates the correlation of the leader LPC and group productivity. A point above the midline indicates a positive correlation, i.e., that a high leader LPC score is associated with high group productivity for that cell. A negative correlation shown as a point below the midline indicates that low LPC leaders have more productive groups in that particular cell.

The heavy dark line connects the median correlations for all studies within a particular cell. As can be seen from the curve, low leader LPC scores are associated with high productivity in the very favorable and very unfavor-

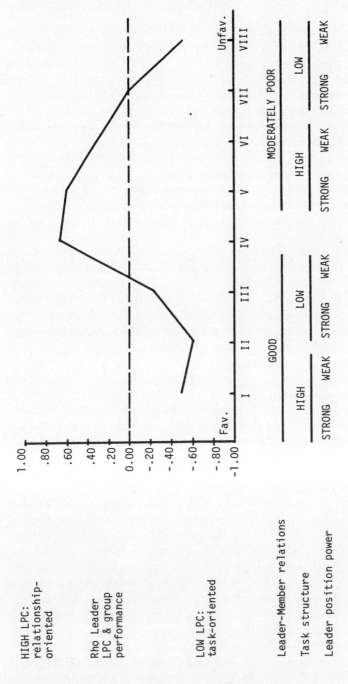

Fig. 7. Fiedler's contingency model. (Adapted from *A theory of leadership effectiveness* by F. E. Fiedler. Copyright 1967 McGraw-Hill, Inc. Used with permission of McGraw-Hill Book Company.)

97

able portions of the dimension (i.e., octant I, II, III, & VIII). High leader LPC scores are associated with high group productivity in the moderately favorable zone of the favorableness dimension (i.e., octant IV, V, & VI). This curve is based on a *post hoc* arrangement of previous research, and no adequate assessment of its validity can be made without examining research which has occurred subsequent to its exposition. The question of the predictive validity of the contingency model will be dealt with in detail in a later section of this chapter.

To understand the significance of the contingency model as a theory and as an instigator of research, it is necessary to examine some of the explicit and implicit assumptions which underly it. The model shares many of the basic assumptions underlying all contingency approaches. The notion that there is no such thing as a universally good leader or one best way to lead is common to all contingency theories. And to a greater or lesser extent, all such theories embody the idea that there is a range of leadership styles or approaches and that different styles are maximally effective in different situations.

The contingency model makes a few further assumptions which are not logically necessary for all contingency approaches. Two of these assumptions are, however, crucial to Fiedler's theory. First, the contingency model maintains that certain leader attributes are stable and enduring and that these attributes must be integrated with situational factors in order to predict leadership effectiveness. In the contingency model, the stable attribute or attributes are embodied in a general orientation towards group activity which is measured through the LPC scale. Although Fiedler (1972b) maintains that the manifestation of this orientation (e.g., behavior) may change with changes in the situation, the orientation itself is central to the individual and relatively unchanging. A corollary of this position is that the behavioral changes which occur in different situations are themselves consistent and predictable from a knowledge of the leader's basic orientation.

The second assumption is the one which serves to make the contingency model unique and separate from other contingency theories. This assumption or set of assumptions underlies the specification of crucial situational variables. The number of potentially important situational variables approaches infinity. However, based on the assumptions and theoretical considerations discussed earlier, Fiedler selected weighted variables and combined a manageable subset of these variables. The dimension of situational favorableness as the leader's potential for influence and control represents the result of those assumptions in the contingency model.

A further assumption regarding situational favorableness concerns the number of elements included in evaluation of the favorableness dimension. In recent, as well as earlier writing (Fiedler & Chemers, 1974a), it is clearly acknowledged that the three variables of leader acceptance, task structure, and position power are not the only variables which might be used to specify situational favorableness. Fiedler (1967) has, at times, integrated the variables of stress, cultural and linguistic heterogeneity, training and experience, leadership legitimation, and others, into specifications of favorableness. Rather, the three standard variables are assumed to represent the most general and most important of the situational variables.

Another extremely important assumption is central to this line of reasoning about the contingency model. Situational favorableness, or potential influence and control, is a general and widely encompassing dimension. It is assumed that almost all variables which affect the leadership position can be subsumed into the favorableness dimension. This is an extremely important assumption for both theoretical and practical reasons.

Based on this general assumption in recent years, Fiedler has been able to incorporate a wide variety of organizational and psychological variables into the contingency model without changing its basic form or direction. For example, the effects of leader training and experience, organizational climate, internal and external stress, and leader intelligence have been integrated into the contingency model and have made important contributions to our understanding of leadership effectiveness.

CURRENT ISSUES SURROUNDING
THE CONTINGENCY MODEL

Having laid out the contingency model in terms of its basic content and underlying assumptions, we can now turn to an evaluation of the model and its recent extensions and formulations. Four major questions with regard to the contingency model are presently active in the literature.

The first question concerns the basic validity of the model. Critiques by Graen, Alvares, Orris, and Martella (1970) and Ashour (1973) will be evaluated in light of recent experimental evidence from our laboratory. [Though not discussed in this chapter, a recent critique by McMahon (1972) also appears relevant in the present context.]

The second general issue concerns limitations and weaknesses of the contingency model. These criticisms do not attack the basic validity of the model, but consider the areas in which the model must be further developed.

The third major issue concerns Fiedler's attempt to incorporate leadership training and experience in the contingency model. We shall report some recent experimental results on the training effect and discuss the usefulness of the approach and its possible future directions.

The last major issue which we will discuss in this chapter concerns the meaning of the LPC score. The discussion will focus on three different attempts to provide a theoretical interpretation of the LPC score. Again we will present data from our laboratory which bear on these issues.

Validity of the Contingency Model

The question of validity is, of course, central to the examintion of any theory. It is an especially important question when applied to the contingency model for two reasons. First, the contingency model is a theory with important and wide ranging implications of both a theoretical and applied nature. Recent revisions have extended both the scope and potential ramifications of the theory. For this reason alone, the validity question is paramount. Further, the contingency model, as it was first fully presented (Fiedler, 1964), was largely based on the restructuring and arrangement of previously collected data. The contingency model, then, is especially susceptible to criticism that it is merely a *post hoc* arrangement of data resulting in a formulation which is conceptually pleasing, but which has no predictive validity. It becomes extremely important, then, to examine research which has occurred subsequent to 1964, and which actually provides a test of the model.

In 1971, Fiedler reviewed several recent laboratory experiments and field studies which either directly or indirectly tested the contingency model. The research reviewed was broken down into separate categories for laboratory and field studies and into studies which test the model in terms of its traditional parameters and those which employ other means for specifying the favorableness dimension. On the whole, the research tends to support the contingency model, but the support is not unequivocal. Table 15, taken from Fiedler (1971b), lists the studies which were direct tests of the model. [Though too recent for inclusion in the table, a field study by Yunker (1972b) is also relevant here].

Fiedler (1971b) assessed the number of correlations which were in the direction predicted by the contingency model curve and found that 34 of 45 correlations were in the predicted direction. By binomial test, this effect was quite significant (p < .01). However, even these evidential data are open to considerable question.

Several criticisms can be levelled at the results presented by Fiedler. Many of the studies yield supportive data only after some reanalysis of the data. In many cases (e.g., Mitchell, 1969) the reanalyses were within normal and acceptable standards. In other cases, such as the Belgian Navy study (Fiedler, 1966), normal procedures for assessing situational favorableness and assigning groups to cells were so seriously deviated from that interpretation is difficult and implied support for the model, equivocal. Furthermore, while most of the results in the validation studies are in the correct direction, few of the correlations reach normally acceptable levels of significance. Also,

TABLE 15

Summary of Field and Laboratory Studies
Testing the Contingency Model

Study	Octants							
	I	II	III	IV	V	VI	VII	VIII
Field studies								
Hunt (1967)	-.64		-.80		.21		.30	
	-.51		.60				-.30	
Hill (1969)[a]		-.10	.29			-.24	.62	
Fiedler et al. (1969)		-.21		.00		.67*		-.51
O'Brien et al. (1969)		-.46		.47		-.45		.14
Laboratory experiments								
Belgian Navy	-.72	.37	-.16	.08	.16	.07	.26	-.37
	-.77	.50	-.54	.13	.03	.14	-.27	.60
Shima (1968)[a]		-.26		.71*				
Mitchell (1969)		.24		.43				
		.17		.38				
Fiedler exec.		.34		.51				
MEDIAN								
All studies	-.64	.17	-.22	.38	.22	.10	.26	-.35
Field studies	-.54	-.21	-.29	.23	.21	-.24	.30	-.33
Laboratory experiments	-.72	.24	-.16	.38	.16	.13	.08	-.33
Median correlations of Fiedler's original studies (1964)	-.52	-.58	-.33	.47	.42		.05	-.43

Note.—Number of correlations in the expected direction (exclusive of octant VI, for which no prediction had been made) = 34; number of correlations opposite to expected direction = 11; p by binomial test = .01.

[a]Studies not conducted by the writer or his associates.

*p <.05.

SOURCE: F.E. Fiedler, "Validation and extension of the contingency model of leadership effectiveness: A review of empirical findings," Psychological Bulletin, 1971, 76, 128–148. Copyright 1971 by the American Psychological Association. Reprinted by permission.

of the studies which provide strong support for the contingency model, none are tests of the full situational favorableness dimension with unchallengeable specification of all relevant variables.

These weaknesses, which are neither unusual in leadership research nor totally invalidating, nonetheless leave the contingency model open to criticism. One source of such criticism was an article by George Graen and his associates which appeared in *Psychological Bulletin* (Graen, Alvares, Orris, & Martella, 1970). It will be discussed in some detail because it represents the most extreme criticism of the contingency model yet offered. [But see also Ashour (1973).] It also highlights several important issues surrounding the question of validity.

Graen and his associates (Graen et al., 1970) reviewed several of the same studies which Fiedler (1971b) later reported as support of the contingency model, but reached drastically different conclusions. Graen et al. asserted that the model was basically without any predictive validity. In essence, they maintained that the contingency model curve was simply an artifact of inappropriate methods of research and data analysis. These authors based their conclusions on a line of reasoning with three specific foci.

First, they maintained that the specification of situational favorableness has been so vague and variable across studies, that any pattern of results could be produced by the careful *post hoc* ordering of data buttressed by convoluted justifications. To support this contention, Graen et al. (1970) focused on a single investigation, the Belgian Navy study, (Fiedler, 1966) which they asserted indicates the manner in which the model is normally tested.

Graen et al.'s second criticism was directed at the use of nonsignificant directional results as support for a theory. They pointed out the dangers inherent in a procedure in which no single study stands as a test of the theory and the pattern of data when taken together is judged by criteria far less stringent than those normally used in scientific inquiry.

Finally, these authors presented data from two laboratory experiments of their own which failed to support the contingency model (Graen, Orris, & Alvares, 1971a; 1971b). In these two experiments, employing 26 and 48 three-man groups, an attempt was made to test the full eight cell favorableness dimension for the relationships of LPC and performance. In neither of these studies did any of the 16 correlations between leader LPC and group productivity reach significance, nor did the correlations follow the pattern predicted by Fiedler.

Fiedler (1971a; 1971b) has addressed himself to Graen et al.'s (1970) criticism. In his rebuttals, Fiedler focused largely on the inadequacy of the experimental tests conducted by Graen and his associates. Fiedler pointed out several methodological weaknesses including extremely weak manipulations of task structure and leader power, inadequate assignment of high and low LPC leaders to conditions, and the inherent difficulties in testing the null hypothesis. Fiedler's criticism of the Graen, et al. (1971a; 1971b) experiments are well founded. They do not, however, answer the more general criticisms which Graen et al. levelled at the problems of specification and analysis in contingency model research.

By placing the arguments of Fiedler (1971a; 1971b) and Graen et al. (1970) in juxtaposition, an avenue of resolution becomes apparent. The validity of the contingency model, both agree, could be tested by a carefully controlled, adequately manipulated experimental test of the full eight-cell model. Such a test was provided in a comprehensive experiment by Chemers and Skrzypek (1972), using 128 cadets at the United States Military Academy at West Point. About six weeks prior to the actual experiment, two cadet companies were administered the LPC scale and a sociometric questionnaire assessing patterns of liking and respect. Thirty-two four man groups were constructed in the following manner.

High and low LPC leaders were randomly chosen from groups of cadets who scored at least one standard deviation above or below the mean of the LPC distribution. Unlike studies of Fiedler's model which have relied on *post hoc* measures of group atmosphere, leader-member relations were independently manipulated in this experiment. Good leader-member relations groups were composed of cadets who had expressed strong liking and respect for each other and the leader on the preexperimental sociometric measure. Poor leader-member relations groups were composed of members who had mutually rejected each other and the leader.

Each group was assigned two tasks varying in structure (order was counter balanced). The structured task consisted of drawing the plan for a barracks building to scale from a set of specifications. The task was broken down into discrete subtasks and a picture of the finished product drawn to a different scale was provided. Thus, the task was exremely high on the elements normally used to specify task structure in contingency model research, i.e., decision varifiability, solution specificity, goal clarity, and goal path multiplicity (Shaw, 1963). The unstructured task required the group to design a program to facilitate an interest in world politics among enlisted men in overseas assignments.

Further, groups were given a manipulation for either high or low leader position power. In the high power condition, groups were informed that after the task, it would be the leader's responsibility to evaluate the performance of each group member and assign a score which would become part of the cadet's permanent service record. Leaders in the low power condition were instructed to act as chairman, and the group was told that the leader had no real power to reward or punish group members.

Thus, leader LPC was carefully assessed, and leaders were assigned to groups in which the variables of leader acceptance, task structure, and leader position power were strongly manipulated. These manipulations yielded the full eight-celled situational favorableness dimension as specified in the contingency model.

Leader LPC and group effectiveness were correlated for each octant of the favorableness dimension. In Figure 8, the resultant correlations are plotted against the curve predicted by the contingency model. The close concordance between the two curves is striking. The rank order correlation between predicted and obtained curve points was .86 (p < .05). Although the overall pattern of correlation coefficients strongly supported contingency model predictions, none of the correlations are individually significant. However, the interaction of LPC, leader acceptance, and task structure is highly significant (F = 6.19, p < .025). This interaction of leader LPC and situational favorableness actually controls about 28% of the group performance variability (Shiflett, 1972).

The Chemers and Skrzypek (1972) study, by virtue of its clean methodology and strong results, provides extremely powerful support for the contingency model curve. It establishes the predictive validity of the model and indicates that experimental studies of leadership can be quite useful.

In another laboratory test of the contingency model, Rice and Chemers (1973b) assigned 18 four-man groups to one of two tasks. Nine groups worked on the barracks drawing task (Chemers & Skryzpek, 1972), and the other nine groups worked on an unstructured task which required groups to make up creative stories, using an ambiguous picture as a stimulus.

Each group was composed on two high and two low LPC college student subjects. No leaders were assigned. Emergent leaders were assessed from sociometric nominations on a postexperimental questionnaire. Fiedler (1967) maintained that situations of emergent leadership, almost by definition, imply low levels of leader acceptance and position power, because group members are competing with one another for leadership positions. By this reasoning, Rice and Chemers's experiment provides a replication of octant VI (low leader acceptance, high task structure, low position power) and octant VIII (low leader acceptance, low task structure, low position power). No differences were found in the number of high or low LPC emergent leaders within or across conditions. However, the correlations between emergent leader LPC and group productivity were extremely close to those predicted by the contingency model. For octant VI, the point prediction extrapolated from the curve is +.30, and the obtained correlation was +.30. In octant VIII, predicted rho is −.43. The obtained correlation was −.40.

Because the specification of leader-member relations and position power were less direct in the Rice and Chemers study than they were in the

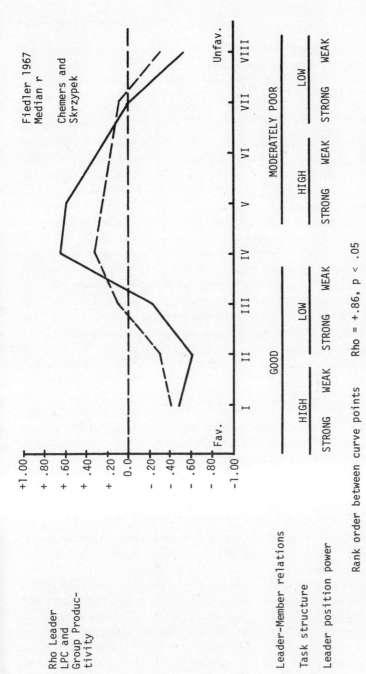

Fig. 8. Comparison of predicted and obtained curves for least preferred co-worker (LPC) and group effectiveness. (Adapted from M. M. Chemers & G. J. Skryzypek, "An experimental test of the contingency model of leadership effectiveness," *Journal of Personality and Social Psychology,* 1972, *24,* 172–177. Copyright 1972 by the American Psychological Association. Reprinted by permissinn.)

experiment by Chemers and Skryzypek, the support for the contingency model is somewhat weaker. Taken together, however, these two experiments make a very strong case for the validity of the contingency model.

Other Criticisms of the Model

Recent validation studies conducted in our laboratory and elsewhere (Hardy, 1971) have supported the basic validity of the model. However, this support does not invalidate certain of the criticisms made by Graen et al. (1970) and others (Ashour, 1973; Kerr & Harlan 1973) including Fiedler's own group (Mitchell, Biglan, Oncken, & Fiedler, 1970).

The present authors are in substantial agreement with the Mitchell et al. (1970) criticisms which focused primarily on inadequacies in the specification of the situational favorableness dimension. Although reasonably objective means are available for the specification of task structure and position power, leader-member relations has been typically assessed after the task session (as in laboratory experiments) or at the time of productivity data collection (as in field studies) via a ten item group atmosphere scale. An inherent confounding in this procedure is that group atmosphere scores might be affected by the activities of the group (e.g., success or failures.) While valid this criticism was made less important by the Chemers and Skrzypek (1972) findings, which closely replicated earlier research while independently manipulating leader-member relations.

Questionnaire measurement, such as the group atmosphere scale, poses a problem in terms of comparability across studies. In any particular study, it may be difficult to specify what score on the group atmosphere scale actually constitutes good or poor leader-member relations. A step toward solving these problems was provided by Posthuma (1970). He established norms for the LPC and group atmosphere scales on the basis of an analysis of thirty different contingency model studies. Although such norms do not eliminate the potential source of confounding discussed earlier, they can be quite useful. For example, in a recent study by Chemers, Rice, Sundstrom, & Butler, (1973), the determination of group location on the favorableness dimension was aided by the use of the Posthuma norms.

A related, more general criticism of the contingency model refers to the extensive problem of the dimensionality and anchoring of the situational favorableness dimension. Each of the three variables which determine favorableness is typically dichotomized into two levels. This procedure results in a ranking of eight different combinations rather than a true continuum. This is conceptually unsatisfying and also contributes to errors in assignment. For example, it is possible for two groups to both have relatively high task structure even though one group's task is considerably more structured than the other's. The same state might exist for leader-member relations or power. These variables are conceptually continuous dimensions rather than ordinal dichotomies. Two groups might be assigned to octant IV of the favorableness dimension, but one group might actually be closer to octant V while the other group is closer to octant III.

If the variables were measured on graded continua and combined via a weighted product, a continuous dimension would result. Any group or set of groups, regardless of the context in which measurement took place, could then be placed at the appropriate point on the favorableness dimension. Admittedly, the development of such weighting procedures represents a major undertaking. While the magnitude of such a task is recognized by the authors, two approaches to this problem appear to hold promise. First, multiple regression procedures may be useful for combining a variety of situational factors into a single, weighted index of favorableness. Second, O'Brien and his associates (O'Brien, Biglan, & Penna, 1972; Oeser & O'Brien, 1967) have proposed that structural role theory offers methods to improve specification of the favorableness dimension. If either approach to improved specification of the favorableness dimension proved successful, it would have the effect of providing anchors for the favorable and unfavorable poles of the dimension, reducing discrepancies across studies, smoothing out the contingency curve, and increasing the applicability of the model for naturally occurring groups.

A final problem of the contingency model deals with situational variables which are not included in the favorableness dimension. Several variables which have, at times, been used to specify favorableness, but are not part of the formal specification include stress, (Meuwese & Fiedler, 1965), linguistic or cultural heterogeneity (Fiedler, 1966; Fiedler, Meuwese, & Oonk, 1961), training, experience (Csoka & Fiedler, 1972), leader status, (Rice & Chemers, 1973b), organizational climate (Csoka & Fiedler, 1972), and others. Of course, many other variables prominent in leadership and organizational research could be added to the list. Contingency model theorists have acknowledged the need to incorporate such variables into the theory (Fiedler & Chemers, 1974a).

The question of the most effective way to include such variables remains unsettled. It was stated earlier that a basic assumption of the contingency model is that the leader's potential for influence and control is the most important aspect of the situation. Such a view would require that additional variables be integrated into a specification of favorableness. This could be accomplished in three possible ways.

First, a new set of variables could replace those presently in use. In light of recent evidence on the validity of the model in both laboratory and field studies, such a drastic change would appear unwarranted. An alternative is to add new variables to the list as needed in the same fashion as they are now used. This is a feasible alternative. However, such an approach could result in a steadily proliferating list of sometimes redundant measures without any means for ascertaining a complete finite set.

A third possibility is to incorporate new variables into the favorableness dimension in terms of how they affect the three variables presently in use. This procedure has already been employed in previous studies. For example, in a study of the effects of human relations leadership training in a crosscultural setting (Chemers, 1969), level of training, rather than a group atmosphere measure, was employed for the specification of leader-member relations. In a recent extension of the contingency model, training and experience have been conceptualized in terms of their effects on the implicit structure of the task.

Leadership Training and Experience

As early as 1970, Fiedler was concerned with the effects of leadership training and experience on group and organizational performance. The organizational literature on leadership training effects has not been very encouraging. Campbell, Dunnette, Lawler, and Weick (1970) reviewed the limited literature on leadership training for organizational effectiveness and reached two general conclusions. They found that in most cases the research on training effects has not been adequate to test those effects due to poor design, absence of controls, and inadequate criterion measures. In the few studies which were adequate to test for training effects, the results were mixed and do not inspire great confidence in the efficacy of leadership training. These general conclusions are in line with those of other writers (Fleishman, Harris, & Burtt, 1955; House, 1967).

Recently, Fiedler (1970; 1972b) has offered a new interpretation of leadership training which attempts to integrate training effects into the contingency model framework. Fiedler maintains that leadership training might usefully be thought of as modifying the situation in which the leader functions rather than modifying the man himself. He argues that a leader's motivational orientation or personal style is likely to be relatively impervious to modification through short term training. On the other hand, training might improve the leader's potential influence and control (i.e., the situational favorableness of his job) by helping to remove ambiguity from his job environment. Leadership training, and to a lesser extent experience over time, provides the leader with standard operating procedures, solutions to difficult problems, and formulas and guidelines for carrying out his duties. Fiedler argues that both human relations and technical training have this effect, even if the effects are manifested in somewhat different domains.

If training is viewed as a modifier of situational favorableness, several important ramifications are seen. The contingency model predicts that an improvement in favorableness will have differential effects depending on the leader's orientation (LPC) and his original position on the favorableness dimension. For example, if a situation for a group of leaders is originally of moderate favorableness, the high LPC leaders are predicted to be more effective than the low LPC leaders. If, however, all leaders receive training which provides enough structure to change the situation into a very favorable one, the low LPC leaders are now predicted to be most effective. Thus, by changing the situation, the effect of training has been to improve the performance of low LPC leaders but decrease the performance of high LPC leaders. The net result of training would be zero, which is theoretically compatible with the reported effects of training on organizational performance. Table 16 summarizes Fiedler's hypotheses regarding training and experience.

In this formulation, experience is thought of as on the job training, or conversely, training is simply experience compressed in time. An interesting side note to this concept is Csoka's (1972) finding that the effects of experience are identical to those of training, but only for intelligent leaders who are able to learn from experience.

Two recent papers (Csoka & Fiedler, 1972; Fiedler, 1972b) have offered evidence to support the training hypotheses. The first set of findings

TABLE 16
Summary of Hypotheses Regarding the Effects of
Training and Experience

Favorableness of situation for trained and experienced leader	Performance level of leaders with adequate training and experience LPC		Favorableness of situation for inadequately experienced leader	Performance level of leaders without adequate training and experience LPC		Predicted effect of training and experience for previously untrained leader
	high	Low		High	Low	LPC
Very favorable	Poor	Good	Moderate	Good	Poor	High decreases Low increases
Moderately favorable	Good	Poor	Unfavorable	Poor	Good	High increases Low decreases
Unfavorable	Poor	Good	Very unfavorable	Good?	Poor?	High decreases Low increases

SOURCE: F. E. Fiedler, "Predicting the effects of leadership training and experience from the Contingency Model: A clarification," *Journal of Applied Psychology,* 1973, *57,* 110-113. Copyright 1973 by the American Psychological Association. Reprinted by permission.

which helped to prompt this extension of the model were reported by McNamara (1968). McNamara studied the effectiveness of elementary and high school principals, using the principals' LPC scores as the independent variable. His preliminary findings showed no effects of LPC on performance. However, when the principals were separated on the variable of experience, extremely significant effects were noted.

Among elementary school principals who were new to the job (i.e., less than three years of experience), high LPC principals were most effective. Among the experienced principals, however, low LPC individuals were most effective. The exact opposite was true for high school principals; low LPC leaders were most effective among new principals while high LPC individuals were most effective among experienced high school principals.

Fiedler's (1972b) explanation of these effects takes the following form: An elementary school is a relatively simple organization. It has a flat hierarchical structure, all the teachers do approximately the same activities, and major policy decisions are made at the superintendent level. Thus, after a few years of experience the principal's job is quite favorable, although it is only moderately favorable for a new and inexperienced leader. Thus, the high LPC leaders perform most effectively in the moderately favorable situation (new principals) while the low LPC leaders perform most effectively in the very favorable situation (experienced principals).

In the secondary schools, the principal's job is much more difficult. The organization is more complex, with departments and department heads, the school is larger, and the principal must deal with difficult to manage teenagers. The job is much less structured and even the leader-member relations are likely to be more strained because of interdepartmental rivalries, cliques, etc. Thus the situation is only moderately favorable for experienced principals (high LPC principals perform well) and unfavorable for inexperienced principals (low LPC principals are most effective). For both sets of data performance differed significantly as a function of the interaction of LPC and experience.

To test the generalizability of these effects, Fiedler (1972b) reanalyzed a considerable body of previous research. Using either training or experience as a conceptual mediator of favorableness, he found some support for his hypotheses in data on general managers and board presidents in a farm cooperative; foremen, assistant postmasters, and superintendents in the postal department; and police patrol sergeants.

Impressive results were also found in several new studies of military personnel (Csoka & Fiedler, 1972). In these studies task structure was not used to determine situational favorableness. Based on Fiedler's proposition that training moderates task structure, groups in these studies were assigned to octants of the favorableness dimension on the basis of a measure of group atmosphere and amount of training. In one study of 55 artillery sergeants all leaders were assumed to have high power, except in the situation where they had neither good leader-member relations nor sufficient training. Under such conditions, the authors maintain, position power is relatively ineffective. Leaders were assigned to octants I, III, V, & VIII on the basis of dichotomized group atmosphere and training variables. The resultant LPC and productivity correlations were consistent with those predicted by the contingency model. These effects were later replicated using the same procedure on groups of army company commanders, petty officers in charge of naval aviation maintenance shops, and army mess sergeants.

How valid is this evidence and how good are the hypotheses offered and conclusions drawn? Like the evidence presented earlier in Fiedler's (1971b) paper supporting the validity of the contingency model, these data have strengths and weaknesses. The data presented by McNamara (1968) and by Fiedler's (1972b) reanalysis of previous research are, by their very nature, quite weak. Reanalyses are always subject to charges of *post hoc* gerrymandering of the favorableness dimension to produce desired results. In fairness, it must be noted that Fiedler did not present the McNamara study or the reanalyses as a test of the hypothesis, but merely as weak but suggestive support for the general notions.

The four field studies of military personnel (Csoka & Fiedler, 1972) are not subject to the same criticisms. Favorableness assignments were made on *a priori* grounds and the real life nature of the samples strengthens the generalizability of the effects. The problem of correlational data still remains, however. Field studies, laudatory for their generalizability and realism, do not allow for causal or directional inferences.

Again, carefully controlled laboratory experiments can answer questions concerning the validity of the model. Such an experiment was undertaken by Chemers et al. (1973) to test the effects of leadership training on group performance. One hundred and twenty college students (80 R.O.T.C. cadets and 40 introductory psychology students) were recruited for an experiment in group performance. The R.O.T.C. cadets participated as a required part of their course work and the psychology students received extra credit in exchange for their participation. Forty three-man groups were randomly constructed, with leaders chosen from the upper and lower third of the distribution of LPC scores. The leaders were always R.O.T.C. cadets, and each group was composed of a cadet leader, one cadet follower, and one psychology student follower.

All groups were brought together for a 45-minute task session. Each group was given 18 cryptograms (coded messages) to solve in a predetermined order. All crypotgrams followed a letter substitution format in which each letter in the English alphabet was substituted for one other letter of the alphabet. Each cryptogram had its own code. Difficulty level was controlled by supplying the group with difficult or key letters. The average decoding time was five to six minutes per cryptogram. A sample cryptogram with solution is shown below.

GKKW   GK   MW   WQK   CWMRFT   WDKCOMZ   GFVTRTJ.   R
----------   -----   ------   --------   ------S----------   ----------S-------   ------R-----. ----

BRSS   NK   OVKCCKO   RT   M   NSMLH   FXKVLFMW
---LL----   -----   ----R-SS----------   -----   ----   -----L------   --------R-----------

MEET ME AT THE STATION TUESDAY MORNING. I WILL BE DRESSED IN A BLACK OVERCOAT.

The deciphering of cryptograms represents a relatively unstructured, intellectual-manipulative task. Its lack of structure results primarily from the fact that there are no clear procedures to follow in obtaining a solution. The task tends to be quite high in "goal path multiplicity" (Shaw, 1963).

Prior to the group task session, half of the leaders received a 30 minute lecture-demonstration-participation training program in cryptogram solution. While decoding procedures are not generally known to the novice, such procedures do exist, and knowledge of these procedures drastically reduces the ambiguity of the task. The training session supplied leaders with information on step by step solution procedures, letter frequencies, frequency and distribution of vowels, double letters, one and two letter words, common endings, etc. Leaders were also given practice in solving three cryptograms similar in form to those used in the experiment.

Leader position power was controlled at a low level by telling the groups that the leader was a coordinator with responsibility for the group's peformance but with no real power to reward or punish group members. Leader-member relations were a priori predicted to be good. In past studies of the contingency model, *ad hoc* laboratory groups were generally found to have high scores on post task group atmosphere measures (Posthuma, 1970).

Given these manipulations, the experiment was designed to replicate octant II (good leader-member relations, high task structure, low position power) for trained leaders and octant IV (good leader-member relations, low task structure, low position power) for untrained leaders (see Figure 7).

However, posttask measures of group atmosphere indicated that the groups had much poorer leader-member relations than expected. Using

Posthuma's (1970) norms for group atmosphere, the Chemers et al. (1973) groups were found to have significantly lower group atmosphere than normal (t = 7.09, p < .001, by t-test against an exact hypothesis (Hays, 1963, p. 311). Post session interviews of participants indicated that the R.O.T.C. cadets had been admonished to perform well by their officer cadre. This generated considerable stress. Further, participants volunteered the information that the assignment of cadet and psychology students to the same groups resulted in some internal group stress as well.

Thus, the experimental manipulations resulted in replications of octants VI and VIII rather than II and IV. (see Figure 7). Based on Fiedler's training hypothesis it was predicted that low LPC leaders would perform best in the untrained leader condition (octant VIII, low favorableness), and high LPC leaders would perform best in the trained leader condition (octant VI, moderate favorableness).

This predicted interaction of training and LPC was found to be extremely significant (F = 24.61, p < .00003). Figure 9 indicates that, as predicted, low LPC leaders had the most productive groups in the untrained leader condition, while high LPC led groups were most productive in the trained leader condition.

This experiment provides extremely strong support for Fiedler's (1972b) hypothesis. The study also provides further support for the basic

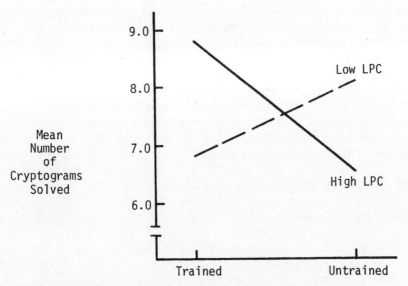

Fig. 9. Interaction of training and LPC on group productivity.

predictive validity of the contingency model. It can be concluded from these findings that training does indeed cause an alteration in the leadership situation, which, when moderated by LPC, has powerful effects on group productivity.

This experiment provides an opportunity to evaluate certain criticisms of the training hypothesis in light of the present results and to conjecture on the implications of this extension of the model. In a recent article, Kerr and Harlan (1973) examined the training hypothesis (Fiedler, 1972b) and offered several points of criticism or clarification. We shall deal with each of these in light of recent findings.

Kerr and Harlan maintained that training and experience effects are really an unimportant addition to the favorableness dimension. They argue that if a situation is favorable, it makes little difference how the situation became so. These authors have missed an important point. Since there is no direct measure of favorableness which is independent of the variables which specify it, any variable which affects favorableness becomes extremely important. Indeed, if we had a "favorableness geiger counter," we would have no need to measure leader-member relations, task structure, etc. However, since no such favorableness meter exists, the measurement of additional relevant variables helps to refine the measurement of favorableness. The inclusion of training and experience both refines and extends the scope of the situational determinants of leadership effectiveness.

In another criticism, Kerr and Handlin were skeptical of the possibility that training has no effect on the leader, himself. They argued that human relations training must surely modify the leader's motivational patterns and indirectly his LPC score. This point is well taken, but it places Kerr and Harlan in the unenviable position of arguing against data from insight. Since the contingency model makes its predictions on the basis of a static LPC score, any change in LPC should reduce the predictability of the theory. The results of the studies by Csoka and Fiedler (1972) and Chemers et al. (1973) indicate that the theory is predictive at a very powerful level.

One qualifier is in order. Most of the studies cited by Fiedler (1972b) involve some form of technical training. Kerr and Harlan (1973) quite correctly pointed out that it is reasonable to assume that human relations training may have very different effects from those of technical training. Leaving aside the question of the general efficacy of human relations training, the effects of such programs might affect leader-member relations more directly than task structure. In this respect, we agree with Kerr and Harlan. Type of training is an important variable which should be examined in future research. Nonetheless, the evidence presented thus far appears to give considerable support to the contingency model explanation of leadership training effects.

The Conceptual Meaning of LPC

We have, until now, assiduously avoided any clear-cut statement about what the LPC scale actually measures. This has been an area of considerable doubt and some controversy. For many years, LPC was correlated with nothing except productivity. As an aside, this is a considerably more acceptable state than that of many personality or motivational measures which have good face and concurrent validity, but which don't predict anything.

At times, researchers in the leadership area have argued that since the exact nature of the LPC construct is vague and confusing, the measure should be discarded. In its place, some argue, we should substitute more familiar measures such as the LBDQ factors of consideration and initiating structure. We feel that such a course of action would be precipitous and ill-advised. The very fact that LPC is a reliable predictor of leadership effectiveness demands that we not discard, but make renewed efforts to understand and possibly improve upon the measure.

Recently there has been a renewed interest in the meaning of LPC. Currently three possible interpretations of LPC are most prominent. Two of these interpretations employ motivational constructs which are assumed to be manifested in leader behavior. The third explanation leans in a cognitive direction and focuses more on perception and information processing than on behavior. Some recent research at the University of Utah has yielded interesting results which may shed some light on this question.

The original interpretation of LPC as an index of motivational characteristics was conceptually quite simple (Fiedler, 1964; 1967). Low LPC leaders, who completely rejected an incompetent co-worker, were thought to be primarily motivated toward successful task achievement. It was assumed that this relatively stable orientation would be manifested behaviorally in terms of high levels of task related or structuring acts. High LPC leaders were considered to be oriented toward and motivated by good interpersonal relations. This motivation was assumed to manifest itself in behavior designed to satisfy that need, specifically high levels of considerate, socioemotional behavior.

This interpretation of LPC is nicely illustrated in recent findings by Rice and Chemers (1973a). They found that low LPC followers rated group atmosphere significantly higher when their groups were highly productive than when they were unproductive. However, low LPC followers' ratings of group atmosphere were unaffected by differences in leader-member relations. On the other hand, the group atmosphere scores of high LPC followers differed significantly as a function of leader-member relations, but were unaffected by group productivity. The original interpretation of LPC also appeared to be supported by empirical findings on the nature of high and low LPC leaders' descriptions of least preferred co-workers (Fishbein,

Landy, & Hatch, 1969), and by their reactions to success and failure on task or interpersonal facets of group functioning (Bishop, 1964; McGrath & Julian, 1963; Myers, 1962). Several studies which have employed descriptions of leader behavior have shown low LPC leaders to be more task oriented and high LPC leaders to be more relationship oriented (e.g., Chemers & Skrzypek, 1972; Hawkins, 1962; Hawley, 1969).

The underlying logic of this interpretation of LPC is that although the leader's behavior, either structuring or considerate, is constant across situations, the situational leadership demands vary. Thus, low LPC leaders are successful in the situations which require strong and directive leadership, that is, the very good or very bad situations. On the other hand, the moderately favorable situations require the subtler, more relationship oriented style of the high LPC leader.

Recently, Fiedler (1972b, 1973a) has offered a new motivational interpretation of LPC. While the original interpretation proposed that LPC is an index of *the goal* that motivates leader behavior, his new interpretation proposes that LPC is an index of a *hierarchy of goals*. Consistent with the earlier interpretation, Fiedler maintained that the primary goal of low LPC leaders is task achievement while the primary goal of high LPC leaders is good interpersonal relations. The new interpretation differs from earlier formulations in that it introduces secondary goals, which become active when primary motives have been satisfied. The secondary goal for low LPC persons is successful interpersonal relations, while high LPC persons are secondarily motivated to attain individual prominence and attention within the group.

This motivational hierarchy hypothesis was prompted by the need to integrate several new findings and data from older studies. Under certain conditions low LPC persons were found to report a greater interest in interpersonal than in task concerns, while the opposite was true for high LPC persons (Bass, Fiedler, & Kreuger, 1964; Bishop, 1964; Fiedler, O'Brien, & Ilgen, 1969; Nealey, [reported in Fiedler, 1972a]). In addition, several studies showed that in situations of high favorableness both high LPC and low LPC leaders deviated from their characteristic forms of leader behavior. In very favorable conditions, low LPC leaders were described as engaging in more relationship oriented behavior while high LPC leaders engaged in more prominence seeking or task oriented behavior (Fiedler, Meuwese, & Oonk, 1961; Meuwese & Fiedler, 1965; Sample & Wilson, 1965; and others).

The motivational hierarchy interpretation of LPC* makes several assumptions which are at variance with earlier interpretations. First, the behavior of both high and low LPC persons is assumed to change with the situation. Under very favorable conditions, low LPC leaders maintain high levels of relationship-oriented or consideration behavior and are also most successful. Under moderately favorable conditions, the high LPC leaders are more considerate and also more successful. Only under very unfavorable conditions does the implied correlation between consideration and success break down. (The word *implied* is used here because none of these studies report direct correlations between leader behavior and success.) This interpretation brings greater concordance between the contingency model findings and those of other researchers concerned with the effects of leader behavior on performance such as the Ohio State (Stogdill & Coons, 1957) and Michigan (Likert, 1961) groups.

A point should be made about the validity of the data used to support either of the above interpretations. Several problems arise in the interpretation of either self report or follower descriptions of leader orientation and behavior. Mitchell (1970a) found extremely low agreement between leader, follower, and observer descriptions of leader behavior in laboratory groups. Likewise, Nealey and Owen (1970) found great disparities in real and perceived use of time by nurses when ratings were made by the nurses themselves, by their superiors, or by an independent observer. Because most studies of leader behavior and LPC have used either leader or member ratings of leader behavior (e.g., Chemers & Skrzypek, 1972), any conclusions must be drawn with caution.

Self-report measures of leader motivation are also suspect. Fiedler (1972a; 1973a) maintains that individuals, when asked to imagine themselves in a leadership situation and describe the behavior they would employ, tend to picture themselves in a very favorable leadership situation. While this may be the case, it is also quite possible that individuals will differ in their imagination of situations. Since situational demands are such powerful determinants of leader behavior, such individual differences in imagination or perception are likely to lead to considerable error in all self-report measures.

A third interpretation of LPC has recently been propounded which conceptualizes LPC as an index of the individual's cognitive complexity (Foa, Mitchell, & Fiedler, 1971; Mitchell, 1970b). Using a modification of Scott's (1963) measure of cognitive complexity which requires individuals to sort and categorize various types of groups, Mitchell (1969) found a moderate correlation (.50) between complexity and LPC. In another measure of the leader's perception of situational factors, Mitchell (1969) asked subjects to rate a series of hypothetical group task situations on situational favorableness. The situational descriptions were systematically varied on the three situational parameters included in the favorableness dimension. In corroboration of the complexity findings, Mitchell reported that high LPC subjects used more information and a more complex procedure for evaluating favorableness than did low LPC subjects. Similar results were obtained by Chemers and Summers (1968).

Thus, LPC is seen as a measure of the individual's degree of differentiation in task situations. A high LPC leader, when asked to rate an individual with whom he had difficulty getting a job done, (i.e., his least preferred co-worker), differentiates between this individual's task performance and personal attributes. The high LPC person is able to rate his least preferred co-worker positively on interpersonal attributes even though he is a poor co-worker. On the other hand, the low LPC person, who gives his least preferred co-worker uniformly low ratings on both task and interpersonal dimensions, is showing a lower degree of differentiation.

As a further test of the differentiation interpretation Mitchell (1970a) divided the LPC scale into three subscales which included items which referred to task performance, items which referred to interpersonal attributes, and items which were not clearly classifiable into task or interpersonal categories. He found that the correlations between these three subscales were significantly higher for low LPC than for high LPC subjects, indicating a lower degree of differentiation for low LPC subjects. In another study, Mitchell and Foa (1969) asked leaders to rate groups with which they had interacted on five scales following an experimental session. The intercorrelations of the five conceptually distinct scales were significantly higher for low LPC leaders than for high LPC leaders.

Foa, Mitchell, and Fiedler (1971) have offered the hypothesis that the situational favorableness dimension can be reconceptualized in terms of the demands which the situation places on the leader to be complex and differentiating. Situations in which the task demands and leader-member relations are congruent (i.e., both favorable for the leader or both unfavorable), call for less differentiation than do situations which offer conflicting demands, such as good leader-member relations but low task structure, or poor leader-member relations with high task structure. These authors argue that the success of low LPC leaders in highly favorable or unfavorable situations and of high LPC leaders in moderately favorable situations is the result of the appropriate matching between the leader's level of cognitive differentiation and the amount of differentiation inherent in the group task situation.

This analysis is provocative. However, the *post hoc* analysis of situations on the basis of differentiation does not provide an adequate test of the hypothesis. This is especially true because of the fact that the same predictions about the relationship between LPC and performance are made by the cognitive differentiation hypothesis and by the motivational hypotheses. So far, the differential, matching interpretation has done no more than apply different terms to the dimensions of the contingency model, i.e., LPC is termed a measure of cognitive complexity and favorableness is relabelled as an index of situational complexity. It remains to be seen if such an interpretation offers any advantages over earlier interpretations.

The results of a recent study by Rice and Chemers (1973b) may shed some light on the value of the complexity interpretation. In this laboratory experiment 32 three-man groups of college students were composed with leaders chosen from the upper or lower third of the distribution of LPC scores. An attempt was made to manipulate leader-member relations in the following manner. Group members in the good relations condition were told that, on the basis of tests administered earlier in the psychology class, the members of this group were highly similar in their orientation toward group function, and they should have a very compatible and effective group. Individuals in the poor relations condition were told that while the two followers were quite similar in their orientations, they were very different from the leader. They were further told that these differences might well lead to an incompatible and difficult group experience. Group atmosphere ratings completed after the task indicated that the manipulation was successful with subjects in the poor relations condition reporting significantly lower group atmosphere scores.

Half the groups were assigned a structured task which required the construction of a tinker toy model from a set of blueprints. The other groups worked on an unstructured task which asked the group to compose an original story in response to an ambiguous picture stimulus. These manipulations yielded four groups with good and poor leader-member relations and high and low task structure. Power was low in all conditions.

All groups were videotaped and trained observers rated the leaders' behavior on three dimensions. The rating scales were modifications of earlier scales developed by Fleishman (1953a) and Carter (1953) and included several new items prepared especially for this study. Factor analyses of the measures indicated three dimensions which were labeled task oriented behavior, relationship oriented behavior, and prominence seeking behavior.

Figure 10 illustrates the observer ratings of high and low LPC leader behavior on the three behavior dimensions. On all three dimensions, there is almost no variability in the behavior of low LPC leaders across situations. The high LPC leaders, on the other hand, show great variability due almost completely to their reactions to differences in task structure. Figure 11 shows the LPC X task structure interactions which are significant on all three dimensions ($F = 6.46, p < .02$ for task oriented behavior; $F = 9.23, p < .006$ for prominence seeking behavior; $F = 5.66, p < .03$ for relationship oriented behavior).

These effects clearly support the differentiation hypothesis of Foa, Mitchell, and Fiedler (1971), and Mitchell (1969, 1970a). Variability in leader behavior across the four cells was compared for high and low LPC leaders, and the F- ratios (with 3/3 degrees of freedom) are 28.88 for task oriented behavior, ($p < .025$), 7.22 for prominence seeking behavior, ($p <$

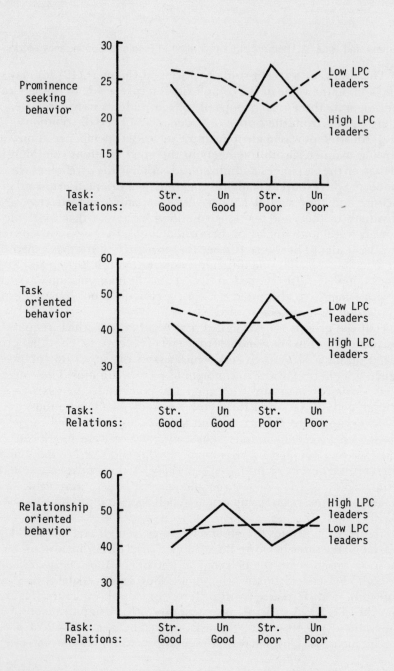

Fig. 10. Observer ratings of high and low LPC leader behavior on three behavior dimensions.

120

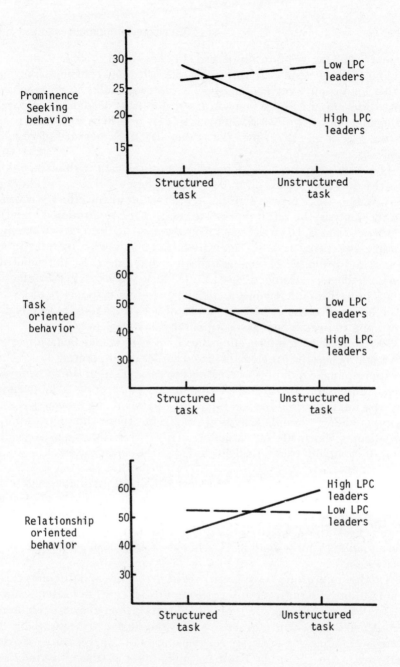

Fig. 11. Significant LPC x task structure interactions for three behavior dimensions.

.10) and 13.02 for relationship oriented behavior, ($p < .05$).

The variance results are consistent with Mitchell's (1970b) earlier finding that high complexity leaders show greater variability in their behavior across different situations than do low complexity leaders. The parallel findings for high cognitive complexity leaders and high LPC leaders support the Foa et al. (1971) hypothesis that LPC is a measure of cognitive complexity.

The results also point to an interpretation relevant to the motivational hierarchy question. Figure 13 indicates that when the leader-member relations variable, which is not a significant interactant in any effect, is dropped from the analysis, the results appear to support the motivational hierarchy hypothesis. That is, from the less favorable unstructured task to the more favorable structured task, the high LPC leaders show an increase in task oriented and prominence seeking behaviors and a decrease in relationship oriented behaviors relative to low LPC leaders. We see, however, that this effect is caused completely by the high LPC leaders' response to task structure rather than a change in the behavior of both high and low LPC leaders in response to overall changes in situational favorableness.

The confusion in interpreting the changes in leader behavior in past studies may reflect the problem discussed earlier of pinpointing and anchoring experimental conditions with respect to their position along the favorableness dimension. In several of the studies supporting a motivational hierarchy interpretation the full range of situational favorableness was not manipulated (e.g., Sample & Wilson, 1965). In others, the specification of favorableness was made on variables such as stress (Meuwese & Fiedler, 1965) which are not traditionally included in the specification of favorableness.

The results of the Rice and Chemers (1973b) experiment suggest that the changes in leader behavior are the result of the high LPC leader's differentiation of and response to changes in task characteristics. These findings lead the present authors to conclude that the complexity-differentiation hypothesis appears to be the most fruitful avenue for future investigation.

Another interesting fact was uncovered in the Rice and Chemers experiment. Although significant and consistent differences in leader behavior were found between high and low LPC leaders, the behaviors themselves were uncorrelated with group activity. This may be due to the possibility that measures of behavior were more reliable and valid than measures of group productivity. On the other hand, it might indicate that our traditional categories of leader behavior and traditional way of measuring leader behavior, i.e., total score on a behavior factor, may not be assessing the most crucial aspects of the leader's behavior. It may be more important to look at changes in the leader's behavior over time or in response to changes in the situation. These results also suggest that it may be useful to look at other categories of leader behavior besides the traditional categories used in our study. The cognitive differentiation interpretation of the contingency model suggests that cognitively related forms of leader behavior may mediate the relationship between LPC and group productivity, e.g., the leader's manner of dealing with equivocality (Weick, 1969), the perception and integration of task and interpersonal demands, patterns of information exchange, etc. Also we may wish to examine the variability in leader behavior matched to the situational demands for differentiation. Future research with these specific foci in mind may help to pin down the elusive link between leader LPC and group performance.

Whichever avenues of future research are chosen, it is clear that the contingency approach must be adopted. The value of the contingency approach in the study of the relationships between LPC, leader behavior, and group productivity was clearly illustrated in the Rice and Chemers (1973b) study. In this experiment, leader behavior differed as a function of situational factors (the task), personal attributes (LPC), and interactions involving individual and situational factors. Such results indicate that a contingency approach, recognizing both situational and personal factors, is necessary for an adequate theory of leader behavior or related leadership processes.

CONCLUSIONS

The research reported in this chapter allows us to reach some relatively strong conclusions. The predictive validity of the contingency model appears to be well supported. Likewise, the recent extension of the model into the effects of leader training and experience promises to be a potentially major advance into our understanding of the leadership phenomenon.

The question of the conceptual meaning of LPC may not yet be fully answered, but the complexity-differentiation hypothesis has received support in several research paradigms and presents a promising new area for contingency model research.

In closing, we should note that the contingency model is not the final answer to the study of leadership effects. Certain leadership phenomena, such as follower loyalty and satisfaction and global organizational effects are not adequately dealt with by the model. Other contingency theories of leadership with different foci will continue to add to our understanding of leadership. We feel, however, that after over twenty years of research the contingency model is alive and well. It is, in fact, still growing and promises to remain a viable source of research ideas and theoretical advances.

Discussant Comments

BY STEVEN KERR

In a recent review of the consideration-initiating structure literature, Kerr, Schriescheim, Murphy and Stogdill (1974, in press) concluded that an important moderator between leader behavior predictors and organizational criteria is the variable "subordinate need for structuring information." It was generally found that the lower the level of subordinate competence, knowledge, and experience, the greater was the subordinates' tolerance of initiating structure and the greater were the positive relationships between structure and subordinate satisfaction and performance. Certain task characteristics, such as ambiguity, increased needs for structuring information as well.

Kerr et al. also found that factors sometimes exist which impair the leader's ability to influence subordinates' satisfaction or performance very much for either better or worse. For example, House, Filley, and Kerr (1971) found generally insignificant relationships between leader behaviors and satisfaction in one of three firms studied, and speculated that the existence of extensive government contracts in that firm may have prevented the leader from exercising discretion concerning rewards, methods, target dates, etc. Rigid bureaucratic rules and regulations, or the existence of tasks which are totally defined by required methodology, may accomplish the same result.

Such factors may be considered to be "substitutes for leadership," since they may reduce subordinate needs for structuring information almost to zero, and thereby neutralize the leader's potential impact upon the attitudes and performance of his work group. The existence of such substitutes for leadership may provide a partial explanation for the claims of some researchers that leadership does not account for very much criterion variance.

A potentially critical substitute, particularly relevant to the samples of scientists (and to a lesser extent, engineers) studied by Farris, is the existence of "professional" standards and methodology. By definition, professionals a) possess expertise, in the form of specialized skills and knowledge usually acquired through academic training; b) demand autonomy to decide *how* their organizational tasks are to be performed and, to some extent, *what* functions they will perform; c) are "cosmopolitans" rather than "locals," identifying more with other members of their profession than with fellow

124

employees within the organization; and d) adhere to codes of ethics and professional self-discipline (Strauss, 1963).

Professionals are often unwilling to be evaluated by hierarchical superiors on organizationally determined criteria. The peer leadership described by Farris typically determines the professional's goals, while his expertise, coupled with the code of ethics, determines his means. Farris has therefore emphasized an important point in stating that "if leadership involves influence on matters of organizational relevance, it can be exerted by any person, *inside or outside* of a formal organization. The persons exerting leadership *may or may not* be in a managerial position" (italics added). Not only when dealing with professional samples, but with any group or situation where leadership substitutes are present, the simple assumption that hierarchical superiors inevitably exert leadership is unwarranted. It is critical, as Farris suggests, to ask not only "*whether* leadership is present at all in a given situation, but *where* leadership is present, and *in what ways*" (italics added).

The matter of "substitutes for leadership" is pertinent also to the research of Chemers and Rice. They claim correctly that their data show strong support for the Fiedler (1967) contingency model in general, and for the position that leadership training and experience affect situation favorableness, bringing about different consequences for leaders high in LPC than for those who are low.

It is less clear that, as claimed by Chemers and Rice, "the inclusion of training and experience both refines and extends the scope of the situational determinants of leadership effectiveness." It has been mentioned elsewhere that

> by increasing the favorableness of the situation you will tend to improve "fits" between leader and situation that are bad, while impairing those that are already good. . . . This is true whether improvement of the situation occurs through experience, training, or for *any other reason*. Furthermore, it is true *regardless of whether the leader is trained or untrained*. . . . The point is that the effects of lack of training or experience will "enter into the equation" by causing the favorableness of the situation score to be lowered. Once this happens, there is no further need to be concerned with the fact that the leader is inexperienced or untrained [Kerr & Harlan, 1973, p. 115].

For evidence of this we need only look as far as Chemers and Rice's own paper. They correctly predicted that "low LPC leaders would perform best in the untrained leader condition (octant VIII, low favorableness), and high LPC leaders would perform best in the trained leader condition (octant VI, moderate favorableness)." However, their hypothesis is not parsimonious. The parts concerning training are superfluous. According to the contingency model, low LPC leaders are *always* supposed to perform best in octant VIII (low favorableness), and high LPC leaders are *always* supposed to perform best in octant VI (moderate favorableness). Since the amount of training in no way alters the prediction, it is a useless appendage to their hypothesis.

The source of their confusion becomes clear when we examine their statement that "the measurement of additional relevant variables helps to refine the measure of favorableness." Certainly it is true that if the training variable were really an *additional* one, largely independent of those components of favorableness which already exist, the refinement claimed by the authors would actually result. However, an analysis of the existing favorableness dimensions has yielded the conclusion that no such independence exists (Kerr & Harlan, 1973). "Adding in" a variable which has already affected favorableness through its effects upon the other components can hardly be said to constitute a refinement and an extension.

Furthermore, it seems foolish to argue, as Chemers and Rice did, for the importance of the training variable that "any variable which affects favorableness becomes extremely important," while claiming at the same time that it is an "extremely important" assumption that "almost all variables which affect the leadership position can be subsumed into the favorableness dimension." Should we therefore conclude that not only is the training variable an extremely important extension to the model, but so are almost all other variables imaginable?

Clearly the authors do not really believe this. For example, the variable "stress" unintentionally emerged as an important part of their experimental induction. Yet despite this fact, and not withstanding that Fiedler (1967) and others have found that stress can exert significant influence upon the model, Chemers and Rice apparently saw no reason to revise their predictions so as to treat stress as an extremely important variable. Instead, they simply allowed it to "enter into the equation" by lowering the favorableness score, and then made predictions wholly consistent with those to be expected in the absence of stress. Why then should training be treated (or thought of) any differently?

It can therefore be argued that, while contingency theory may bring new insight to the literature on leadership training, the leadership training variable is simply one of many which is subsumed within situation favorableness, and cannot be said to constitute an important extension and refinement of that dimension.

It is also less clear that "leadership training might usefully be thought of as modifying the situation in which the leader functions *rather than* modifying the man, himself" (claimed by Fiedler and cited by Chemers & Rice; italics added). The effect of leadership training and experience on LPC scores still seems to be unclear, with some studies showing LPC to be fairly stable over time, while others (e.g., Stinson & Tracy, 1972) claim rather sizable changes as a result of experience or training. Fiedler himself has cautioned that LPC stability "depends to a considerable degree on the intervening experience of the men [1967, p. 48]."

More important is the point that, even if we assume for the moment that LPC is virtually immune to change by training or experience, this does *not* mean that the leader is not changed. What seems to have been forgotten is that LPC is *not* considered to be a measure of leader behavior, but is instead claimed to measure some properties of the leader's motivational system. No one seriously argues that the leader's motivational system affects work group performance *directly*. Rather, there is considerable evidence (e.g., Sample & Wilson, 1965) that leaders with different LPC scores exhibit different behaviors in a given situation, and it is these behaviors which subsequently affect subordinate performance. The question of LPC stability then becomes academic because, whether or not leadership training and experience can change the leader's motivational system, they are certainly able to change his behavior. In fact, to the extent that they do *not* change his behavior, by what magic do they change either situational favorableness or work group performance? (Theoretically, situation favorableness could be changed by the mere fact that the leader was perceived to be more experienced, or to have undergone training. Examination of the method for scoring favorableness, however, leads to the conclusion that in the absence of behavioral change, alterations in the situation favorableness score would probably be trivial.)

Once it is recognized that the leader *is* changed by experience and training, we must account for data that "confirm" a flawed hypothesis. It is certainly not being suggested that logic and intuition are adequate substitutes for data. However, we ought to explore alternate explanations for the failure of training and experience to improve leader effectiveness systematically. In addition to the hypothesis of Chemers and Rice (which seems to have been confirmed so far as their own study is concerned, although they failed to include any postexperiment measurement of LPC) that the situation is changed but not the leader, the following hypotheses are proposed:

1) Training and experience change both the leader and the situation. In this case good leaders would continue to be good, and leaders whose performance was poor prior to training would continue to be poor. This is because the old "mismatch" (say, a task motivated leader in a situation of medium favorableness) might simply be replaced by a new one. "Human relations" training, for example, might cause the task motivated leader to be more relationship motivated, or at least to behave as though he was. At the same time, such training might improve leader-member relations enough to render the situation highly favorable. In such a case, no change in ovreall performance would result.

2) Training changes neither the situation nor the leader. This might be the case, for example, with relatively low IQ trainees. A stupid person would

not be expected to learn from his experiences, or from training, and would therefore behave after training as he did before.

3) Training changes the leader but not the situation. This is particularly likely when "substitutes for leadership" exist. Many times "professional" values and expertise, company policies, or office politics may prevent the "changed" leader from exhibiting his new behavioral repertory. Here again, no change in overall performance would be expected to result.

One other point which seems open to question is concerned with the current interpretations of LPC as measuring some motivational properties of the respondent. Chemers and Rice state that "the low LPC rater is effectively saying that 'if I cannot work with you, you are a bad or unworthy person." The implication is that first the respondent decides upon the person whom he will describe (that is, the person with whom "he had the most difficult time in getting a job done"), and then he thinks of the individual with reference to bipolar adjective scales. The further implication is that these adjectives are not the basis for the choice of the individual being described. This assumption is critical, because only if the adjectives are unrelated to the job which the respondent and his ratee had difficulty in getting done is the notion of LPC as a measure of motivational properties tenable. To the extent that the adjectives are the cause of the ratee being selected, LPC becomes merely a tautological device. If I select my least preferred co-worker precisely because of many of the characteristics described on the LPC, and then I rate him negatively on these characteristics, what have you learned about my motivational system?

Obviously, this dilemma is best prevented by compiling a list of adjectives which are unlikely to be related to the performance of most tasks. Some of the adjectives on the lists provided by Fiedler (1967) and his associates seem satisfactory in this regard (e.g., cold, rejecting), but others seem quite likely to be job relevant. The clearest example of such an adjective is *inefficient*, and others might include *unfriendly*, *uncooperative*, and *quarrelsome*. These last three might be extremely job relevant in some situations, such as those involving extensive interdependence, and irrelevant in others. Other adjectives (such as *stupid*, cited by Chemers and Rice, could become relevant in cases of high task complexity. It seems unclear, therefore, to what extent LPC is a measure of motivational properties, and to what extent it is a factual statement of the reasons for selection of the least preferred co-worker. Particularly when task characteristics cause many adjective sclaes on the LPC to be job relevant, its use as a measure of motivational properties is likely to be confounded. [A study by Fishbein, Landy, & Hatch (1965), along with a recent note by Fox, Hill, & Guertin (1973), reporting LPC factor analysis results may be of some interest here.]

In closing, two sidelights seem worth mentioning. First, it appears that leaders are being haphazardly selected to attend training programs. The overall failure of training to improve leader effectiveness must mean that as many effective leaders are being sent off to be trained (and, according to the contingency model, to be ruined) as ineffective ones. Were this not the case, the overall effects of training would have been positive.

Finally, some words should be said in support of unintelligent leaders. Many studies have shown relatively dull leaders to perform as effectively as bright ones, and in fact the relatively low IQ leaders discussed in Chemers and Rice's paper were somewhat more effective. Furthermore, unintelligent leaders are probably cheaper to acquire and to retain. Most importantly, engineering the job to fit the manager is less difficult when the manager is dull. This is because a bright person who is placed in a situation of appropriate (for him) favorableness will quickly learn from his experience, and will inadvertently create too favorable a situation for a good "fit." An unintelligent leader, on the other hand, will not "benefit" from his experience, and so will continue to perform effectively.

Human relations theorists have long maintained that tasks are, unfortunately, designed by organizations to be so simple that unintelligent employees can perform them best. It now begins to appear that efficiency may be further increased by hiring unintelligent managers as well.

5

Contingent Aspects of Effective Management Styles

BERNARD M. BASS and ENZO R. VALENZI

INTRODUCTION

Two dimensions of managerial behavior consistently reappear in prescriptive analyses of leadership. It is argued that participative approaches are more effective than directive approaches in a wide variety of organizational situations (Likert, 1961; McGregor, 1967). Furthermore, authors describing "organizations of the future," based on observable trends in approaches to organization design, note increasing requirements for managers with skills in interpersonal relations, power equalization, social influence, and collaboration, as opposed to the rational, analytical, impersonal, and rule oriented skills required of managers in bureaucratic "mechanical" organizations (Bennis, 1967).

Nevertheless, evidence is mixed with regard to the utility of participation as opposed to direction. In the past 30 years, most survey studies have found that participative rather than directive managers are more likely to have more productive departments. But when controlled experiments have been performed, participative managerial behavior did not turn out to yield higher productivity (Sales, 1966). Explanations of these diverse results have been given in terms of task and organizational variables, as well as variables associated with the attitudes, values, goals, and styles of managers and subordinates. Additional explanations focus on method of investigation, suggesting that questionnaire data are more likely to reflect the effects of spurious variables than are well-controlled experiments. It may also be that only effective organizations can afford to be participative rather than vice versa.

Many of these studies appear to assume that participative approaches imply personal strategies while directive approaches imply the use of positional influence, but as Bass (1960) noted, it takes power, often positional power, to be a participative supervisor. At the same time, a personally powerful, charismatic leader can be highly directive.

From a partial review of available evidence, Bass and Barrett (1972) suggested that the tendency to pursue participative or directive approaches depends on 1) numerous aspects of a manager's own history, attitudes, values, and goals; 2) similar aspects about his subordinates; 3) the environment external to the manager's organization; 4) specific attributes of top management; 5) the organizational climate and structure in which the group supervised is embedded; and 6) various requirements of the task being supervised.

An overall purpose of our program of research was to test and modify a model accounting for the tendency of managers to be directive, participative, or to pursue styles in between such as manipulative, delegative, and consultative. In doing so we would examine the situational determinants affecting these tendencies as well as their differential effectiveness under varying contingencies. The model would link investigations in survey and laboratory, hopefully becoming a more faithful replica of reality as we proceeded. Ultimately, a sufficiently complex model could be developed which could form a beginning for a formal, testable, theory of leadership.

An integrated series of surveys and experiments is in progress building upon a preliminary survey of the literature on the tendencies of supervisors to be directive or participative as a function of the personality of the supervisor and his subordinate, the external and internal organizational environments, and the task to be accomplished (Bass & Barrett, 1972). The first review was followed by a more comprehensive updated concentration of how person, organization, environment, and task influence leader behavior (Valenzi, Miller, Eldridge, Irons, Solomon, & Klaus, 1972). These two reviews led directly to a selection of what were judged as the most reliable, valid, and popularly employed measures of organizational, environmental, and task variables and leader behavior. These measures were incorporated in a survey administered to 177 middle and upper level managers in industrial organizations and 153 managers and subordinates from military and service organizations who described the behavior of their supervisors. Analyses of this survey to be summarized here isolated dimensions of consequence which affect leader style and effectiveness. A second analysis yielded a hierarchy of dimensions of leader behavior consistent with a theory of leadership as a function of task demands. Another portion of the survey made it possible to test a theory of management style consistent with a systems view of power and information differences between superior and subordinate. It also uncovered the extent to which managers are seen to employ a variety of styles. The transitional model as it now stands in Figure 12 is still fairly primitive.

THE MANAGER-SUBORDINATE SYSTEM

A manager and his subordinates are viewed as an open social system of two persons. The two-person system is open to a variety of informational and power inputs from its environment which are enumerated in Figure 12. The inputs stem from organization, group, task and personal sources. What takes place within the two-person system can be described in terms of four variables: the power difference between manager and subordinate, their information difference, the structure of the system, and the objectives of the manager. These in turn condition which managerial style will be most appropriate for effective functioning of the two-person system. Such effectiveness is measured by how well objectives have been attained and the degree of satisfaction with various aspects of the system. These outputs act on the environment of the two-person system and subsequently affect inputs from the environment.

To transform inputs into outputs, two flows occur within the system, one of power, the other of information. A cycle of events is completed of inputs, transformations, and outputs. The outputs result in a new wave of inputs and a next cycle. The relations within the system grow and become more intricate with repeated cycles to accomplish transformations (Katz & Kahn, 1966). Figure 12 shows the main elements of the system we wish to model.

At the beginning of a designated cycle of events, the energy or power available to the manager and to the subordinate can have been established by outside authority, or by expectations of legitimacy which each has brought with him to the system. The manager may have such power over the system as the power to override or veto any decision his subordinate makes, to grant or deny promotion or salary increases to his subordinate, to reverse the priorities of his subordinate, to control the size of his subordinate's budget, or to get higher authority's support for what he, the manager, wants to do.

Similarly, the subordinate may have various amounts of power including the power to bring outside pressure to support what he, the subordinate, wants, to do the opposite of what the manager wants him to do; to maintain final control over his own plans, assignments, and targets regardless of what his manager thinks about them; to submit his own requests to higher authority ignoring his manager; or even to nominate or vote for who will be his superior. Organizational, group task, and personal inputs can contribute to the manager or subordinate's power.

Informational differences between managers and subordinates may be due to differences in ability, readiness, personality, education, and so on. Or the differences can be positional—due to the difference in access to available information, or location in a larger communication network (Bass, 1960).

The structure is given by the formal and informal relations between manager and subordinate. Formal relations—relations between occupants of positions regardless of who they are personally—exist between the manager and his subordinates which make it possible to predict more readily each other's behavior. The manager may be formally required to issue directives; the subordinate may be formally required to follow them. Where such formal relations do not fix completely how manager and subordinate will work together, a developmental process takes place between the manager and his particular subordinate. Informal relations emerge, relations which depend on the two individuals more than on the positions they occupy (Bass, 1960).

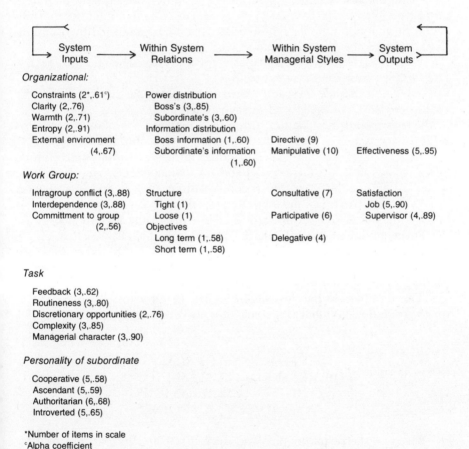

Fig. 12. Model of manager-subordinate system, number of survey items in most current survey, and alpha coefficients.

Such structures can be described as tight or as loose. The system may be highly constrained by a formal structure of relations or by informal legitimacies so that mutual predictability is high and further system development is unlikely. Both manager and subordinate may be bound by rules, constrained by regulations, by time demands, by schedules over which they have no control, by fixed requirements for methods and solutions. Behavior within the system may thus be highly programmed. Or, contrarily, the system may have little orderliness and predictability to it, lending itself to much adaptation, change, and development. The structure is seen as a consequence of organizational, group, task, or personal variables.

Equally important is describing whether the manager has long and/or short-range goals; whether he is concerned more about the development and growth in the effectiveness of the system or more in immediate maximization of goal attainments. These objectives are conditioned by organizational, group, task, and personal inputs.

Five managerial styles are proposed for study based on literature review and factored scale development studies to be described: *directive, manipulative, consultative, participative*, and *delegative*. We postulate that the probability of the occurrence of each for effectively functioning systems is a joint effect of the power and information differences between the manager and his subordinate as well as their structural relation and objectives.

As seen in Figure 12, we need to look empirically at how system outputs (effectiveness and satisfaction) depend on management styles. But these styles are a function of within-system relations (power and information distributions, structure, and objectives). These in turn depend on what impacts on the system from outside of it. Empirically we can also short-circuit the model ignoring the black box within it. That is, we can ask if we attain better empirical correlations between system inputs and system outputs and within system styles without recourse to the *deus ex machina* of needing to know anything about the within-system relations.

The numbers in parentheses in Figure 12 refer to the results of the survey scale development which are described below.

DEVELOPMENT OF SCALES
FOR MEASURING SYSTEM INPUTS,
WITHIN SYSTEM RELATIONS,
AND SYSTEM OUTPUTS

Based on the review by Bass and Barrett (1972), eight sets of variables were selected for inclusion in our first questionnaire as potential contingencies of leader behavior. They were: biographical, leader behavior per se, organizational structure, task, work group, personality, work unit effectiveness, and satisfaction variables. A second literature review was completed for each variable set (Valenzi, et al., 1972) built around a number of suggestions from the literature about contingent relationships between leader style and situational variables. Because there already were a large number of survey instruments available, they were used as sources of items for the further development of scales to measure situational variables and leader behaviors.

The questionnaire was designed according to the following format. Items were collected from already existing instruments and some new items were written and classified according to the eight sets of variables emerging from the literature reviews. All items were cast into five point or six point Likert formats except for the effectiveness and satisfaction items which were on five point scales consistent with the content of the items. Items belonging in the same set were placed consecutively with their separate instructions defining the content of that group of items and how to respond to them. This encouraged a common frame of reference for all subjects.

Response bias was controlled in two ways. First the wording of the items was such that scoring directions were reversed for some of them to lessen the effect of the acquiescence response style—the tendency of some respondents to agree with a statement when in doubt about it. Secondly, except for biographical information, the order of the seven sections was varied independently across questionnaires so that possible order effects would not be systematic. Care was taken in assembling the questionnaires to ensure that each section appeared in the first, second . . . seventh place approximately an equal number of times.

A total of 288 items, not including biographical items, was included. The number of items per section was as follows: task, 28; leader behavior, 73; effectiveness and satisfaction, 16; work group, 52; organizational, 36. Sixty-four personality items were also included.

Because a questionnaire was desired that would be useful for surveys in different kinds of organizations, a deliberate attempt was made to secure respondents from a heterogeneous sampling of organizations. Accordingly, completed questionnaires were obtained from four manufacturing firms (n = 178 middle and upper level managers), a U.S. Army reserve unit (n = 80 enlisted men), and four social service and volunteer organizations (n = 67) for a total sample size of 325.

All subjects were volunteers and anonymity of response was guaranteed. Questionnaires were distributed in several ways. Army reserve questionnaires were obtained in groups of 20–30 at the regular drill meeting, social service and volunteer respondents as well as some managers received questionnaires in person but returned them through the mail, and other managers both received and returned questionnaires through the mail. One group of managers (n = 24) completed the questionnaires as part of a management training exercise. All respondents were instructed to answer items from the perspective of subordinates describing their boss's behavior, the effectiveness of their work unit, and their organizational environment.

Because the initial pool of items drew upon many sources that differed with respect to theoretical and methodological rationale, scale construction started with factor analytic procedures rather than conventional item analysis. Each questionnaire section, except for biographical information, was subjected to a principal components analysis with varimax rotation. For each section, scales were constructed to measure those factors that accounted for the largest amount of variance. To construct a scale those items were selected that had the largest factor loadings—typically these were larger than .40. A total score was computed for those items by summing the scores on the five-point scales and item-total correlations computed for each item. Coefficient alpha, an internal consistency estimate, was computed for each scale, and items were added until an acceptable internal consistency was attained or until no further increment in coefficient alpha was possible.

The factored scales which emerged, their number of items, and coefficient alphas are shown in Figure 12. As can be seen, acceptable internal consistencies were obtained with a relatively small number of items per scale.

The revised form of the Management Styles Survey (MSS) is somewhat unique in that it contains scales with adequate psychometric properties to measure a large number of variables shown to be relevant for the description of effective mangerial behavior.

Data collection is currently underway in a number of diverse organizations to check on the stability of the scales and on potential bias arising from the inadequate sampling of subjects. In this stage of the research an important modification in the nature of the data obtained will be made. Besides requiring respondents to describe the behavior of their superiors, we will also obtain self-descriptions from superiors and their own boss's descriptions of the same superior. Thus a single individual will be described at three organizational levels: by his subordinates, by himself, and by his superior.

MEASURING MANAGERIAL STYLES

What factors appear in leader behavior depend upon the initial content analyzed as well as the posited number of factors. A most popular solution has been Fleishman's (1973) two factor initiating structure and consideration based on a series of studies at Ohio State which identified these two as most salient among a larger list. The closest styles in management to initiating structure are direction, task direction, structuring, production emphasis, and authoritarian leadership. Conceptually, such direction can be given by a superior with or without reasons. Presumably, if he gives reasons he is exhibiting some consideration for his subordinates, which may raise him in Fleishman's second factor of consideration. Elements in initiating structure, direction, structuring, include: trying out new ideas on subordinates, making attitudes clear, assigning subordinates to particular tasks, making sure each subordinate understands what he is to do, insisting subordinates follow standard operating procedures, maintaining definite standards of performance, talking about how much is to be done, seeing that subordinates work to full capacity, emphasizing the meeting of deadlines, deciding in detail what shall be done and how it should be done (Fleishman, 1973; Halpin & Winer, 1952; Hemphill, 1950; Hemphill & Coons, 1957).

Many other behaviors could be conceived as included in direction, such as Suttell and Spector (1955) offered, which included: instructing, supervising, informing, ordering, and deciding.

Bass (1960) argued that these leader behaviors could be attributed to the leader's ability, knowledge and power, and various sources of power such as the power from one's position or status in the organization and the power from one's person or esteem regardless of position. More such direction would be expected from leaders, the more they had knowledge and power.

Consideration included seeing that subordinates are rewarded for a job well done, keeping subordinates in good standing with those in higher authority, expressing appreciation for good work, stressing the importance of satisfaction among subordinates, maintaining and strengthening the self-esteem of subordinates by treating them as equals, making subordinates feel at ease when talking with the leaders, remaining easily approachable, putting subordinates' suggestions into operation, and getting the approval of subordinates on important matters before going ahead. At the other extreme on the same dimension were inconsiderate supervisors who frequently demanded more than could be done, who criticized subordinates in front of others, who treated subordinates without considering their feelings, who "rode" subordinates for making mistakes, and who frequently deflated the self-esteem or threatened the security of subordinates by acting without consulting them, refusing to accept suggestions, and refusing to explain actions (Fleishman, 1953a, 1973).

When a three factor solution of 79 leader behavior items was completed by John Miller (1974), to be described below, consideration broke into two factors which hindsight suggests takes us back to the fundamentals of ideology about social influence. One may subscribe to a Machiavellian view of what is required to change people, which calls for manipulation, playing with social credits and debits, and pursuing a political approach to change. This includes: withholding or timing the release of information, maintaining social distance, bluffing, publicly supporting but privately opposing particular points of view, agreeing to act but delaying or postponing action, forming alliances, and generally negotiating with subordinates (Bass, 1968; Christie & Geis, 1970).

On the other hand, in agreement with those pursuing a more angelic view of man like social theorists Jefferson, Emerson, Dewey, and more recently the human relationists and group dynamicists, there are supervisors who emphasize participation and consultation. Typical behaviors seen in this social approach include: open, frank, candid communications, shared decision making, open and complete commitments, establishing mutual goals, fostering mutual trust, organizing group discussions (Bass, 1968).

Note again that conceptually two managerial styles flow from this behavior: consultation and participation. In the former, the leader discusses matters with his group or his subordinate, then decides based on such consultation. Presumably, subordinates feel they have participated in the decision to the extent they feel their contributions have made a difference. In full participation, a consensual decision is pursued.

A fifth style—delegation—is a form of leadership which requires recognition and analysis as another useful managerial style.

In the main survey 300 respondents completed 72 leader behavior items assembled from standard sources such as the LBDQ. The 73 items were first subjected to a principal components factor analysis. Kaiser's (1958) eigenvalue criterion was employed to select the first 12 principal components for varimax rotation. The results of this solution were consistent with familiar orthogonal factorizations of leader behavior items, although it was clear that certain factors were neither conceptually nor empirically independent (i.e., they had high item loadings in common).

Relationships among factors were investigated in two ways. First, a hierarchical description (Zavala, 1971) was generated by rotating successively two, then three, then four, and so on, up to 12 principal components, using the varimax (orthogonal) rotation algorithm. At each level, interpretable solutions reflecting familiar leader behavior factors emerged. The two-factor solution clearly paralleled consideration and initiating structure, although the label "consideration" was rejected as a motivational inference appropriate to only a subset of the items defining this factor.

Other clearly identifiable factors discovered in previous research emerged successively: production and goal emphasis and close supervision split apart as subfactors of initiating structure in the four-factor solution. Participating (cf. Heller & Yukl, 1969 re decision-centralization) emerged at level six, information sharing at level seven, and supporting (the narrowly interpersonal interpretation of consideration) at level eight, enforcing rules and procedures emerged as a subfactor of close supervision at level nine.

A second approach to the factor structure, rather than "top-down," was to carry out a higher order factor analysis (Schmid & Leiman, 1957) by calling for oblique (in this case, oblimin) rotations of the 12 principal components stipulated by Kaiser's criterion, then factoring the matrix of factor intercorrelations. This procedure directly produced two clusters of factors. Although the interpretation of higher order factors with reference to original items is not typically straightforward (cf. Cattell, 1966), these two clusters clearly confirmed the "top-down" hierarchical analysis. The three primary factors loading most significantly on the first higher-order factor were consideration, power equalization (or decision decentralization) and abdicating (negative of demanding). The three primary factors loading most highly on the second were: production emphasis, directive, controlling, and inflexible.

The five scales assembled to measure the five styles of the model in Figure 14 were built with the information gained from these factor studies. Thus, the nine-item scale of direction contained nine initiating structure items; the ten-item scale of manipulation contained five items from a manipulating and influencing factor; and so on. The scales now available deal with the following contents:

Direction: Telling subordinates what is expected of them, seeing that they work to capacity, emphasizing meeting deadlines, setting standards, ruling with an iron hand, encouraging uniformity, scheduling subordinates' tasks, telling subordinates to follow rules and regulations, changing subordinates' duties without first talking it over with them.

Manipulation: Doing personal favors for subordinates, changing behaviors to fit the occasion, persuading, promising, making subordinates compete with each other, timing the release of information, making political alliances, maintaining social distance, bending rules, reassigning tasks to balance the work load.

Consultation: Being candid and open to questions, listening to subordinates, trying out subordinates' ideas, giving advance notice of changes.

Participation: Sharing decision making, making attitudes clear, arranging meetings, putting group suggestions into operation, treating subordinates as equals, being approachable and friendly.

Delegation: Exhibiting confidence in subordinates, leaving members free to follow their own course, permitting subordinates to make their own decisions.

Before these scales were assembled, a survey of 110 of the 300 respondents was completed in which the five styles were defined for the respondents borrowing from Heller and Yukl (1969) and only one or two global ratings of each style were requested. For instance, the respondent merely had to indicate how frequently his boss consulted with his subordinate. The format is shown in Figure 13.

When the correlations between scales are calculated (see Table 17), these global ratings form a hierarchy indicating that a single general factor underlies them. They form a continuum: consultation, joint decision mak-

In reaching a decision within his authority and of consequence to you and or your subordinates, how frequently does your boss:

Decide without a detailed explanation?	0	1	2	3	4	5
Decide, then give a detailed explanation?	0	1	2	3	4	5
Consult with his subordinate(s) before deciding?	0	1	2	3	4	5
Bargain, negotiate an exchange, deal or contract?	0	1	2	3	4	5
Decide jointly with his subordinate(s)?	0	1	2	3	4	5
Delegate the decision to his subordinate(s)?	0	1	2	3	4	5

In the above, 5 = always, 4 = very often, 3 = fairly often, 2 = sometimes, 1 = seldom and 0 = never. These adverbs were determined by magnitude estimation and the numbers bear an absolute relation to each other. *Never* is at absolute zero. Very often, for an average respondent, is literally seen as about twice as frequent as sometimes; seldom is about half as frequent as sometimes.

The within systems variables use similar magnitude estimation alternatives so that values from the various within systems scales can be multiplied.

Fig. 13. Example of format used for scales.

ing, delegation, manipulation, direction with reasons, direction without reasons.

The continuum also is related to satisfaction with supervision. The correlations between management style and satisfaction are positive for consultative, participative, and delegative styles, and zero or negative for the manipulative and directive styles.

As can be seen in Table 17, the frequency with which a manager is seen to employ a given style is related to subordinate satisfaction with supervision. The most frequently used styles are those that have positive correlations with satisfaction and the less frequently used styles have zero or negative correlations with satisfaction. The latter finding suggests that within system management styles may be sensitive to feedback from the system outputs as indicated by the model.

A number of reasons can be offered for this outcome in contrast to the relative independence of leader factors such as emerge for the LBDQ or as will be described in more detail later. [However, though there was some early evidence suggesting independence of LBDQ dimensions, the House-Dessler chapter as well as material in Fleishman and Hunt (1973) cast doubt on such independence.]

First, we are dealing with an ipsative response pattern. One cannot say that one's boss always consults and always directs. To be consistent, if he frequently does one thing, it is less likely he can frequently do everything else. Second, we are dealing with a global measure. Detailed behavioral descriptions of consultation, say, can hang together as a factor independent

TABLE 17

The Correlation Hierarchy among Global Ratings of the
Frequency with which Managers Employ Various Styles

Style	Style					
	Consul-tation	Partici-pation	Dele-gation	Manipu-lation	Direction With Reasons	Direction Without Reasons
Consultation		.68	.26	.24	-.09	-.49
Participation	.68		.36	.20	-.25	-.43
Delegation	.26	.36		.17	-.15	-.30
Manipulation	.24	.20	.17		.10	-.08
Direct with reasons	-.09	-.25	-.15	.10		.12
Direct without reasons	-.49	-.43	-.30	-.08	.12	
Correlation of Style and Satisfaction with supervisor	.40	.44	.30	-.07	-.19	-.31
Mean frequency that style is reported	3.10	2.65	2.46	1.88	1.97	1.90

of, say, a pool of manipulative items even though consultation and manipulation lie on the same global continuum. Furthermore, the typical analysis, principal factors, and varimax rotation must produce such a result, i.e., independent factors. [But see Glass & Maguire, 1966.] Third, it may be useful, at times, to locate a manager on such a continuum, recognizing that as we will show he is likely to exhibit a variety of styles. Presumably, location on such a continuum would be less forecast by situational compared to personal traits where personal factors imply some generalized tendencies of the manager. To sum up, we asked a global question here and obtained a global answer.

The extent to which each management style was seen to be used by a manager was correlated with the extent he was seen to have more power, P, and more information, I, than his subordinate. Standardized multiple regression equations were calculated for all 110 managers surveyed with these global methods as well as for those 55 above the median in effectiveness as assessed by a factored set of seven scales of work unit and organizational effectiveness and for those 55 below the median.

Results were as follows for direction:

Direction (A)	$= .03P + .07I$	$R = .07$
Effectives only: A	$= .12P + .05I$	$R = .14$
Ineffectives only: A	$= .22P + .04I$	$R = .12$

Our first expectations were that for effective managers, increased power and information would contribute to increased directiveness. While the betas for the effective managers were in line with such expectations, results failed to attain statistical significance.

For manipulation, results were as follows:

Manipulation (M)	$= -.22P - .07I$	$R = .23 (p < .05)$
Effectives only: M	$= -.21P - .15I$	$R = .27$
Ineffectives only: M	$= -.23P - .02I$	$R = .23$

We expected that manipulation would be greater when effective managers were highly informed but lacked power. Actually, for effectives and ineffectives, a significant relation at the 5% level supported the contention that manipulation is greater when both power and information are lacking. The same trend appeared for effective managers.

For consultation, results were as follows:

Consultation (C)	$= .09P - .14I$	$R = .16$
Effectives only: C	$= .24P - .28I$	$R = .35 (p < .05)$
Ineffectives only: C	$= -.03P - .02I$	$R = .03$

Our expectations were initially that for effective managers, more power coupled with less information would associate with greater amounts of consultation. Results were in line with such expectations and significant at the 5% level.

For participation or joint decision making, we obtained:

Participation (J)	$= .06P - .16I$	$R = .15$
Effectives only: J	$= .16P - .35I$	$R = .37 (p < .05)$
Ineffectives only: J	$= .01P - .01I$	$R = .02$

Results support the contention that participation goes along with more power in a leader. It takes power to permit subordinates to participate yet remain effective as a manager. But such participation is also seen to reflect lack of information in the manager as well. Results are significant for effective managers at the 5% level.

We expected that where power and information favored the subordinate, more delegation would be employed. This occurred, but for ineffective managers only. Results failed to attain statistical significance.

$$Delegation\ (D) \qquad = -.13P -.01I \qquad R = .13$$
$$For\ effectives\ only:\ D \quad = -.10P +.10I \qquad R = .13$$
$$For\ ineffectives\ only:\ D = -.17P -.08I \qquad R = .18$$

The structural tightness of constraints within the manager-subordinate system was assessed by two questions for the 110 managers:

How frequently is your boss bound by rules, constrained by regulations, by time demands, by schedules over which he has no control, by fixed requirements for methods and solutions?

$$0 \qquad 1 \qquad 2 \qquad 3 \qquad 4 \qquad 5$$

How frequently are you and your subordinates bound by rules, constrained by regulations, by time demands, by schedules over which you have no control, by fixed requirements for methods and solutions?

$$0 \qquad 1 \qquad 2 \qquad 3 \qquad 4 \qquad 5$$

As was expected, tight constraints went with more direction and manipulation and less consultation, participation and delegation, but no correlations were significant.

Short run rather than long run objectives were a combined measure based on the difference between the following two scales:

How frequently does your boss concentrate on short run results, quick payoffs, maximum productivity at minimum costs now?

$$0 \qquad 1 \qquad 2 \qquad 3 \qquad 4 \qquad 5$$

How frequently does your boss concentrate on long range payoffs, the development of your subordinates and you, the creation of a capable and effective operation for the long run?

$$0 \qquad 1 \qquad 2 \qquad 3 \qquad 4 \qquad 5$$

Again, as expected, more short-run objectives coincided, but not significantly, with direction and manipulation and greater long run objectives with consultation ($r = .25$ $p < .01$), participation ($r = .20$, $p < .05$) and delegation (n.s.).

We will not attempt to interpret these data nor complicate our model with these data in mind. They merely are pilot results suggesting that generally we may be moving along the right track. We will repeat the analyses with more reliable measures of managerial style before regarding our testing of these relations as sufficient for interpretation and use in increasing specifications of the relations between within-systems variables and managerial styles. Future analyses will be done with the multiitem scales of managerial style noted in Figure 14 with reliabilities which will be hopefully at satisfactory levels for establishing firmer signficiant relations between within system variables and management styles.

A simple yet important question is whether a manager pursues one style or many. If he concentrates on one, it argues for the importance of personality in contrast to situational demands. It puts a premium on selection and classification. On the other hand, if managers tend to use different styles on different occasions, it argues for attaching greater importance to situational analyses with a premium placed on training. If the same manager uses a variety of styles and if different situations call for different styles, then what is required is that managers know how to use those styles they don't ordinarily employ, and learn on which occasions one style is more appropriate than others.

The answer seems to be very clear. Few managers are seen to use only one style; most are seen to use a variety of styles. Hill (1973a; 1973b) looked at 124 middle and first level supervisors in the United Kingdom. Only 14% of the supervisors were seen as likely to use the same one of four styles in four hypothetical situations. We obtained even sharper results when we asked 124 subordinates in our survey to describe how frequently their superiors actually used five styles. A manager was classified as exhibiting a *single* managerial style if the subordinate responded to only one of the scales of Figure 13 with a "very often" or "always" and the remainder with "never" or "seldom." A manager was classified as exhibiting a *dual* approach if the subordinate answered on two scales of style with "very often" and/or "always" and the remainder with "never" or "seldom." A manager was classified as exhibiting a *multi*managerial approach if the subordinate answered on at least three scales with "sometimes," "fairly often," "very often," and/or "always." Subordinates' response patterns not meeting any of the above schemes were designated as unclassifiable. Of 124 subordinates, 3 or 2.4% indicated that their boss exhibited a single style, 1 or 0.8% indicated that their boss exhibited a dual approach, 117 or 94.4% indicated that their boss exhibited a multistyle approach and 3 or 2.4% were unclassifiable.

As Heller and Yukl (1969) reported earlier, we also find that the most frequently reported style is consultation (see Table 17). The gaps between the mean frequency of consultation and participation and between participation and direction were statistically significant at the .001 level. Thus the average for consultation was close to fairly often (=3.00) while the average for direction was close to sometimes (=2.00).

RELATIONS BETWEEN SYSTEM INPUTS, MANAGEMENT STYLES AND SYSTEM OUTPUTS

The variables in the organizational, work group, and task subsets together specify the environment in which the boss and subordinate are required to function. While the complete model postulates that the impact of the environment on effective managerial behavior is conditioned by the distribution of power and information between boss and subordinate, the present analysis short circuits the complete model and deals with variables of environment, leader style, and output (satisfaction and effectiveness).

Three analyses were performed on the factored scales of the 288 item survey questionnaire from the 325 respondents to explore relationships

TABLE 18

Multiple Regression of Management Styles with Output Variables

Management Style	Satisfaction with Supervisor		Job Satisfaction		Work Unit Effectiveness	
	Beta Weight	R^a	Beta Weight	R^a	Beta Weight	R^a
Participative	.45**	.58**	.18*	.29**	.03	.24**
Directive	.26**		.18*		.23**	
Manipulative	.08		.05		-.06	

Note.—df for multiple Rs are 3/155. The multiple regressions were as follows:

Satisfaction with supervisor = β_1 (Participation) + β_2 (Direction) + β_3 (Manipulation)

Job satisfaction = β_1 (Participation) + β_2 (Direction) + β_3 (Manipulation)

Work unit effectiveness = β_1 (Participation) + β_2 (Direction) + β_3 (Manipulation)

[a]Multiple correlation between the three leader style variables and output variable.

*p < .05

**p < .01

among the variables of interest. First, three multiple regression analyses were completed to see the pattern of how frequently a manager employed three management styles for which preliminary versions of factored scales were available: direction, manipulation, and participation. How they related to two satisfaction scales as well as a work unit effectiveness scale was calculated. Second, the sample was split at the median as nearly as possible on each systems input (Figure 14) and zero order correlations between each of the three styles and each systems output were computed. Third, because the three output variables of satisfaction and effectiveness were correlated with each other, second order partial correlations between outputs and management styles were also computed as a control on the halo effect. Thus, for example, the common variance effects of job satisfaction and satisfaction with supervision were removed from correlations between management style and work unit effectiveness.

Table 18 shows the multiple regression of the pattern of these factored management style scores against output. It can be seen that satisfaction with supervision was most strongly linked to the profile of three styles with a multiple R of .58 (p < .01). The other outputs, although significant at the .01 level, were less strongly associated (R = .29 and .24).

Most important, clear evidence was seen in the beta weights showing the differential contribution to output of participation, direction, and manipulation. Participation was associated with satisfaction with one's supervisor (p < .01) but not unit effectiveness; direction was associated with both (p < .01), and manipulation with neither.

The relationship of a directive leader style to work unit effectiveness became more convincing when analyses disclosed that for subsamples based on differential systems inputs to be described below, the effect transcended most subsample splitting. Of 13 splits, 11 maintained significant positive correlations between a directive leader style and effectiveness for either high or low subsamples, regardless of how they were different on system inputs. In other words, a directive leader style was consistently and positively related to effectiveness.

The total sample of 325 was split into high and low subsamples on the basis of their scores on each systems input (excluding the four personality variables) listed in Figure 14. For each subsample, correlations were computed between each management style and each output with the expectation that, if found, significant differences between the correlations for low and high subsamples would demonstrate the strongest evidence for contingent relationships.

Contingent effects were most evident for the output, satisfaction with supervision. Table 19 summarizes the important effects. Of 13 systems inputs analyzed, four revealed significant differences between low and high subsamples. Directive supervision was seen as more satisfying when the

TABLE 19
System Inputs that Make a Difference in
Management Style–Satisfaction with Supervisor Relations

System Input	Zero-order correlations between management style and satisfaction with supervisor			Partial correlations between management style and satisfaction with supervisor (Holding constant effectiveness and job satisfaction		
	Partici-pative	Direc-tive	Style Mani-pulative	Partici-pative	Direc-tive	Mani-pulative
Commitment (Group)						
Low	.51	.45	-.10*	.50	.35	-.05
High	.58	.31	.25*	.48	.24	.17
Entropy (Organization)						
Low (Organized)	.52	.16*	.01	.43	.13*	.00
High (Disorganized)	.51	.50*	.16	.52	.43*	.12
External Environment (Organization)						
Low (Influence)	.44	.21*	.11	.39	.10*	.09
High (Influence)	.61	.53*	.05	.59	.40*	.00
Management characteristics (Task)						
Low (Planning, Coordinating)	.55	.25*	.04	.50	.21*	-.05
High (Planning, Coordinating)	.49	.61*	.15	.44	.49*	.21

Note.—Sample size in low and high subsamples ranged from 70 to 90.
*Difference between the correlations is significant at the .05 level.

organization was seen as disorganized (high entropy), the external organization environment exerted strong influence on work activities, and the tasks required a high degree of planning and coordinating the work of others. These are especially interesting results because they suggest that under certain conditions directive supervision can be seen as satisfying. Manipulative supervision was seen as more satisfying when commitment of members to the goals of the group was high.

Because the three output variables were correlated with each other (supervisory satisfaction and job satisfaction, .54; job satisfaction and work unit effectiveness, .45; supervisory satisfaction and work unit effectiveness, .36), partial correlations analogous to the zero order correlations were computed except that two of the three output variables were held constant. For example, the partial correlation between participation and job satisfaction would partial out the common variance effects of work unit effectiveness and supervisory satisfaction from both variables in the correlation. This was a severe restriction on the correlations because it assumed that all the common variance among the four variables was the result of a general halo effect, which may not be the case.

Comparing the partial correlations of Table 19 with the zero order correlations for supervisory satisfaction, the main difference was the disappearance in significance of the contingent effect of the systems input of commitment, in the partial correlation analysis. The other systems inputs, entropy, external environment, and management characteristics had similar effects in both analyses.

There were no contingent effects revealed in the zero order correlations for job satisfaction. But the situation is quite different for the partial correlations. Four systems inputs revealed significant differences between the partial correlations for low and high subsamples on one management style or another (Table 20). Under conditions of a relatively high degree of organization (low entropy) but loose constraints and highly routine tasks, a participative leader style was positively correlated with job satisfaction and negatively correlated otherwise. Ordinarily the sign reversal would signify an especially strong contingent effect analogous to intersecting profiles or a disordinal interaction (Lubin, 1961) in the context of an experimental design analysis. The absolute values of the correlations are relatively low however and should be cautiously interpreted. Tasks low in planning and coordinating the work of others had a positive correlation with a manipulative management style. A negative correlation appeared for tasks high in planning for others.

Three systems inputs had significant contingent effects on the correlation of managerial style with work unit effectiveness (Table 21). When the level of interpersonal conflict among group members was high, a directive leader style had a positive correlation with work unit effectiveness while there was no correlation for low intragroup conflict. A directive leader style also had a positive correlation with effectiveness for tasks high on coordination and planning of the work of others and zero correlation otherwise. In the partial correlation analysis there was only one significant contingent effect of a systems input variable and no clear pattern was discernible among the remaining correlations.

TABLE 20
System Inputs that Make a Difference in
Management Style–Job Satisfaction Relations
(With Supervisor Satisfaction and Effectiveness Partialled)

		Style	
System Input	Participative	Directive	Manipulative
Entropy (Organizational)			
Low (Organized)	.17*	.03	.06
High (Disorganized)	-.17*	-.06	.03
Constraints (Organizational)			
Loose	.22*	.02	.05
Tight	-.27*	.03	.06
Routineness (Organizational)			
Varied	-.21*	.02	.04
Routine	.14*	-.03	.06
Management characteristics (Task)			
Low (Planning, Coordination)	-.03	.06	.26*
High (Planning, Coordination)	-.03	-.13	-.19*

Note.—Sample size in low and high subsamples ranged from 67 to 89.

* Difference between the correlations is significant at the .05 level.

AN EXPERIMENTAL PARADIGM IN CONTINGENT ASPECTS OF MANAGERIAL STYLE

We have completed data gathering (although not analysis, as yet) of an experiment which hopefully will become the first in a series. We manipulate the power difference between manager and subordinate and measure their difference in information to obtain within systems data. Five managerial styles are role played by the manager and the outputs of satisfaction as well as objective goal attainment are measured. By selecting subjects from different organizational settings, we may be able also to collect systematically data on systems inputs.

The standardized research instrument, PAXIT, is an exercise developed by Shackleton, Bass, and Allison (1973). The exercise requires a

TABLE 21
System Inputs that Make a Difference in
Management Style–Unit Effectiveness Relations

System Input	First-Order Correlations Between Management Styles and Work Unit Effectiveness		
	Participative	Style Directive	Manipulative
Intragroup Conflict (Group)	-.02	.04*	-.08
Low			
High	.11	.31*	.01
Entropy (Organizational)			
Low (Organized)	.36*	.14	-.05
High (Disorganized)	.06*	.18	-.02
Management Characteristics (Task)			
Low (Planning, Coordination)	.11	.09*	-.10
High (Planning, Coordination)	.06	.37*	.03

Note.—Sample size in low and high subsamples ranged from 62 to 89.

*Difference between correlations is significant at the .05 level.

subject first to choose by himself a list of 10 items from a list of 100 that he considers are the 10 most essential items to enable a crashed pilot of a small light airplane to survive in a hostile environment. The respondent repeats this procedure five times, each with concern for surviving in a different geographical area: mountains, cold water, tropical rain forest, warm seas, and the Arctic in winter. A respondent's score is based on the number of items which he considered essential that a panel of survival experts debating the same problem also considered essential. Thus five scores are available for each individual—one for each of the five geographical areas.

In our first experiment, the subjects were 76 NROTC students at the University of Rochester. Each subject completed PAXIT individually, and then a second time in pairs. The individual scores on PAXIT allowed a calculation of the base level of information for each individual, for each of the five areas, based on the scoring procedure outlined above. The power variable was manipulated by instructions.

All subjects were incorporated into dyads, with one of the pair assigned the role of leader and the other the role of his assistant. The assistant was always a freshman student, while the leader was an upperclassman—a sophomore or junior. Since the structure of the NROTC organization was such that the upperclassmen are given a great deal of responsibility for organization of NROTC activities, while the freshmen are essentially given none, the experimenters capitalized on this arrangement and thus the leaders were legitimate managers of the two person system in the experiment. We were simulating an ordinary, but temporary boss-subordinate relation. What was also required, however, was a manipulation of power such that in some cases the subordinate's power could be considered as greater than the manager's. This was accomplished by an evaluation procedure. In 50% of the dyads, the assistant was given a four-page evaluation questionnaire of exactly the same design and format as that currently used by NROTC staff to evaluate students. In the remaining 50% of dyads, the leaders received this questionnaire. Subjects were told that one of the pair—the evaluator—would evaluate the other on his behavior during the experiment, and that the resulting scores would be placed (as they really were) on both the individual's and the NROTC company records. The full support of NROTC staff was obtained for using this procedure. This evaluation procedure can be seen to endow the evaluator with real power.

Each of the leaders was instructed in how to role play five leader styles—participation, manipulation, consultation, delegation and direction. Each leader discussed each of the five subproblems of PAXIT with his assistant, each time role playing a different style. Five orders were employed to balance out order effects.

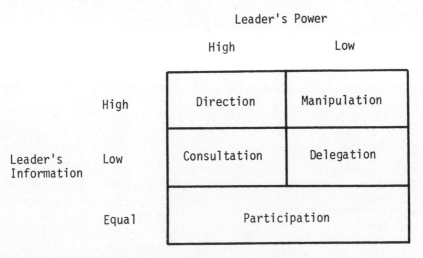

Leader's Power

		High	Low
	High	Direction	Manipulation
Leader's Information	**Low**	Consultation	Delegation
	Equal	Participation	

Fig. 14. Style most likely to be effective as a function of the power and information difference between leader and assistant.

A measure of the amount of relevant information available to leader and subordinate was based on their initial individual scores on each of the five PAXIT scales. The change in score from the average of the scores of the leader and subordinate, to the final score based on the results of the discussion between leader and subordinate, was used as a measure of the success of the dyad's interaction.

Analysis of results is in process. The hypothesis of interest is that the most appropriate leader style for effective functioning will be a function of the difference in power and information between the leader and subordinate.

Specifically, the hypotheses under test state that each of five styles will be most effective in each of five combinations of power and information, as shown in Figure 14, where leader's power and information are stated in relation to subordinate's power and information.

We need obviously to relate system inputs to within system variables. We need to design studies where input, internal, and output variables are each measured independently. We need to initiate cross lagged research to tease out cause-effect relations. We need to experiment with subjects drawn from different organizational settings to provide different systems inputs. Given time and resources, all these can be done. We believe we have made a start with our identification and distillation of relevant sets of variables with their associated measurements both in survey and experimental settings. Our model is still mainly a primitive listing of variables, but as our empirical work advances, strong inferences will be substantiated, enabling us to increase the model's complexities, specifying relations between variables and feedback loops.

Discussant Comments

BY ERICH P. PRIEN

I have been reading the research literature and doing a bit of research during the past several years. It has occurred to me that there are some common threads running through what I have read. One of these threads is reflected in the statement or phrase, "More research is needed." What authors really mean here is that somehow they neglected to ask the right question or they failed to measure the salient variables in the study. Another one that I read occasionally is, "Confirmation awaits further research." What they really mean to say here is that they attempted every conceivable statistical analysis, every manipulation, and finally they came up with an improbable value—something that was significant. They don't know what to do with it, but nonetheless, they did get something significant. My favorite one is: "We don't know what we are doing, but we are doing it very carefully, and hope you will be pleased with our unintelligent diligence [Wherry, 1957]."

More than 20 years ago, Harold Guetzkow (1951) said at a symposium that one of the problems in social psychology was that they lacked a unique vocabulary and that the discipline had to beg, borrow, and steal terms and concepts from other disciplines in psychology. More recently I suggested that one of the problems in industrial-organizational psychology was that we lack a standard set of terms or a standard set of instruments. A number of other people have suggested this also [e.g., Triandis, 1966]. I contend that these conditions—the lack of standard terms, the lack of standard instruments—seriously limit our efforts to integrate results of different studies, and thus they interfere with our progress. The detrimental effect is magnified by our seeming reluctance to legitimately use the output of other disciplines, not only of psychology but disciplines such as sociology, education, and so forth. Now my own position is, "if you want to see what's ahead of you, then you ought to get up on someone else's shoulders."

The point is that we collectively appear to be unduly resistant to either innovating, adapting data from these other disciplines, or to collaborating with our own peers. We arrive at different conclusions on the basis of our research, particularly so when we piecemeal one variable at a time. I have seen study after study looking at leadership or manager performance or any other phenomenon where one researcher takes one variable as a moderator, another takes another variable, and so on. They use their own instruments, they use slightly different terms, and it is difficult if not impossible to go across these studies to piece together a description of where we are at the present time.

Now as I read the Bass-Valenzi chapter, what they are saying is that if we want to understand a particular phenomenon, then it is essential that we study that phenomenon—here leadership—within the total natural context. Look at all variables. Look at the complex, rather rich complex, of environmental characteristics, job characteristics, person characteristics. When we do that, then we will increase our understanding of this particular phenomenon. Now there is considerable evidence, I think, that if we go into additional studies there is a relationship between what people will do and the environment in which they perform. Environments can be described, and we have linked these characteristics directly to individual behavior. Jobs also have definable characteristics and there is evidence of linkage to individual behavior and, of course, individual differences do exist and we have linked these to differences in behavior. Bass and his associates appear to be implementing a comprehensive design to obtain simultaneous measures of a total set of the variables representing the logical, relevant domains. Eventually (as is pointed out in the Bass and Valenzi chapter) they will increase the scope of their sampling to ensure that they have covered the full range of each of these variables.

Now, I want to raise some specific questions, questions that I had possibly because I would have done some things a little differently.

1) Are Bass and Valenzi suggesting that leadership be cast as a dependent variable rather than as an independent variable?

2) If the answer to this is "yes," then I would ask a question—what are the target variables for research and/or intervention?

3) If they are building instruments based on past research, based on their literature survey, then why do they ignore the complexities of some domains and ignore others altogether? Particularly important are the functions that supervisors or managers perform. These are not task characteristics, but an inventory of the functions that they perform. Is this not a relevant domain?

In my own synthesizing of studies of measures of manager functions, I identified 14 different dimensions (see Prien & Ronan, 1971). Also in synthesizing results of studies of organization structure and climate, about 14 different dimensions were identified (see Ronan & Prien, 1973). Some of these dimensions characterized what could be called structure and some characterized climate. Now in Figure 12, in the Bass and Valenzi chapter, only five organization characteristics are identified. The ones that are used there do resemble—at least the labels are the same—the ones that could be derived if some published studies were consulted (see Ronan & Prien, 1973). Obviously Bass and Valenzi are working within the same domain but ignoring, I think, some of the richness of that domain. When this question was raised with Bass, his answer was that they selected the variables that appeared to have some relationship to leadership as reflected in prior studies. This is a good technique, but my contention is that perhaps we haven't done the right studies to illustrate the relationship between some of these other dimensions and leadership, and that excluding these other dimensions may be premature. So, while the design is elegant, I would have preferred more of a concession; I would have preferred that they had gotten up on the shoulders of the people who preceded them in this area to take a better look at what's coming in the future.

One other comment regarding the Bass-Valenzi chapter concerns the criterion problem. My own personal view is that while the focus on the system inputs is very appropriate, there is a disproportionate underemphasis on system outputs. I am very reluctant to accept as a measure of effectiveness the judgments or the perception of a particular subject within that system; especially when he is the subject that is giving the data on supervisory or manager style. [A similar point is also discussed in the volume covering the first leadership symposium.]

4) Finally, how do I intervene? Of course as a practitioner I am concerned with intervention. If I want to change system outputs, what variables do I concentrate on within this total complex?

General Discussion

The general discussion following the Bass and Valenzi chapter and Prien's responses centered upon the important variables to include in any model attempting to predict individual or organizational criteria. Discussion concentrated on Prien's comment that the functions that supervisors and managers perform should be included in a model such as that of Bass and Valenzi. Prien pointed out that the results of diary and observational studies indicated considerable variance in the actual activities of managers and that some managers spend as little as 4% or 5% of their time in the interpersonal contacts with subordinates emphasized by Bass and Valenzi. The rest are spent in other managerial functions. Bass welcomed Prien's comment and agreed that the question of the extent to which a manager's style depends upon the amount of time he must spend on such activities as investigating, staffing, and processing information represented a critical area that needed attention. [The process variables discussed by Olmstead in the next chapter appear particularly germane here.]

Bass also pointed up an additional related concern that is missing in much of the work currently being done. He was concerned about the linkages due to the functional demands that develop as a consequence of membership in a particular department. He indicated, for example, that in most of the studies with which he had been involved, he had on the one hand been looking at organizational variables (such as, is this an engineering department or a research and development department?) and on the other hand looking at the behavior of individuals. However, little attention was paid to the relationships between the department names and their functions and the behavior of individuals in those departments, such as the Taylor chapter on technology and behavior has done.

House reinforced this concern with the impact of the technology on the leadership style available to the supervisor. He suggested that this point is probably underestimated in most of the research being done. Consistent with Kerr's earlier discussion, House indicated that there are some kinds of leadership styles that just simply are not available to some supervisors as a result of technological parameters. He pointed out that this has been showing up in the teaching of supervisory styles that are compatible with the organizational climate within which the supervisors must operate. He suggested that perhaps it was more than just climate that precludes certain styles and that it may be the engineering of the job itself that precludes some styles. He went on to say that this point has implications not only for training and leadership but also for intervention strategies. For example, we have human engineering and job engineering from the production point of view, and we might begin thinking of organizational engineering from the point of view of producing greater compatibility with what theoretically are desirable leadership styles. As Fiedler (1967) has suggested, perhaps one could have a greater impact on productivity by engineering the work situation than by engineering the leader. [Kerr's earlier comments about substitutes for leadership also appear relevant here as do functional equivalency and equifinality notions; see Katz & Kahn (1966); Triandis, (1966)].

Korman suggested that this organizational engineering was possible only if one knew the mechanisms by which it operates. In anticipation of one of the key points in his overview, he indicated that there are at least five separate kinds of mechanisms by which technology can operate and suggested that the dilemma we are facing is that in the study of variables like technology we have not paid attention to these mechanisms, and because this has not been done they are not understood and therefore cannot be used for organizational engineering.

Prien suggested there is a great need for crossdomain research in industrial psychology, and a strength of the Bass-Valenzi chapter was its attempt to be more comprehensive and to include variables which at the present time we do not have strong support for including in the model. Advances in knowledge will come only if we attempt to go beyond what present theory dictates.

6

Leader Performance as Organizational Process: A study of Organizational Competence*

JOSEPH A. OLMSTEAD

Historically, the importance of mission related performance in leadership has been a somewhat neglected issue. Recently, however, there has been increased recognition that, at least in goal oriented organizations, effective performance of mission related activities by individuals in leadership positions may be as important as the more commonly studied "maintenance" or "human relations" aspects (Bass, Cooper, & Haas, 1970). Especially when organizations are viewed from the perspective of open systems theory (Katz & Kahn, 1966), the mission related performance of individuals who occupy nominal leadership roles becomes critical, because those who occupy such positions are also responsible for organizational achievement and survival. Much of their influence upon their organizations is exercised through activities directed toward these objectives.

The study reported here was concerned with the performance of teams of middle level leaders in a military organization and with a test of theory concerned with the relation of certain mission related processes to the effectiveness of organizations. The study was the first phase of a program designed to identify critical leadership functions within complex organizations and was intended to lay the foundation for future studies of the effects of leadership upon what will be termed here *organizational competence.*

*The research reported in this chapter was performed at HumRRO Division No. 4 under Department of Army contract; the contents of this chapter do not necessarily reflect official opinions of the Department of the Army.

CONCEPTUAL APPROACH

Bennis (1966), probably the most articulate critic of customary ways of studying behavior in organizations, has concluded that conventional approaches are "out of joint" with the recently emerging view of organizations as adaptive, problem solving systems. He argued that "the main challenge confronting today's organization . . . is that of responding to changing conditions and adapting to external stress [p. 46]; and that there is a need for studies which reveal the processes by which the organization, through its members, searches for, adapts to, and solves its changing problems. Bennis further concluded that the methodological rules by which an organization approaches its task and interacts with its environments are the critical determinants of effectiveness and, without an understanding of these dynamic processes, knowledge about organizational behavior is woefully inadequate. Building upon this position, Bennis has proposed that the major concern should be with "organizational health," defined in terms of "competence," "mastery," and "problem-solving ability," and has postulated a number of criteria or "ingredients" of organizational health (1966, pp. 52–54).

A number of other theorists (Altman, 1966; Katz & Kahn, 1966; Schein, 1972) have adopted similar views of organizational behavior. This swing to a process emphasis signals a significant new development in ways of thinking about organizations. If the views of these theorists are correct, it would appear that the processes through which organizational adaptation occurs should be a significant subject of analysis and that it would be important to learn precisely how these processes influence and contribute to the effectiveness of organizations.

The study reported here was designed to test some of the concepts of Bennis (1966) and Schein (1972) and to learn whether the processes performed by individuals at various levels of organizational leadership contribute to effectiveness. The concepts which follow were starting points for the study and established the basic framework for data collection.

The concept of *organizational competence* is intended to encompass within one term the processes used by organizational systems to cope with their environments. It was hypothesized that organizational competence is a major operational determinant of organization effectiveness. When effectiveness is the final outcome (goal achievement, mission accomplishment, etc.), competence is the ability of the organization to perform the critical operational functions (processes) that lead to the achievement of effectiveness. When the organizational processes which compromise competence are performed well, they enable an organization to cope with problems arising in its operational environments. When performed poorly, they may negate many of the positive effects contributed by efficiency in other areas of endeavor.

It was further hypothesized that the ability of an organization to maintain competence under change and pressure from its environments is closely related 'to its ability to sustain effectiveness. If the processes break down when the organization is subjected to the stress of external pressures, effectiveness will be impeded. On the other hand, if the processes continue to function adequately, effectiveness should be maintained or enhanced.

Two of Bennis's (1966) "ingredients of organizational health" and an additional one suggested by Schein (1972, p. 118) were adopted as components of competence. Thus, organizational competence was defined in terms of the following competence components:

1) *Reality testing* (Bennis, 1966): Capacity to test the reality of situations facing the organization—the ability of the organization to search out, accurately perceive, and correctly interpret the properties and characteristics of its environments (both external and internal), particularly those properties which have relevance for the functioning of the organization.

2) *Adaptability* (Bennis, 1966): The capacity to solve problems arising from changing environmental demands and to act with effective flexibility in response to these changing demands.

3) *Integration* (Schein, 1972): The maintenance of structure and function under stress and of a state of relations among subunits such that coordination is maintained and the various subunits do not work at cross purposes.

In order to evaluate the competence of an organization, it was necessary to measure the components of which competence is comprised. The problem was to find a method for converting these broad components—reality testing, adaptability, and integration—into elements that would be susceptible of measurement.

It appeared that the various stages of Schein's (1972) adaptive-coping cycle closely resembled the components hypothesized as comprising competence. In short, the cycle, with modifications, appeared to be a feasible basis for operationalizing organizational competence.

Accordingly, the following seven processes were derived from Schein's adaptive-coping cycle to serve as bases for analyzing organizational competence:

1) *Sensing:* The process of acquiring information about the external and internal environments by the organization.

2) *Communicating information:* The process of transmitting information that is sensed to those parts of the organization that can act upon it.

3) *Decision making:* The process of making decisions concerning actions to be taken as a result of sensed information.

4) *Stabilizing*: The process of taking actions to maintain internal stability and integration which might otherwise be disrupted as a consequence of actions taken to cope with changes in the organization's environments.

5) *Communicating implementation*: The process of transmitting decisions and decision related orders and instructions to those parts of the organization that must implement them.

6) *Coping actions*: The process of executing actions against an environment (external or internal) as a consequence of an organizational decision.

7) *Feedback*: The process of determining the results of a prior action through further sensing of the external and internal environments.

It is important to note that each of the processes is related to one of the components of Competence. The relationships are as follows:

Competence Component	*Organizational Process*
Reality testing	Sensing; Communicating information; Feedback.
Adaptability	Decision making; Communicating implementation; Coping actions.
Integration	Stabilizing.

Thus, each component of competence is comprised of one or more organizational processes which can be measured and whose quality of performance can be evaluated.

METHOD

The method of study employed extremely elaborate simulation and data reduction procedures. Here, space limitations do not permit a full description of the methodology. Accordingly, only a summary of aspects considered relevant for understanding the results will be presented. (Details of the methodology appear in Olmstead, Christensen, & Lackey, 1973.)

The study focused upon the activities of members of command and control groups in U.S. Army infantry battalions. In terms of systems theory, these groups constitute "leading systems" (Katz & Kahn, 1966, p. 63) and, accordingly, are critical to the performance of their organizations.

The overall method was to simulate the activities of an infantry battalion engaged in combat operations in Southeast Asia. The specific method of simulation was one-sided role playing in which officer subjects filled the roles of 12 key positions in the battalion. Each simulated battalion was exposed to a series of events, extending over a period of eight hours, to which it was required to respond. Although activities of the subjects were uninterrupted over the entire period, the simulation was designed in three administrative phases which differed in the intensity of environmental pressure. *Pressure* was defined in terms of task load as determined by frequency and complexity of inputs. Ten 12 man groups of subjects participated, thus providing for 10 replications of the simulation.

Figure 15 shows the simulated organization and indicates those levels and units occupied by players and experimenters respectively. From Figure 15, it can be seen that subjects occupied three levels in the simulated organization. The levels were 1) battalion commander, 2) battalion executive officer and staff officers, and 3) company commanders.

Experimenter/controllers filled roles at higher (brigade) levels, lower (platoon) levels, and adjacent units. Through the use of preplanned and scheduled inputs, experimenter/controllers created a dynamic and realistic situation which provided continual environmental changes and placed stringent requirements for rapid and flexible organizational responses upon the members of the simulated organization.

Early in the exploratory phase of this study, it was recognized that an organizational simulation is a highly complex situation which requires careful planning if control is to be exercised and data are to be efficiently recovered. Accordingly, a method for controlling inputs and for recovering data was developed. The method is based upon the concept of a *probe*. A probe is a problem which is designed to stimulate a particular subsystem of the organization and about which data can be recovered separately from data concerned with other probes. Thus, probes can be planned to challenge all different subsystems and to cover a wide spectrum of problems and activities.

Operationally, a probe is a set of inputs consisting of one or more messages designed to provide information about the problem or to stimulate action by the organization concerning the problem. A single input about a probe is a *probe element*. In this study, probes consisted of from one to fifty probe elements. Taken together, probe elements concerning a single probe make up a pattern of information about the problem. However, elements pertaining to a single probe can be inserted at different points in the organization, at different times, and by different sources; they possess an unfolding quailty which requires the organization to assemble all of the information about a probe and interpret it properly before it can act upon it correctly.

Except for a very small number of contingent inputs, all probe elements in the simulation were scheduled to be inserted in the same numbers and at the same times for all experimental groups. Through this means, there could be assurance that all groups were exposed to the same experiences and, therefore, that data would be comparable across groups.

The scenario was designed to present 128 interlocking probes which consisted of 376 probe elements. In multiple element probes, time from

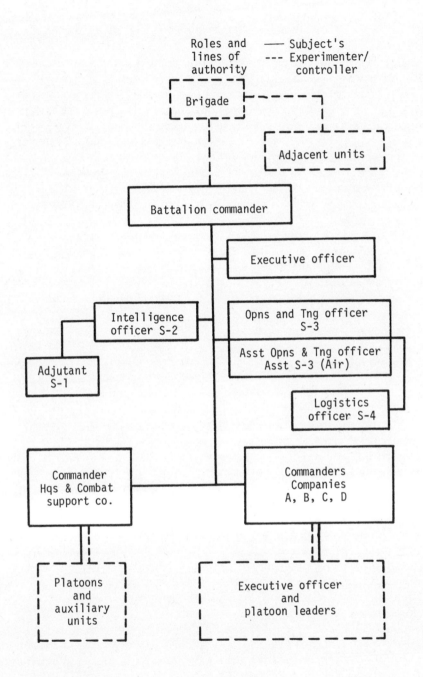

Roles and   —— Subject's
lines of   ‑‑‑ Experimenter/
authority   controller

Brigade

Adjacent units

Battalion commander

Executive officer

Intelligence officer S-2

Opns and Tng officer S-3

Asst Opns & Tng officer Asst S-3 (Air)

Adjutant S-1

Logistics officer S-4

Commander Hqs & Combat support co.

Commanders Companies A, B, C, D

Platoons and auxiliary units

Executive officer and platoon leaders

Fig. 15. Organization of the simulated battalion.

163

introduction of the first input to insertion of the last element for a single probe varied from several minutes to over three hours. Furthermore, elements pertaining to a single probe might be inserted by several controllers into different points within the simulated battalion, thus requiring considerable communication among players before a complete and accurate view of the problem could be achieved. Since probes varied in numbers of elements and in lapsed time for completion of scheduled inputs, each group worked on numerous probes concurrently. Once inputs were inserted, players were free to react spontaneously—to handle the problems in any way they chose. The research staff made no attempts to control player responses or to influence problem solutions.

The research design included a requirement for exposing participants to different degrees of environmental pressure in the three operational phases of the simulation. To manipulate pressure according to the design, three input characteristics were varied across phases. They were 1) frequency of inputs to which players were required to respond; 2) complexity of probes, in terms of number of elements comprising a probe; and 3) importance of probes for mission accomplishment and unit survival.

Table 22 shows input characteristics for the simulation.

Communication within each simulated organization could be accomplished by written message, simulated radio, and face-to-face conversation. All communications in these modes were monitored continuously by 1) tape recording for the radio and face-to-face conversations and 2) retention of copies of all written messages. Accordingly, a complete record of all communications was available for each of the ten experimental groups.

Sixteen tape recording channels were required to monitor the nine radio nets and seven face-to-face transmissions that were possible. Recorders operated continuously throughout the operational phases of the simulation and generated 108 hours of tape per group. For the ten groups, 1,080 hours of tape recordings were available for transcription, reduction, and analysis. The communications were the bases for analyses of organizational competence, organizational effectiveness, and communication patterns within the experimental groups.

Experimental subjects were 120 combat experienced infantry officers ranging in grade from senior major to first lieutenant. Subjects were randomly selected, within the restrictions stated below, from nonstudent officers stationed at Fort Benning, Georgia. Within each group, the senior officer was assigned the role of battalion commander. Accordingly, the ten battalion commanders were majors, nine of whom had served on brigade or battalion staffs in combat units in Southeast Asia. Wherever possible, players were assigned to battalion staff roles on the basis of prior experience related to the position. In approximately 90% of the cases, players who were assigned to staff roles had prior experience as a principal or assistant staff officer in a

TABLE 22

Characteristics of Simulation Inputs

Input characteristics	Phase			Total simulation
	1 Low pressure	2 Moderate pressure	3 High pressure	
Probes (problems)	51	31	46	128
Probe elements (messages)	77	91	208	376
Probe complexity (N probe elements/ N probes)	1.51	2.94	4.52	2.94
Input rate (N probe elements/minutes)	0.57	0.67	1.54	0.93
Mean probe weight (Importance)[a]	2.43	3.68	4.43	3.45

[a]Probes were judged by military experts on scale of 1 to 7, based on "importance for mission accomplishment."

relevant activity. After completion of assignments to battalion command and staff positions, the remaining officers were assigned to be company commanders.

The sources of data were tape recorded and written communications of each experimental group. Reduction of communications data required preparation of typed transcripts of the communications of each group; development of "probe manuscripts," which contained all communications by a group pertaining to each probe; and analysis of probe manuscripts to evaluate both competence and effectiveness of each group.

The analysis of organizational competence included 1) content analysis of each unit of communication to identify the processes that were performed, and 2) assignment of a score to each unit on the basis of predetermined criteria of quality of process performance. To evaluate organizational effectiveness, a combat experienced, field grade officer analyzed each probe manuscript and, using preestablished criteria, assigned a score based on outcome of the probe in terms of contribution to mission accomplishment. It should be emphasized that scoring operations for competence were performed independently from those for effectiveness, and that criteria, procedures, and scoring personnel were different for the two variables.

The results of these data reduction and evaluation procedures, which required more than 12 months to accomplish, were two sets of scores for each group, which scores represented organizational effectiveness and various elements of organizational competence. With regard to organizational effectiveness, the data for each group included a probe effectiveness score of 128 for each probe. These scores served as the basic units from which phase and simulation effectiveness scores were developed. A group's phase effectiveness scores were the sums of its probe effectiveness scores within the respective phases, and its simulation effectiveness score was the sum of its three phase effectiveness scores.

With regard to organizational competence, the basic element was a process score, one or more for each unit of communication. From these were developed a number of scores representing larger units of analysis. Thus, a probe process score was the sum of all scores for a particular process within a specific probe. A probe process score was derived for each separate process on each probe.

The research design also provided for computation of scores for phases and for the entire simulation. A score for each phase was obtained by summing relevant probe scores within the phase, and simulation scores were sums of scores for the three phases.

Process scores were computed by probe, phase, and simulation for each

TABLE 23
Summary of Organizational Activities

	Phase 1		Phase 2		Phase 3		Total simulation	
	Mean	S.D.	Mean	S.D.	Mean	S.D.	Mean	S.D.
Contacts (frequency)	467.20	36.30	354.30	39.93	555.80	39.33	1,377.30	91.83
Rate of contacts[a]	51.91	4.03	39.37	4.44	61.76	4.37	51.01	4.37
Contacts per probe	9.16	0.71	11.43	1.29	12.08	0.86	10.76	0.72
Scoring units (frequency)	595.10	35.10	424.20	46.19	781.40	50.19	1,800.70	99.88
Scoring units per probe	11.67	0.70	13.68	1.49	16.99	1.09	14.07	0.78
Total contact minutes	306.37	38.40	248.23	26.37	374.02	31.51	928.63	81.01
Contact minutes per probe	6.01	0.75	8.01	0.85	8.13	0.69	7.25	0.63
Minutes per contact	0.66	0.06	0.70	0.05	0.67	0.04	0.68	0.05
Minutes per unit	0.52	0.06	0.59	0.04	0.48	0.03	0.53	0.06

[a]Rate = number of contacts per 15 minute period.

of the seven processes outlined in the conceptual framework. In a similar fashion, competence component scores were sums of relevant process scores, and competence scores were obtained by summing the scores for the three competence components.

RESULTS

Table 23 summarizes group activity in the simulation. Data concerned with contacts indicate the level of activity within the groups. For the total simulation, the mean of over 1,377 contacts per group and the mean rate of 51 contacts per 15 minute period show that the simulation generated a high level of activity, which is typical for command and control personnel in operations of the type depicted in the simulation.

Of particular significance for the analysis of competence are the data concerned with scoring units. Mean scoring units per group was 1,800.70 and group mean units per probe was 14.07. It is apparent that each group produced a very large number of units, thus permitting a high level of confidence that scores developed from them are genuinely representative of the groups' performances.

Table 24 summarizes frequencies of occurrence and scores for the major variables and subvariables for the total simulation. For all entries except effectiveness, responses were free to vary, i.e., no ceiling existed for the frequency with which any process could be performed. Therefore, frequency of process performance by a group reflected that group's unique propensity for performing processes and was not controlled by any design features other than number of inputs, which was constant for all groups. On the other hand, effectiveness scores for the simulation were summations of the scores on each of the 128 probes and, accordingly, frequency of these scores for every group was 128 with a maximum possible score of 6,400 (128 X 50).

Two aspects of the data are especially noteworthy. First, the groups did not perform stabilizing and feedback actions to any great extent. Reasons for failure to perform these actions can only be conjectured; however, scrutiny of probe manuscripts suggested some possible explanations. With regard to stabilizing, it appears that the participants simply did not perceive the necessity for performing such actions. Stabilizing involved those activities which were executed as supplemental to coping actions and which were intended to counter possible unstable effects within the organization which might result from a coping action. Thus, performance of a stabilizing action required anticipation of potential negative effects at the time a decision was made to take a coping action. In turn, such anticipation required individuals to maintain a perspective oriented toward the future welfare of the organi-

TABLE 24
Summary of Frequencies and Scores for
Major Variables and Subvariables

Variable	Frequency		Score	
	Mean	SD	Mean	SD
Effectiveness	128.00	0.00	3,214.49	198.00
Competence	1,800.70	99.88	17,179.79	1,570.85
Competence components				
Reality testing	1,013.40	70.01	9,889.78	908.90
Adaptability	783.90	55.94	7,222.51	741.23
Integration	3.40	5.93	67.50	107.17
Processes:				
Sensing	568.70	41.68	5,832.15	599.11
Communicating information	443.60	45.55	4,029.62	395.52
Decision making	261.20	20.56	2,908.96	380.31
Stabilizing	3.40	5.93	67.50	107.17
Communicating implementation	288.60	39.40	2,174.19	236.75
Coping actions	234.10	25.77	2,139.35	206.30
Feedback	1,10	1.52	28.00	39.94

zation. Apparently, this future oriented perspective did not operate during the simulation reported here.

The paucity of feedback scores appears to be due to the nature of the scoring system. By definition, feedback was limited to those activities which were designed to obtain information about the outcomes of prior coping actions and which were planned organizational operations, i.e., the results of identified formal decisions rather than the spontaneous actions of individuals. Inspection of the probe manuscripts revealed that individual officers sometimes inquired about the outcomes of coping actions or took some spontaneous action to evaluate outcomes; however, since designation of an activity as feedback required definite linkage back to a formal organizational decision to obtain information about outcomes, spontaneous individual actions were scored as *sensing*. It, therefore, appears that actions to evaluate outcomes did sometimes occur but were not scored as feedback. Since few formal organizational decisions were made to obtain information about actions, the result was a minimum of feedback scores for the various groups.

The second noteworthy aspect of the data summarized in Table 24 is the difference between frequencies for the various processes. Sensing was more than twice as frequent as decision making, which illustrates the fact that a single decision often leads from multiple sensing events. Communicating information occurred less often than sensing, which illustrates that selectivity often occurs in the transmission of information from those who have sensed it to those who must make decisions about it.

Communicating implementation occurred more often than decision making; however, the difference between these two processes is somewhat misleading as an indicator of the number of linking communications required for implementation of decisions. By definition, communicating implementation was coded only when a linking, or relaying, communication was interposed between decision maker and action taker. The fact that, even under these conditions, more communicating implementation occurred than decision making suggests that many single decisions required numerous linking communications in order for them to be implemented. Finally, the fact that fewer coping actions occurred than decision making suggests the possibility of aborted or unimplemented decisions. This eventuality will be examined later.

Frequency and Effectiveness

At the beginning of the study, it was conjectured that one possible determinant of organizational effectiveness might be frequency of process performance. Accordingly, a zero order correlation between frequency of occurrence of all processes and simulation effectiveness scores was computed. The result was a coefficient of .33, which is not significant ($N = 10$). It is concluded that effectiveness is not related to the total number of processes which are performed by an organization. If competence is related to effectiveness, the source must lie elsewhere than in the frequency with which an organization performs its critical processes.

Competence and Effectiveness

Table 25 shows intercorrelations between the major variables and subvariables. For this study, the most important finding is concerned with the relationship between organizational competence and organizational effectiveness. The obtained coefficient of .93 is highly significant ($p < .01$) and indicates a strong relationship between the two variables. Under the conditions of this study, competence accounted for 86% of the variance in effectiveness. Therefore, it appears that competence was a principal determinant of organizational effectiveness.

TABLE 25
Intercorrelations: Major Variables and Subvariables

Variable	1	2	3	4	5
1. Effectiveness	1.00	.93	.96	.79	.11
2. Competence		1.00	.94	.92	.33
3. Reality testing			1.00	.73	.10
4. Adaptability				1.00	.43
5. Integration					1.00

Note.—Significance, 8 degrees of freedom:

$p < .05 = .632$

$p < .01 = .765$

Zero order correlations of competence components with effectiveness resulted in coefficients of .96 for reality testing, .79 for adaptability, and .11 for integration. Thus, both reality testing and adaptability were related significantly to effectiveness; however, the relationship of integration to effectiveness was quite small and not significant. This lack of relationship is explained, in part, by the few occurrences of stabilizing, the one process of which integration is comprised. The results concerning stabilizing and integration are deemed to be inconclusive because of insufficient data.

A multiple correlational analysis between the competence components and effectiveness resulted in a corrected coefficient of .94. Beta weights were .79 for reality testing, .25 for adaptability, and −.08 for integration. Relative contributions to effectiveness were 76% for reality testing and 20% for adaptability, while the contribution of integration was negligible (.008%). It is apparent that reality testing and adaptability were critical determinants of organizational effectiveness. It is also apparent that reality testing contributed more than adaptability, which demonstrates the importance of information acquisition and information processing to the effectiveness of organizations.

Organizationl Processes

Table 26 shows intercorrelations between effectiveness, competence, and the various organizational processes. For all processes except stabilizing and feedback, correlations with effectiveness were significant beyond the .05

level. Sensing produced the highest correlation (.92), communicating information was second highest (.83), and decision making, communicating implementation, and coping actions were somewhat lower and approximately equal (.70, .71, .72).

The high intercorrelations for many of the processes suggest a dependency linkage between them. Those processes which comprise the adaptive-coping cycle were not conceived to be independent and, indeed, the data in Table 26 verify this conception. In many instances, effective performance on one process depends upon the quality of processes that precede it in the cycle. This demonstrates the necessity for good performance on all processes if full competence and, hence, effectiveness is to be achieved.

An interesting exception in the data is the relation of all subsequent processes to communicating information. This process is highly correlated with sensing (r = .72), as would be expected since communications should be dependent upon the quality of the information that is acquired. However, it is noteworthy that processes which follow communicating information in the cycle are not significantly correlated with it, even though some relationships

TABLE 26
*Intercorrelations: Effectiveness, Competence,
and Processes*

Variable	1	2	3	4	5	6	7	8	9
1. Effectiveness	1.00	.93	.92	.83	.70	.11	.71	.72	.03
2. Competence		1.00	.95	.72	.86	.33	.77	.77	.18
3. Sensing			1.00	.72	.79	.32	.58	.65	.06
4. Communicating information				1.00	.30	-.33	.58	.47	-.08
5. Decision making					1.00	.63	.59	.67	.37
6. Stabilizing						1.00	.14	.17	.49
7. Communicating implementation							1.00	.68	.29
8. Coping actions								1.00	.18
9. Feedback									1.00

Note.—Significance, 8 degrees of freedom:

   p < .05 = .632

   p < .01 = .765

are indicated. On the other hand, communicating information is highly correlated with effectiveness (r = .83). It appears that this process may have
contributed something unique to the variance in effectiveness, which "something" was not related to any processes other than sensing.

To explore these relationships further, a multiple correlation was computed with the seven processes as independent variables and effectiveness as
the criterion. Neither the obtained R (.97) nor the corrected R (.86) met the
.992 value required for significance with the two degrees of freedom that
were permissible. However, of more interest for the present discussion are
the obtained Beta weights for the various processes and the percent which
each process contributed to effectiveness. Table 27 summarizes the results.

It is apparent that each of the five processes which produced significant
zero order correlations probably contributed to effectiveness in important
degrees. It is also apparent that, once again, the importance of reality testing
(sensing, communicating information, and feedback) was confirmed. However, the most striking point for this discussion is that communicating
information contributed 43.9% to effectiveness, more than twice the contribution of the next highest process. This finding reinforces the probability
that communicating information made a unique contribution to effectiveness, whereas the other four significant processes each contributed a smaller
amount of unique variance but also contained a common factor which
influenced effectiveness.

Multiple correlation results are likely to be unstable in view of the small
number of groups involved. However, despite instability, the results are

TABLE 27
*Summary of Multiple Correlation between
Processes and Effectiveness*

Process	Beta	Percent Contribution (Beta x r from Table 26)
Sensing	.2130	19.3
Communicating information	.5317	43.9
Decision making	.1948	14.0
Stabilizing	.1142	1.2
Communicating implementation	.0740	5.0
Coping actions	.1555	11.5
Feedback	-.1147	0.4[a]

[a]Though technically this value should be negative, it is recorded as positive to facilitate its interpretation as a percent contribution.

sufficiently strong to indicate the probable existence of important relationships between the processes and effectiveness.

Effects of Pressure

To determine whether pressure affected the competence of some groups differently than that of others and whether such differential effects influenced effectiveness, mean probe competence scores of the five most effective groups and the five least effective groups were compared.

Figure 16 illustrates graphically the differential effects of pressure upon the two classes of groups.

Competence of the high effectiveness groups was better than for groups with low effectiveness under all pressure conditions. A groups by phases analysis of variance showed significant differences between the competence of the two classes of groups and between phases. Interaction between groups and phases was not significant, indicating no difference in the direction of pressure effects upon the two types of groups. For both high and low effectiveness groups, competence in phase II deteriorated from that in phase I and, for both groups, some recovery occurred in phase III. These similarities in the directions of pressure effects account for the finding of no interaction between groups and phases.

However, of very special significance for understanding the relationships between pressure, competence, and effectiveness are 1) differences in the gradients of competence degradation between phases I and II, and 2) differences in the amount of recovery in phase III. (It is recognized that interpretations of gradients is risky when no interaction indicates the possibility of differences due to chance; however, observation of the groups indicated the occurrence of actual differences in performance, attributable mainly to variations in direction and coordination by battalion leaders. For further elaboration, see Olmstead et al. [1973].) These differences appear clearly in Figure 16, which shows that competence deteriorated for both groups during phase II. However, for the high effectiveness groups, the degradation in competence amounted to an average of 11.30 points per probe, whereas scores for low effectiveness groups decreased by 22.10 points. Obviously, the change in mission and operations and the increase in pressure which occurred in phase II affected competence of the low groups much more than that of the high groups.

Figure 16 also shows that high effectiveness groups recovered competence in phase III to within three points of their original phase I level, despite the extremely intensive high pressure conditions. On the other hand, low effectiveness groups never made much of a recovery. A modest increase in competence for these groups can be seen for phase III; however, under high pressure, these groups continued to function at a greatly reduced level of competence and never approached their original performance.

The degradation in competence which occurred in phase II for both groups illustrates a phenomenon which is common in complex organizations. At the beginning of phase II, the battalion received a directive for preparation and movement into a new area of operations where the unit was to perform a different mission. This assignment was a radical change from the routine activities to which the battalion had been accustomed and the change, coupled with the increased pressure of phase II, resulted in deterioration of organizational processes. Some deterioration in process quality is a common occurrence in organizations when radical changes in goals or in situational demands are experienced. However, the critical considerations in terms of enduring organizational health are the extent of deterioration and whether competence can be recovered without serious damage to effectiveness.

Thus, three aspects appear to account for the reduced effectiveness of the low groups. First, throughout all phases they performed at a level of

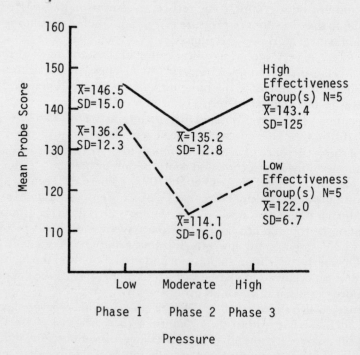

Fig. 16. Mean probe competence scores for high and low effectiveness groups.

competence which was consistently below that of the high groups. Second, when faced with the change in mission and operations, competence deteriorated much more drastically for the low groups. Finally, after deterioration in competence occurred, low groups could not recover under increased pressure and, therefore, continued to function at a reduced level. The above aspects probably account for the scores in overall effectiveness of the low groups.

A similar analysis for competence components (not shown) revealed that reality testing deteriorated with change in mission and increased pressure, but recovered for both classes of groups. Patterns of reality testing were similar, although performance was consistently better for high effectiveness groups. On the other hand, patterns for adaptability were different. For high effectiveness groups, scores for adaptability remained essentially the same throughout the three pressure phases. However, adaptability scores for low effectiveness groups showed a continual degradation as pressure increased. Therefore, it appears that effectiveness of low groups was less because of 1) consistently lower performance of reality testing and 2) a breakdown in adaptability processes under increased environmental pressure.

Aborted Decisions

In complex organizations, where many decisions are made at high levels but implemented at lower ones, numerous opportunities exist for breakdowns in process performance to occur between points of decision and points of intended execution. When a breakdown occurs, a decision may never be implemented as intended. Such aborted decisions can have serious consequences for effectiveness.

In this study, *aborted decisions* were defined as those decisions which were communicated to someone for action but upon which no action was ever taken. Figure 17 shows the effects of pressure upon abortion of decisions by the five high effectiveness and the five low effectiveness groups. It is clear that, throughout the simulation, low groups aborted more decisions. However, of special significance is the large increase in decisions aborted by the less effective groups under the high pressure conditions of phase III. Whereas mean aborted decisions in phase II were 2.8 and 4.2 for the high and low effectiveness groups respectively, high groups had 3.2 incomplete decisions in phase III, an increase of only .4; but, in that phase low groups aborted an average of 11.8 decisions, which is an increase of 7.6 per group.

It is apparent that, under the stress of high environmental pressure, processes for implementing decisions more frequently broke down in the low effectiveness group. On the other hand, implementation processes functioned much more reliably in the high effectiveness groups.

The findings indicate a probable major cause of reduced effectiveness in organizations. Even though decisions may be of the best, when an organization cannot maintain all of its other adapting processes (communicating implementation, coping actions) under pressure, problems, although solved, may never be overcome. In short, at least adequate performance of all processes is necessary in order for effectiveness to be achieved.

Locus of Process Performance

An important consideration for both organizational analysis and training involves the points wthin an organization where the various processes are, or should be, performed. Table 28 and the following comments are presented to illustrate that process performance is often specific to position and level within an organization and that the conceptual framework makes it possible to determine where the processes are usually performed and would permit evaluation of the quality of such performance either in terms of individuals or of units. Table 28 summarizes the frequency with which each

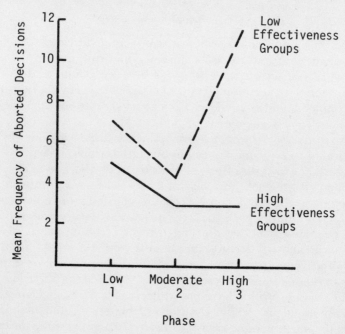

Fig. 17. Aborted decisions of high effectiveness and low effectiveness groups.

process was performed by the different positions within the simulated battalions.

The data show that requirements for process performance differ according to level and position in an organization. In general, sensing and coping actions occur most often at points which are in contact with the environments. With regard to external environments, these points are always at the boundaries of the organization; however, the location of the points may differ according to the type of organization. For example, in military tactical units (Table 28), sensing of much of the external environment and most actions intended to cope with it are performed by individuals at low organizational levels, because they are in most direct contact with the tactical environment. This might also apply in retail sales organizations where a principal component of the external environment consists of "walk-in" customers. On the other hand, in nontactical military units and certain internally focused types of governmental and civilian organizations, e.g., universities, low level personnel may not sense or execute external coping actions at all because the principal external environment may be other organizations whose representatives must, of necessity, be contacted only by higher level personnel. With regard to internal environments, sensing and coping actions may be performed by occupants of any position, but, even here, the most accurate sensing and the most critical coping actions will occur at those points which are in contact with most of the organization's members, e.g., at first line leadership or supervisory positions.

Decision making may occur at any level and usually does. However, because of the nature of their particular responsibilities, occupants of some positions make more decisions than others, e.g., line as opposed to staff positions. Furthermore, the numbers of decisions that are required may be greater at lower levels than at higher ones. On the other hand, decisions made at higher levels are usually more complex, more widely applicable, and more far-reaching in time than those made at lower levels.

Finally, communicating information is performed most often by individuals who have sensed changes in the environments, usually by personnel at the boundaries of the organization. An exception is individuals who occupy special coordinating roles, as, for example, the S-3 (operations officer) in the present study. On the other hand, communicating implementation may occur anywhere, but it is performed most often by individuals intermediate between decision makers and implementers and, therefore, it occurs most frequently within internal organizational channels.

Thus, it appears that requirements for the performance of particular processes differ by level and position. Furthermore, patterns of process performance will differ according to type of organization, nature of mission, and character of critical environments.

TABLE 28

Frequency of Process Performance by Position

Position	Sensing		Communicating information		Decision making		Stabilizing		Communicating implementation		Coping actions		Feedback	
	M	SD	M	SD	M	SD	M	SD	M	SD	M	SD	M	SD
Bn Commander	17.6	3.6	26.4	6.8	25.1	44.8	.1	.3	26.2	9.3	2.4	2.1	0	0
Bn Exec. Officer	3.9	2.4	14.7	7.1	13.3	8.5	.1	.3	28.1	13.6	2.9	2.8	0	0
S1	15.9	3.7	20.2	8.6	9.6	3.9	0	0	30.3	13.3	7.7	3.2	0	0
S2	22.2	3.7	36.5	12.9	8.2	3.7	.1	.3	13.0	5.9	3.4	2.5	0	0
S3[a]	46.7	10.2	69.9	11.8	35.6	8.2	.2	.4	56.4	10.2	15.3	6.1	.2	.6
S4	18.6	3.7	26.8	9.0	19.8	8.2	0	0	31.9	6.1	14.4	7.0	0	0
Commander, Hq & Cbt Sup Co.	66.3	13.6	43.8	12.4	16.3	6.6	.8	1.2	19.7	8.3	33.3	8.2	.1	.3
Commander Mvr Co.[b]	93.2	15.4	47.9	10.7	32.8	9.1	.5	1.2	17.2	6.0	36.3	10.1	.1	.3

Note.— N = 10 except for Commander, Maneuver Company

[a]Includes Assistant S 3

[b]Mean and standard deviation for commanders of all maneuver companies (N = 40).

DISCUSSION

The results of the research are clear. Strong relationships were found between effectiveness, competence, and most of the processes that were studied. The fact that high, significant correlations were obtained despite the small number of groups (10) included in the study attests to the probable actual strength of the relationships between the variables. Furthermore, confidence in the results can be greater than that usually placed in statistics based upon an N of 10 because each group's scores were derived from very large numbers of observations, which should have the effect of reducing error variance considerably.

Military tactical units are examples par excellence of organizations which must continually adapt to fast changing environmental conditions. Furthermore, the comparatively short and clearly demarcated time frames characteristic of combat operations usually encompass most of the activities which occur over extremely long periods in more conventional organizations, thus permitting intensive examination of complete cycles of events critical to the units. On the other hand, except for the activities in which they engage and the stresses common to combat, tactical units are surprisingly similar to other organizations in their fundamental operating characteristics.

For the above reasons, it is concluded that the study described here is a fair test of the conceptual framework and that the results confirm it as a valid and viable approach to the analysis of behavior within organizations. Competence is concerned with the quality of performance of personnel who occupy leadership positions within an organization and, accordingly, is an important factor in effectiveness.

The results also demonstrate the importance of competence for the ability of organizations to adapt rapidly changing conditions in their environments and to cope with intense environmental pressures. The results show that the quality of process performance is affected by both change and pressure. They also show that organizations which maintain competence in the face of change and pressure are more effective.

Maintenance of competence in the event of change involves the ability of an organization's members to rapidly and correctly identify modified aspects of its environments, to attach the correct meanings to such changes, to correctly decide upon necessary modifications in operations, and to execute them in accordance with the decisions and available knowledge about the environments. In short, the leaders of an organization must continually evaluate the reality of its total situation and adapt activities to the specific demands of that situation. When the quality of process performance is high, information is current and accurate, decisions are made promptly and with full consideration of all available information, and actions are executed as intended and in full coordination. Under these conditions, the organization is alert for all contingencies and flexible in adapting to them.

Maintenance of competence under pressure involves ability of organizational leaders, as a group, to continue adequate performance of critical processes under the stress imposed by increased frequency, variety, complexity, and difficulty of environmental demands. At present, the reason why organizations differ in their abilities to maintain competence is not fully clear, although it is suspected that one major source lies in the leadership provided to the command and control group.

Some informal observations made during the study provide support for the above suspicion. Although evaluation of leadership style was not a part of the design, two quite different approaches to leadership were observed among commanders of the simulated battalions, and these approaches seemed to be related to effectiveness of the groups. Thus, most commanders of the five low effectiveness groups seemed to practice a very centralized style of leadership, in which they established early the requirement that all information and most decisions must be referred to battalion headquarters for resolution, and they reinforced this requirement by their actions throughout the exercise. On the other hand, most commanders of high effectiveness battalions permitted considerable latitude to subordinates from the beginning. The upshot was that different patterns of process performance were established early in the simulations and continued throughout. In low effectiveness groups, the overall pattern was for company commanders to push most decisions upward and to rely heavily upon battalion level personnel for guidance in their activities. Conversely, company commanders in high effectiveness groups made many more independent decisions and managed their affairs without nearly so much reliance upon superiors.

The payoff with respect to these different patterns came during the intensive pressures of phase III. Under near overload conditions, company commanders in low effectiveness groups continued to try to push decisions upward. The result was clogging of radio nets, long delays in obtaining important decisions, and, as noted earlier, the abortion of many decisions. On the other hand, following the patterns which had been previously established in their high effectiveness groups, company commanders made even more independent decisions than before, directed their units with less guidance from above and, in general, gave attention to meeting the demands of the situation as they arose. The result was that these battalions functioned more effectively.

The principal contribution of this study is a concrete demonstration of the importance of organizational competence as a determinant of effectiveness, of the relative contributions of the various processes, of the systematic relationships that exist among them, and of the ways in which change and pressure affect their performance. It is now apparent that competence plays a critical role in the performance of organizations and, accordingly, warrants major attention in efforts to improve effectiveness.

Competence is the ability of an organization to continually and accurately sense the properties of both its external and internal environments, to internally process the information that is sensed, and to flexibly adapt its operations so as to cope with its constantly changing environments in accordance with its goals or missions. The capacity of an organization to identify, solve, and adapt to operational problems derives in part from the formal body of policies and procedures intended to guide decisions and actions, in part from the adequacy of techniques and equipment, and in part from the technical skills of individual personnel. However, neither the logic of decisions, the adequacy of techniques and equipment, nor the skills of individuals in executing technical operations are sufficient to result in a controlled and directed system of organizational decision and action. A remaining critical element involves performance of organizational processes concerned with the coordination of activities and the integration of information and decisions. An organization is a problem solving, decision making system in which the basic purpose is to take directed, unified action in an environment that presents a continuous flow of uncertainty situations. In such a system, the means whereby information, decisions, and actions are brought into conjunction involve a complex interplay between positions and between levels. This constant interplay is the essence of organizational competence.

Despite this emphasis upon an organization as a problem solving, decision making, action taking system, it is apparent that competence ultimately reduces to the judgments and actions of key leaders, both individually and collectively. It depends upon skills in acquiring and interpreting information; choices concerning to whom acquired information is to be communicated, as well as the accuracy and completeness of the communications; decisions concerning ways to cope with unusual or unanticipated situations; and the execution of actions resulting from such decisions—all performed at a high level of sensitivity and coordination.

In many organizations, the quality of process performance is not very good because, in order to control variability and thus insure reliability, leaders tend toward regulated and formal responses. They tend to prefer the certainty of standardized procedures and, accordingly, give little attention to performance of processes, which are less strictly formulated. However, overreliance upon standardized responses tends to result in organizational rigidity, whereas, in the fast changing environments of today, to be effective an organization must maintain a high level of flexibility. This quality is essential in uncertainty situations, and it has its source in what has been called here *organizational competence*.

Although most people who have given much thought to leadership are aware of organizational processes, little has been done about them in any systematic way. The conceptual framework presented here under the rubric of organizational competence seems to offer one means for overcoming the problem. This study has demonstrated that organizational competence is a feasible means for opening the "black box" of an organization and for examining its internal functioning. Accordingly, competence has relevance for both research and application. With respect to research, the concepts of competence, its components, and its processes offer a practical framework for understanding the dynamics of organizations. With respect to application, competence provides a systematic and concrete framework upon which realistic training and organizational development can be based.

Discussant Comments

BY T. O. JACOBS

Rather than critical evaluation, since I have a professional relationship with the author, the purposes of the present discussion are:

1) To identify what I perceive to be the primary contributions of the chapter itself.

2) To relate these purposes to the purposes of the present symposium, given that the relationship might possibly appear tenuous at the outset.

3) To develop the relevance of the specific findings of the paper, in the context of other organizational psychology literature, at the same time emphasizing a further need for integration of crossdisciplinary findings.

4) To identify possible further directions, both to extend the findings of the present chapter and to integrate the type of research therein reported with the type generally being treated in other papers in this symposium.

At least three points appear highly noteworthy in Olmstead's work. First, there is a focus on macro variables, as opposed to micro ones, and an apparently successful operationalization of these macro variables. Second, these variables, the organizational processes in the adaptive coping cycle, have been shown to be related to organizational competence. Finally, the integration of these performances, as they relate to organizational competence, has been assessed during a period of organizational stress, with highly interesting results. The significance of each of these will be discussed in turn.

The focus on macro variables stands in rather sharp contrast to the plethora of studies focusing on micro variables, with which our existing psychological literature abounds. The significance of a macro focus would seem to be logically apparent when one notes that one great source of relevance for the study of influence processes is their seeming significance for the outcomes, either good or bad, of formal organizations. Phenomenologically, formal organizations appear to be given birth, grow, live, and sometimes die. Organizational outcomes are highly significant to organizational members, and to the society as a whole. Indeed, the increasingly widespread recognition of the significance of findings from real-world organizations may be inferred from the increasing tendency of social scientists to study influence processes (including leadership) in existing formal organizations rather than in small groups in the laboratory.

The question, of course, really addresses an assessment of the significance of leadership behavior—or, more appropriately, the behavior of superordinates. This, of course, is basically the criterion question, about which more will be said later. For present purposes, it seems reasonable to assert that the superordinate does impact on the outcomes of the organization. While his ability to influence individuals may be mediated through face-to-face contacts, it seems logical that there should be something more. For example, the various studies of organizational climate seem to be one approach to assessing what that "something more" might be.

It seems reasonable to assert that the superordinate achieves results in formal organizations through a kind of multiplier function. That is, his influence consists not only of what he himself is able to do or influence others to do directly, but perhaps more importantly what he causes to happen indirectly within his organization and how he seeks to achieve these indirect effects. In this regard, I am thinking of such more general phenomena, with which the organizational literature abounds, as authority, delegation, centralization, control, and so on. These are functional attributes of organizations. A satisfactory outcome in this "multiplier function" probably depends in part on the superordinate's possession of a model or cognitive map of what is good/effective, together with the requisite skills to implement that model. Unfortunately, most of the research and organizational development work has focused on micro processes, which provide a model to the individual of effective interpersonal relationships. Very little has been done to develop and provide the superordinate, especially the high level executive, a model consisting of macro variables, which would characterize the internal activities of the organization itself in some meaningful fashion.

This is why the quantification of process variables, as they relate to competence, was listed as the second salient contribution of the present chapter. If one indeed thinks at the level of the organization as a whole, especially in an open systems framework, he must indeed become concerned with the organization as an acting entity, in competition with other acting entities. Appropriately, and this question will also be addressed later, one might inquire whether the superordinate's activities to move the organization as a whole can appropriately be called leadership. If yes, then it would appear that the focus on organizational process variables, referred to above as macro, might be the cognitive map needed by senior superordinates, given that research can provide a generalizable set of findings about these processes. The importance of such a cognitive map cannot be understated. Most useful theories of organismic behavior include a provision for feedback loops. Without feedback loops, it seems highly unlikely that learning, whether individual or organizational, can occur. The maladaptiveness of micro variables as a resource for developing feedback models is intuitively evident. If, for example, one focuses on LPC (Fiedler, 1967), then one is confronted with what Fiedler assumes to be an invariant characteristic of the individual, relatively immune to feedback. If one observes initiating structure and consideration, then one must ask in whose eyes, and under what conditions? If it is in the eyes of the subordinate, the superordinate who most needs the feedback may be least able emotionally to accept it.

A further criticism of micro variables is that they tend to be drawn from static or cross-sectional studies more often than not. Unfortunately, there is no clearcut evidence that information gained from static or cross-sectional work generalizes well on a longitudinal basis. In fact, Vroom (1966) makes the point that dynamic methods may very well yield relationships which are quite different from those yielded by static methods, and which are more "common sense." Zand (1972) studied initial level of shared trust, and found that it constitutes a dynamic input variable to interaction. With low initial shared trust, there was a spiraling deterioration of effectiveness in interaction in a decision making simulation, and with high trust, there was a spiraling increment. The point is that identification of such variables and assessment of their significance require a longer involvement among the participants in a situation than normally is allowed in the usual laboratory experiment. A most dramatic illustration of this kind of finding, from a different area of study, is Zimbardo's study of role relationships in a simulated prison environment (Haney, Banks, & Zimbardo, 1972). At the risk of extrapolating beyond the data, it is inviting to assert that identification of crucial organizational processes can only be identified and verified in the same kind of context, as was done in the present study.

The third salient set of findings in the present study consist of observed changes in organizational performance as stress—in the form of time pressure—increases. In particular, these were found to be a decrease in adaptability processes, and an increase in aborted decisions. Perhaps at the risk of being redundant, one might again observe that these findings provide some insight into the kind of organizational process deterioration that occurs when organizations are stressed, which, in turn, should provide some basis for theory construction and experimentation to identify the reasons why such process failures occur.

It would be inappropriate to criticize the concept of contingency theories of leadership. The developing literature strongly suggests that contingency approaches probably will, at least eventually, produce major advances in our understanding of human behavior in organizations. However, it does seem appropriate to examine with some suspicion the types of variables that, with few exceptions, presently are being investigated. Korman's (1966) review casts doubt on organizational development efforts which focus on dimensions of initiating structure and consideration. While a number of studies suggest that consideration may moderate structure, or vice versa, one can only wonder if a variable can be salient if manipulating it in a real world environment produces little subsequent effect. Perhaps the answer lies in a more basic evaluation of what is being tapped by measuring instruments and research methods. On the independent variable side, just as an example, Mitchell (1970b) used a multitrait/multimethod approach for studying interpersonal behavior, task oriented behavior, and group atmosphere in 35 three-man groups, in a 30-minute construction task. He obtained data from leaders, members, and outside observers. In this study, the evidence for construct validity was not good, with only one construct validity correlation being significant at the .05 level. This suggests the possibility that leadership, as an interpersonal process, may well be subject to construct validity questions, as well as to contingency questions. [For a somewhat less pessimistic view see House (1973a); Kerr & Schriescheim (1973); Schriesheim & Kerr (1973).]

On the dependent variable side, one feels constrained to inquire what constitutes an adequate criterion. While criterion questions do seem to be clearly beyond the scope of the present symposium, one might inquire how contingency theories can be meaningfully tested in the absence of demonstrably acceptable criteria. That the presence of demonstrably acceptable criteria is in doubt is indicated by the variety of criterion measures to be found in the literature, which range from measures of job satisfaction through quantitative measures at the individual level (individual productivity, sick leave, unexcused absences, etc.), to more global measures such as profitability, resource monopolization (Katz & Kahn, 1966), and superior bargaining position (Yuchtman & Seashore, 1967), to mention only three. Problems with these criteria are that subjective measures are undoubtedly open to multitrait/multimethod criticisms, objective data at the individual level typically show low correlations with anything, and the more global measures may be too abstract.

Organizational competence, as a dependent variable, may not be much of an improvement because of the difficulties involved in measuring it. However, that problem aside, it and the processes thus far described appear to offer a great deal of promise as a generalizable, i.e., technology free, type of criterion which may be more proximal than the more ultimate ones, and more suitable for purposes of structuring feedback to organizational superordinates. In fact, this suggests one possible extrapolation from the present study, which would be to use measures of organizational processes as dependent variables in testing contingency models. Examination of what happens to various processes as different experimental conditions are established might give considerably sharper insights into the kinds of environmental and organizational contingencies that impact on the action of leadership variables.

One of the most interesting findings to emerge from the present study is the difference between high effectiveness organizations and low effectiveness organizations. While this may to some extent be capitalization on chance, differences found between them could perhaps be found replicable. It will be recalled that Olmstead thought centralization of authority was one factor differentiating between high and low effectiveness units. It is certainly reasonable to believe that might have been the case. In the present study, if centralization is a causal factor, examination of differential effect on process performance is revealing indeed. At least four purposes are served by organizational control systems: to prescribe routine procedures in order to save the time of decision makers; to prescribe review procedures, thereby establishing authority rights; to reduce uncertainty about what is required; and to reduce the superordinate's reliance on power as an influence basis.

However, in the present study, degree of complexity and routineness was held constant. It thus appears as though variations in centralization might have been serving two more general kinds of functions. One might have been depersonalized superordinate-subordinate relationships, which might serve defensive purposes for the position incumbent. Moment and Zaleznik (1963) underscored the defensive purposes served by some kinds of leader behavior. A second important purpose, for the highly effective leader, would be to make explicit the organization's requirements, so as to facilitate consensus on relative role requirements, and reduce the need for resorting to position power in interactions with subordinates.

Other research suggests, however, that there might be a negative pole to the second of these two. It is probably important to recognize that individual behavior within organizations is a product, at least to some extent, of preorganizational behavior. Social exchange theory suggests that power is an important end in itself for most people. Further, the more insecure an individual is (power deprived) the greater utility power should have. One might postulate, therefore, that less effective superordinates would tend to develop broader power bases for themselves, all other things equal. Information control is a source of power, being a scarce resource. (Control of scarce resources, if they are in demand by others, leads to development of a power base.) A number of studies of information nets suggests that centrality produces a perception of leadership (Goldberg, 1955; Leavitt, 1951). Thus, the less effective superordinates may have tended to overcentralization as a way of enhancing their own outcomes. However, centralization may be counterproductive. Mulder (1960) pointed out that centralized nets are characterized by vulnerability. Landsberger (1961) found that centralization tends to cut horizontal contacts which are essential for intraorganizational coordination. Finally, Gerard (1957) found that high status in a laboratory experiment induced control oriented behavior.

Obviously, further research would be necessary to test hypotheses of this sort. However, if they were confirmed, it would seem that the kind of diagnostic information provided by process analysis would be considerably more suitable as a feedback medium for position incumbents than feedback about personality or personal behavior, which might tend to generate defensive reactions. Further, the opportunity to continue observing such processes, once sensitized to them, might provide the superordinate with a continuing source of feedback concerning the effectiveness of his own leadership actions. One would suspect this kind of feedback is in remarkably short supply in current organizational environments.

Clearly, it would be of substantial value to know how leader behaviors contribute in one way or another to process performance. While hypotheses could be drawn, and hypotheses have been drawn in the preceding material, this kind of future research is strongly suggested. Indeed, one would have enjoyed having information relative to the leader's substantive role in the present study, with high effectiveness and low effectiveness organizations contrasted. It would be indeed interesting to examine the applicability of contingency models, considering that examination of impact on process performance might be a more precise diagnostic tool than more global measures. This, in turn, suggests the possible utility of incorporating process variables of the type examined in this study in contingency models.

Another clear question is whether the present findings generalize to other kinds of organizations and other kinds of structures. There is a growing body of literature relating structural variables to organizational performance. One might also inquire about the interactions between leadership variables, structural variables, and process variables. [A number of references cited in the Taylor chapter and the discussion by Osborn appear relevant here.]

Finally, it seems worthwhile to reemphasize the apparent value of simulation for study of organizational process. It would have been extremely difficult to perform Olmstead's research within an existing, real-world organization. Of course, these findings might not generalize to real-world organizations. However, assuming that they do, one wonders what other kinds of process variables or relationships remain to be discovered through the use of veridical simulations under carefully controlled conditions and on subjects other than college sophomores.

7

Contingency Approaches to Leadership: An Overview

ABRAHAM K. KORMAN

Any attempt to integrate in a meaningful fashion the diversity of papers presented at this conference is, clearly, a difficult proposition. The reason is, I believe, that the papers presented here and the discussion they stimulated are reflective of the situation that exists in leadership theory today. Thus, on the one hand, there has been a great leap forward in the complexity and sophistication of theoretical formulations and the range of the variables which have come under consideration. On the other hand, in this great leap forward, there has also been a neglect of some basic considerations which are necessary in the formulation of adequate conceptual frameworks. Such neglect, I think, has occurred more as a result of omission, rather than commission, but the result has been the same. Finally, most of all, and perhaps the most dominant theme of all, the amount of solid empirical research increases every year, an increase which is obviously desirable for attempts at theoretical integration, but which also poses problems.

In order to illustrate these general beliefs, my integrating remarks will take the form of first attempting to specify what I think would be some desirable steps in the development of leadership theory and, in particular, contingency leadership theory, the concern of this symposium. Once these specifications are set forth, I will then try to point out both where I think those concerned with contingency leadership theory, as reflected in this symposium, are beginning to meet these criteria and where I think movement still needs to take place.

1) In developing contingency variables, there needs to be theoretical and empirical concern with the mechanism by which the contingency variable is hypothesized to be having its effects.

The significance of this point is, I would submit, great for both theoretical and administrative purposes. It is important in a theoretical sense because a theoretical statement is, essentially, an argument that certain variables (which we call independent variables) have their effects on dependent variables as a result of operating through certain mechanisms. In this sense, then, a theoretical statement about a contingency variable which does not specify the mechanism through which the effect on the dependent variable occurs is not a theoretical statement at all. (In this case the dependent variable is a leader characteristic-performance correlation. This argument is developed further, below.)

This point is also important administratively because, as we will see, a given variable can operate in ways not thought of. Hence, we lose the ability to utilize the results of a given contingency model in an administratively practical way by manipulating the contingency variable or by understanding what will happen when it occurs without direct intervention, unless we know the mechanisms by which the contingency variable operates. The point can be illustrated in a concrete manner by considering, for example, the technology variable, a commonly hypothesized contingency variable (see Woodward, 1965). There are at least five different mechanisms by which technology may affect human behavior. One mechanism is that different levels of technology may lead to different arousal levels in the individual. There is an increasing body of literature concerning the behavioral significance of different arousal levels (Korman, 1974, in press; Scott, 1966). Secondly, technology may operate as an influence on behavior by directly constraining it in some manner. Such constraints then influence behavior in the future as a function of either reinforcement (Breer & Locke, 1965) or as a result of cognitive attribution (Bem, 1970; Festinger, 1957). Administratively, then, if an administrator wanted to manipulate the contingency variable or predict what would happen at different levels of technology, given the type of leadership ideology in the organization and the mechanism was the arousal processes, a direct control of/or just considering technology alone might be sufficient. On the other hand, considering technology alone might be inaccurate, insufficient, or even inappropriate if the effect on behavior has come from the attribution that was made in response to the technology, rather than the technology alone. What the administrator would then have to do in order to affect and control the behavior would be to concern himself with understanding and perhaps intervening in the attribution process, not the technology, and this is a different variable. The argument becomes even more complex when we realize that technology may also have effects by other mechanisms such as: a) social influence—Glass and Singer (1972) have shown that noise levels have different effects on behavior depending on the socially manipulated frame of reference within which one interpets the noise; b) differential self-and-other evaluation—individuals often use environmental cues in order to assess the value of oneself and others (Korman, 1971); c) "exposure" effects—the exposure to any type of environment may lead to increased sensitivity to that environment and the influence of any of its characteristics (cf. Gavin, Korman & Greenhaus, 1973; Korman, Greenhaus, & Gavin, 1973).

How, then, does technology influence behavior? What must an administrator look to to understand and/or manipulate? How can he control these other possible mechanisms which may also influence behavior and, thus, confound his understanding and/or manipulations? How can a theorist deal with analogous problems? Clearly, these are questions with which any contingency model must deal.

An examination of the presentations at this symposium suggests that, in fact, such concerns are beginning to be recognized. Thus, for example, the House and Dessler chapter attempts not only to specify a set of contingency variables that are hypothesized to moderate the usefulness of different forms of leader behavior, but it also argues that these contingency variables operate by affecting the expectations and values of the employees involved. Such changes in expectancies and values are then assumed to influence behavior (an expectancy x value model of behavior is assumed). The House and Dessler approach is a good illustration of how this criterion might be met in contingency leadership theory, as is the research Taylor has reported here on the differential behavioral significance of technology as a function of the ideology of the organization. Finally, there are Kerr's discussant remarks concerning some of the problems of Fiedler's contingency model. In addition to the other questions raised in regard to Fiedler's work, Kerr has suggested that a real problem in the Fiedler approach is the lack of knowledge as to how some of the basic theoretical constructs work and the mechanisms by which they operate. All in all, then, there is movement toward meeting this very important criterion, a movement which I applaud.

2) The utilization of personality constructs as contingency variables will have to be redirected. Future work will need to use constructs that relate more specifically to work behavior. In addition, better measurement is needed.

At the risk of offending many of the personality oriented theorists in this area and those of us (including myself) who were trained to believe in the significance of personality differences for behavior, I would suggest that future work in this area needs to be redirected. My reason for this statement stems primarily from the excellent monograph by Walter Mischel a few years ago (1968) which concerned itself in large part with reviewing the evidence which exists as to the reliability of personality tests over time and over different situations. The question is a crucial one since a measure that does not correlate with itself cannot possibly correlate with any other variable. It is significant, then, that Mischel found little evidence for such reliability. Correlations between separate administrations of the same personality test over different situations were found to be quite low, a finding supported by the independent research of Entwhistle (1972) and, in this symposium, by Bass and Valenzi. How does one interpret such findings? One interpretation is that we have been using the wrong constructs and that better measurement would be achieved with different personality constructs. A second interpretation is that the personality constructs are meaningful and significant; we just have poor ways of measuring them. Finally, a third interpretation is that we measure personality very well; it is just that personality is not very important compared to situational determinants of behavior. Which is the better explanation? Until we find out, it does not matter since, for all three, the implications are the same. Using personality variables as contingency variables may not be very fruitful at this time since either a) we do not have the right constructs, b) we have the right constructs but we do not measure them very well, or c) we have the right constructs and we do measure them well; it's just that personality is not very important in influencing behavior as compared to situational determinants.

My own guess is that if there is a future in using personality variables, it will lie in the first explanation, and, to some extent, the second. My reason for this optimism stems from the work of Ghiselli (1971). Using personality type constructs of organizational and work relevance, rather than "general personality variables," his research on the personality determinants of managerial success has been a model of careful construct definition and measurement validation and systematic research. The result has been a continuing succession of meaningful, replicated findings.

Perhaps, then, if the personality constructs offered as contingency variables are more situationally defined (i.e., organizationally and work relevant) and the measures developed construct validated in the way that Ghiselli has worked with his, the problems stemming from Mischel's work can be avoided. (It is my belief, incidentally, that the Fiedler model has suffered greatly from the failure to pay attention to this question early in the research. As a result, we still do not know how to interpret the Fiedler findings. Fortunately, as the Chemers and Rice chapter indicates this problem is now being attended to and some answers should be forthcoming soon.)

However, it needs to be pointed out that the Ghiselli research may be a rare occurrence and it is conceivable that another interpretation of the Mischel, Entwhistle, and Bass and Valenzi findings may generally be a better one, that is, we have the right personality characteristics and we are measuring them quite adequately and quite reliably. It is just that the determinants of the behavior reflected in personality test scores that stem from the personality are not as important as the situational influences in the situation where the test measurement is taking place. Hence, the result is a low test-retest correlation on the test. Can personality be that unimportant? I, frankly, doubt it. Yet, it is conceivable and research needs to be undertaken to investigate this possibility, regardless of our preconceptions.

3) The development of contingency models of leadership has to move from a static view of the leadership process to a longitudinal view of a changing dynamic process which may call for different behavior at different times in reference to the same people.

Conceptually, the argument here is a simple one. Basically, to say that "Given Situation A, Leader Type A is best; Given Situation B, Leader Type B is best" is to deny an increasing body of literature which is concerned with the cognitive, emotional and attitudinal changes in people as a result of their interactions with different types of environments over time (cf. Bem, 1970; Breer & Locke, 1965; Festinger, 1957). Thus, while we do not know the answer to such questions as the conditions under which reinforcement facilitates these environmental effects on people (Breer & Locke, 1965) as opposed to debilitating them (Bem, 1970; Festinger, 1957), there is little doubt that these effects take place. Hence, they need to be taken account of in leadership theory, instead of making the implicit assumption that assigning individuals to an appropriate leader will solve the problem in the long run as well as the short.

Recognition of this is, I think, increasing and was evidenced at this symposium, most directly in Taylor's examination of the effects of technology at different points in time. In addition, Farris's entire conceptualization reflects his previous work illustrating how performance outcomes may affect the choice of a leadership pattern, as well as the reverse. It is my opinion that we need much more of this perspective, even though the longitudinal equations which will be needed will undoubtedly be quite complex in nature. [Greene (in press) has begun to address this issue.]

4) It is becoming clear that any conceptual difference between the "contingency variable" and the indpendent variable is moot at best. Perhaps, in the interest of greater theoretical clarity and administrative value, the distinction should be eliminated.

Conceptually, the point here is that there really is no such thing as a contingency variable. All it is is an independent variable whose dependent variable happens to be the correlation between two other variables (e.g., some leader characteristic behavior and some criterion measure). This is a point of view which I found expressed quite often at the symposium, and it is one with which I am in considerable agreement. It seems to me that this is a very good way of thinking for several reasons. First, it leads us to think of the contingency variable as a variable that can be manipulated for theoretical and administrative value, the value being in this case the optimizing of the value of some leader behaviors and/or characteristics which we either already have or wish to encourage in the organization. Secondly, it helps both to test the model theoretically and use it in an administrative sense since, if the contingency variable is a linear one, a two-variable design is being used and a prediction is being made that increases on the contingency variable (i.e., the independent variable) will lead to increases on the dependent variable (i.e., the effectiveness of a given type of leader behavior). The results are, therefore, interpretable theoretically and can be used administratively. They do not lend themselves to the ambiguity surrounding the type of contingency model that predicts different relationships on an a priori basis as a function of different environmental variables whose parameter variation may be unknown. The problem is that not knowing such parameter variation means the results of all such a priori tests are theoretically ambiguous and administratively meaningless (Korman, 1973a; 1973b).

In essence, then, we should be thinking of "degree of technology" or "degree of batch process technology," or "degree of authoritarian ideology, etc. as independent variables affecting behaviors, like any other independent variable. However, this still would not help the difficulties inherent in curvilinear hypotheses, such as the Fiedler model. The problem here is that parameter variables need always be known beforehand in order to theoretically interpret the findings of such models and adequately use them administratively.

5) The need for better measurement in leadership theory is a matter of prime necessity. Measurement and theory go hand-in-hand and the development of one without the other is a waste of time for all concerned.

An excellent illustration of this point is the examination by Tosi and his associates of the Lawrence and Lorsch questionnaire in a recent issue of *Administrative Science Quarterly* (Tosi, Aldeg & Storey, 1973). I will briefly summarize his findings concerning the adequacy of this questionnaire in a construct-validity sense. Briefly, the existence of such validity is, to quote Twain, "Greatly exaggerated." To be more blunt, it has none that I can see, judging from the reported findings. What does this say for all the conclusions based on the Lawrence and Lorsch questionnaire? The articles written? The recommendations made? Frankly, I don't know, although I could make some guesses. The point is *not* that adequate measurement is "nice." It is *necessary, crucial*, etc. Without it, we have nothing.

Along this dimension, the chapters in this volume are, I think, fairly typical. Some of the researchers present work based on measures they have studied extensively in other contexts. Others are just beginning to pay some attention to these questions. Perhaps conferences of this nature will move recognition of this point along to more satisfactory levels.

6) Theory, contingency or otherwise, is to help and guide research, not to control it. We should not become so invested in any theory, particularly our own, that it "strangles" us and we ignore the major goal of our work, the understanding of behavior.

It is not difficult to find cases in the history of all theory, whether administrative science, organizational behavior, physics, chemistry, or others, where such "strangling" has taken place. As far as I am concerned, this is tragic. It is tragic for the field since the strangling effect leads to a loss of knowledge as the theorist seeks to protect his ego by only undertaking that research and interpreting those data which will support him. It is tragic for the individual as his ego defense pressures become more and more dominant in his cognitive and emotional processes, with a consequent loss in his ability to function adequately in a theoretical and empirical sense. I can only agree very much with Bass in his plea for us to be open to new ways of thinking, new conceptualizations, and new ways of looking at problems. The theories we use, and I think we need some frameworks to help us whether or not they are sophisticated enough to call a theory, are there to help us. They should not become so much part of us and we should not become so invested in them that we lose the objectivity, the freshness of viewpoint, and the openness of spirit that characterizes a healthy, growing, viable theoretical field.

General Discussion

General discussion following Korman's overview revolved around two issues. The first issue was related to the value of personality as a predictor of leader effectiveness. The discussion began with reference to the Standard Oil of New Jersey Early Identification of Management Potential (EIMP) (1961 and followup report, Sparks, 1966) as an example of predictiveness based in part on personality measures. The point was that perhaps personality variables should not be entirely dismissed as predictors of leader effectiveness. Attention was called to an article by Korman (1968) that reviewed the literature relevant to managerial effectiveness and indicated several things: 1) the Standard Oil EIMP was not a predictive study it was a concurrent study [for a detailed review of EIMP see Campbell, Dunnette, Lawler, & Weick, 1970]; 2) personality tests never predict managerial performance; and 3) the only thing that appeared to predict management performance was clinical judgment. Another speaker suggested if we go back and look over identification of management potential programs what we will begin to find is that the person who looks good to the psychologist in the assessment setting also happens to be the one who looks good to the manager who is providing the criterion data (Grant, Katkovsky, & Bray, 1967). What one gets is agreement between individuals that one person looks good or looks bad and that is interrater reliability, not validity. The assessment concept appears to work because the person who can impress the psychologist is going to impress the manager. He has an effective interpersonal style and the psychologist has learned to look for this as it predicts a successful management rating. It was also suggested that assessment of "successful" managers in this way did not necessarily lead to effective organizational performance. What is needed is a way of determining effective and not just successful managers. [We should note here that even if one could determine and develop truly "effective" managers, it does not necessarily follow (because of differences in the unit of analysis) that their organization would be effective. This is, of course, a major thrust of the discussant comments relating to the chapters by House and Dessler and by Olmstead, as well as a key point stressed by systems theorists, such as Kast and Rosenzweig (1973).]

A final opinion held that personality tests are a big "snow job" that psychologists have been perpetuating. There do appear to be interpersonal styles which are consistent from situation to situation, but it may be that the amount of variance that is accounted for is so minimal and so hard to get at that perhaps it is not worth the bother.

A second major theme of the general discussion following Korman's overview pertained to the various approaches to the study of leadership. Although this theme appeared throughout the symposium, prolonged discussion was generated when it was suggested that the various papers and commentaries during the conference indicated there was a shift needed in the study of leadership. It was pointed out that alternative models had been presented, for example, the Bass and Valenzi chapter, suggesting experimental or total research trying to identify virtually all the variables involved, and another approach by House and Dessler suggesting precise attempts to identify, manipulate, and measure a few specific variables. The question was raised as to which approach was more fruitful.

One stream of response indicated that it was a matter of preference for the researcher. Whether or not study results are acceptable is a matter of concensus that shifts over time and we may find an approach that does not distinguish itself at first but several years later yields some brilliant insights.

One discussant indicated a preference for research only in areas where precision identification and measurement of variables was possible but pointed out that this approach was not feasible without some general studies which suggested what to measure.

In addition, one function of science is to increase understanding, but there are also practitioners who seek to intervene. The kind of theory that is suitable for understanding may not be what is needed for intervention into a specific situation, and there is a tendency to overlook this in our different models.

Another respondent suggested that we also are in error by viewing the environment as a residual variable. Much the same situation exists in the comparative management literature where if one finds differences between two nations, these differences are called cultural differences and dismissed. He wondered if we are not doing the same thing with our leadership models in that any one model includes only a small portion of the environment. Perhaps we will not move ahead until we start specifying—clinically or nonclinically—the larger factors. Some integration is needed. Psychologists examine many kinds of individual difference factors but little about organizational characteristics and environment. The sociologist, on the other hand, does not look at individual differences—it is very frustrating to compare studies. [The Hunt, Osborn, & Larson (1973) study is one that does make a beginning attempt at such integration.]

Another speaker suggested that one cannot do it all at once; the researcher has to pick out those things that interest him most and work on them. There is always going to be unexplained variance. It is not possible or desirable to attempt monstrous research designs where all the variance sources are isolated. First, such studies are difficult financially and practically. Secondly, any time one of these studies is done there is so much specific variance one gets a limited time-place conclusion. Even if every source of variance is isolated, all we can say is that this was the case at the XYZ company in Cleveland, Ohio, on such and such a date. What does this really communicate?

It was suggested that there was a definite split in approaches to the study of leadership between those with micro models and those with macro models. The question of how can we build on each other's work if this split continues was raised. The problem appears to be that everyone is going his own way. [In this we appear to have advanced little since Triandis's (1966) discussion of this issue.] Another speaker suggested that if one reads across the literature in education, sociology, psychology, an intuitive integration can be done.

It was argued that such an integration is difficult due to the fact that many studies are of a single organization, i.e., British firm, insurance company, heavy metals, etc. But we can begin to see a repetition of dimensions across all of these studies. It is possible to come up with a taxonomy that will describe structure and type and does not require a hundred variables. We are down to approximately 14–16 variables that describe the environment or its existence as it is perceived (Prien & Ronan, 1971; Ronan & Prien, 1973). It is not an impossible task to include these kinds of measures in a single study.

References

Allen, T. J., & Cohen, S. I. Information flow in research and development laboratories. *Administrative Science Quarterly*, 1969, *14*, 12–19.

Altman, I. The small group field: Implications for research on behavior in organizations. In R. V. Bowers (Ed.), *Studies in behavior in organizations: A research symposium*. Athens, Ga.: University of Georgia Press, 1966.

Andrews, F. M., & Farris, G. F. Supervisory practices and innovation in scientific teams. *Personnel Psychology*, 1967, *20*, 497–515.

Ashour, A. S. The contingency model of leadership effectiveness: An evaluation. *Organizational Behavior and Human Performance*, 1973, *9*, 339–355.

Bales, R. F. *Interaction process analysis: A method for the study of small groups*. Reading, Mass.: Addison Wesley, 1950.

Bales, R. F., & Slater, P. E. Role differentiation in small decision making groups. In T. Parsons & R. F. Bales (Eds.), *Family, socialization and the interaction process*. New York: Free Press of Glencoe, 1955.

Bass, A. R., Fiedler, F. E., & Kreuger, S. Personality correlates of assumed similarity (ASo) and related scores. (USPHS Tech. Rep. No. 19) Urbana, University of Illinois, Group Effectiveness Research Laboratory, 1964.

Bass, B. M. *Leadership, psychology, and organizational behavior*. New York: Harper, 1960.

Bass, B. M. How to succeed in business according to business students and managers. *Journal of Applied Psychology*, 1968, *52*, 254–262.

Bass, B. M., & Barrett, G. V. *Man, work and organizations: An introduction to industrial and organizational psychology*. Boston: Allyn & Bacon, 1972.

Bass, B. M., Cooper, R., & Haas, A. (Eds.), *Managing for accomplishment*. Lexington, Mass.: D. C. Heath, 1970.

Beer, M. *Leadership, employee needs, and motivation*. Bureau of Business Research, No. 129. Columbus: Ohio State University, 1966.

Bem. D. J. *Beliefs, values and human affairs*. Belmont, Calif.: Brooks-Cole, 1970.

Benne, K. D., & Sheats, P. Functional roles and group members. *Journal of Social Issues*, 1948, *4*, 41–49.

Bennis, W. G. *Changing organizations: Essays on the development and evolution of human organizations*. New York: McGraw-Hill, 1966.

Bennis, W. G. Organizations of the future. *Personnel Administration*, 1967, *30*(5), 7–19.

Bishop, D. W. Relations between task and interpersonal success and group member adjustment. Unpublished master's thesis, University of Illinois, 1964.

Blake, R. R., & Mouton, J. S. *The managerial grid*. Houston, Texas: Gulf, 1964.

Blauner, R. *Alienation and freedom*. Chicago: University of Chicago Press, 1964.

Bowers, D. G., & Seashore, S. E. Predicting organizational effectiveness with a four-factory theory of leadership. *Administrative Science Quarterly*, 1966, *11*, 238–263.

Breer, P., & Locke, E. A. *Task experience as a source of attitudes*. Homewood, Ill.: Irwin-Dorsey Press, 1965.

Bright, J. R. *Automation and management*. Boston: Harvard Business School, Division of Research, 1958. (a)

Bright, J. R. Does automation raise skill requirements? *Harvard Business Review*, 1958, *36*(4), 85–98. (b)

Burack, E. H. Industrial management and technology: Theory and practice. Unpublished manuscript, Illinois Institute of Technology, 1969.

Campbell, J. P. Dunnette, M. D., Lawler, E. E., III, & Weick, K. E. *Managerial behavior, performance, and effectiveness*. New York: McGraw-Hill, 1970.

Carter, L. F. Leader and small group behavior. In M. Sherif & M. O. Wilson (Eds.), *Group relations at the cross roads*. New York: Harper & Row, 1953.

Cartwright, D. Determinants of scientific progress: The case of research on the risky shift. *American Psychologist*, 1973, *28*, 222–231.

Cattell, R. B. (Ed.) *Handbook of multivariate experimental psychology*. Chicago: Rand McNally, 1966.

Cattell, R. B., Saunders, D. R., & Stice, G. F. The dimensions of syntality in small groups. *Human Relations*, 1953. *6*, 331–356.

Chadwick-Jones, J. K. *Automation and behavior: A social psychological study*. New York: John Wiley, 1969.

Chemers, M. M. Cultural training as a means for improving situational favorableness. *Human relations*, 1969, *22*, 531–546.

Chemers, M. M., Rice, R. W., Sundstrom, E., & Butler, W. M. Leader LPC, training, and effectiveness: An experimental examination. Unpublished manuscript, University of Utah, Department of Psychology, 1973.

Chemers. M. M., & Skrzypek, G. J. An experimental test of the contingency model of leadership effectiveness. *Journal of Personality and Social Psychology*, 1972, *24*, 172–177.

Chemers, M. M., & Summers, D. S. Group atmosphere and the perception of group favorableness. (Office of Naval Research, Tech. Rep. No. 71)

Urbana, University of Illinois, Group Effectiveness Research Laboratory, 1968.

Child, J. Organizational structure, environment, and performance: The role of strategic choice. *Sociology*, 1972, *6*, 1–22.

Child, J., & Mansfield, R. Technology, size, and organizational structure. *Sociology*, 1972, *6*, 369–393.

Christie, R., & Geiss, F. *Studies in Machiavellianism.* New York: McGraw-Hill, 1970.

Collins, B. E., & Guetzkow, H. *A social psychology of group processes for decision-making.* New York: John Wiley, 1964.

Cooper, R. Man, task, and technology. *Human Relations*, 1972, *25*, 131–157.

Couch, A. S., & Carter, L. A factorial study of the rated behavior of group members. Paper presented at the meeting of the Eastern Psychological Association, Atlantic City, April 1952.

Crossman, E. R. F. W. *Automation and skill.* London: Her Majesty's Stationery Office, 1960.

Csoka, L. S. Intelligence: A critical variable for leadership experience. (Office of Naval Research Tech. Rep. No. 72–34) Seattle, University of Washington, Organizational Research Group, 1972.

Csoka, L. S., & Fiedler, F. E. The effect of military leadership training: A test of the contingency model. *Organizational Behavior and Human Performance*, 1972, *8*, 395–407.

Cyert, R., & March, J. *A behavioral theory of the firm.* Englewood Cliffs, N.J.: Prentice-Hall, 1963.

Davis, L. E., & Taylor, J. C. Technology, organization, and job structure. In R. Dubin (Ed.), *Handbook of work, organization, and society.* New York: Rand McNally, 1973, in press.

Davis, L. E., & Valfer, E. S. Studies in supervisory job design. *Human Relations*, 1965, *19*, 339–352.

Dessler, G. A test of the path-goal theory of leadership. Unpublished doctoral dissertation, Baruch College, City University of New York, 1973.

Dubin, R. Supervision and productivity: Empirical findings and theoretical considerations. In R. Dubin, G. C. Homans, F. C. Mann, & D. C. Miller (Eds.), *Leadership and productivity.* San Francisco: Chandler, 1965.

Emery, F. E., & Trist, E. L. Sociotechnical systems. In F. E. Emery (Ed.) *Systems thinking.* Middlesex, Penguin, 1969.

Engelstad, P. H. Socio-technical approach to problems of process control. In L. E. Davis & J. C. Taylor (Eds.), *Design of jobs.* Baltimore: Penguin, 1972.

Entwhistle, D. To dispel fantasies about fantasy-based measures of achievement motivation. *Psychological Bulletin*, 1972, *77*, 377–391.

Etzioni, A. *Modern organizations.* Englewood Cliffs, N.J.: Prentice-Hall, 1964.

Evans, M. G. Extensions to a path-goal theory of leadership. Unpublished manuscript, University of Toronto, Faculty of Management Studies, 1972.

Farris, G. F. Organizational factors and individual performance: A longitudinal study. *Journal of Applied Psychology*, 1969, *53*, 87–92.

Farris, G. F. Organizing your informal organization. *Innovation*, 1971, No. 25, pp. 2–11.

Farris, G. F. The effect of individual roles on performance in innovative groups. *R & D Management*, 1972, *3*, 23–28.

Farris, G. F. The technical supervisor: Beyond the Peter principle. *Technology Review*, 1973, *75*, 26–33.

Farris, G. F., & Butterfield, D. A. Control theory in Brazilian organizations. *Administrative Science Quarterly*, 1972, *17*, 574–585.

Farris, G. F., & Lim, F. G., Jr. Effects of performance on leadership, cohesiveness, influence, satisfaction, and subsequent performance. *Journal of Applied Psychology*, 1969, *53*, 490–497.

Faunce, W. A. Automation in the automobile industry. *American Sociological Review*, 1958, *23*, 401–407.

Festinger, L. *A theory of cognitive dissonance*. Evanston, Ill.: Row-Peterson, 1957.

Fiedler, F. E. A contingency model of leadership effectiveness. In L. Berkowitz (Ed.), *Advances in experimental social psychology*. Vol 1. New York: Academic Press, 1964.

Fiedler, F. E. The effect of leadership and cultural heterogeneity on group performance: A test of the contingency model. *Journal of Experimental Social Psychology*, 1966, *2*, 237–264.

Fiedler, F. E. *A theory of leadership effectiveness*. New York: McGraw-Hill, 1967.

Fiedler, F. E. Leadership experience and leader performance: Another hypothesis shot to hell. *Organizational Behavior and Human Performance*, 1970, *5*, 1–14.

Fiedler, F. E. A note on the methodology of the Graen, Orris, and Alvares studies testing the Contingency Model. *Journal of Applied Psychology*, 1971, *55*, 202–204. (a)

Fiedler, F. E. Validation and extension of the Contingency Model of leadership effectiveness: A review of empirical findings. *Psychological Bulletin*, 1971, *76*, 12–148. (b)

Fiedler, F. E. Personality, motivational systems, and behavior of high and low LPC persons. *Human Relations*, 1972, *25* 391–412. (a)

Fiedler, F. E. Predicting the effects of leadership training and experience from the contingency model. *Journal of Applied Psychology*, 1972, *56*, 114–119. (b)

Fiedler, F. E. Personality and situational determinants of leader behavior. In E. A. Fleishman & J. G. Hunt (Eds.), *Current developments in the study of leadership*. Carbondale: Southern Illinois University Press, 1973. (a)

Fiedler, F. E. Predicting the effects of leadership training and experience from the contingency model: A clarification. *Journal of Applied Psychology*, 1973, *57*, 110–113. (b)

Fiedler, F. E. Style or circumstance: The leadership enigma. In F. E. Kast and J. E. Rosenzweig (Eds.), *Contingency views on organization and management*. Chicago: Science Research Associates, 1973. (c)

Fiedler, F. E., & Chemers, M. M. *Leadership and effective management*. New York: Scott Foresman, 1974.(a)

Fiedler, F. E., & Chemers, M. M. Leadership and management. In J. W. McGuire (Ed.) *Contemporary management: Issues and Viewpoints*. Englewood Cliffs, N.J.: Prentice-Hall, 1974. (b)

Fiedler, F. E., Meuwese, W. A. T., & Oonk, S. Performance of laboratory tasks requiring group creativity. *Acta Psychologica*, 1961, *18*, 100–119.

Fiedler, F. E., O'Brien, G. E., & Ilgen, D. R. The effect of leadership style upon the performance and adjustment of volunteer teams operating in a stressful environment. *Human Relations*, 1969, *22*, 503–514.

Fishbein, M., Landy, E., & Hatch, G. Some determinants of an individual's esteem for his least preferred co-worker: An attitudinal analysis. (Office of Naval Research Tech. Rep. No. 21) Urbana, University of Illinois, Group Effectiveness Research Laboratory, 1965.

Fishbein, M., Landy, E., & Hatch, G. A Consideration of two assumptions underlying Fiedler's contingency model for the prediction of leadership effectiveness. *American Journal of Psychology*, 1969, *4* 457–473.

Fleishman, E. A. The description of supervisory behavior. *Journal of Applied Psychology*, 1953, *37*, 1–6. (a)

Fleishman, E. A. The measurement of leadership attitudes in industry. *Journal of Applied Psychology*, 1953, *37*, 153–158. (b)

Fleishman, E. A. A leader behavior description for industry. In R. M. Stogdill & A. E. Coons (Eds.), *Leader behavior: Its description and measurement*. Bureau of Business Research, No. 88. Columbus: Ohio State University, 1957.

Fleishman, E. A. Twenty years of consideration and structure. In E. A. Fleishman & J. G. Hunt (Eds.), *Current developments in the study of leadership*. Carbondale: Southern Illinois University Press, 1973.

Fleishman, E. A., & Harris, E. F. Patterns of leadership related to employee grievances and turnover. *Personnel Psychology*, 1962, *15*, 43–56.

Fleishman, E. A., Harris, E. F., & Burtt, H. E. *Leadership and supervision in industry*. Bureau of Educational Research, No. 33. Columbus: Ohio State University, 1955.

Fleishman, E. A., & Hunt, J. G. (Eds.) *Current developments in the study of leadership*. Carbondale: Southern Illinois University Press, 1973.

Foa, U. G., Mitchell, T. R., & Fiedler, F. E. Differentiation matching. *Behavioral Science*, 1971, *16*, 130–142.

Fox, W. M., Hill, W. A. & Guertin, W. H. Dimensional analysis of the least preferred co-worker scales. *Journal of Applied Psychology*, 1973, *57*, 192–94.

Friedmann, G. *The anatomy of work*. Glencoe, Ill.: Free Press, 1961.

Gardell, B. *Produktionsteknik och arbetsgladje* (Production technology, alienation, and mental health; with English summary). Stockholm: Personaladministrativa radet, 1971.

Gavin, J., Korman, A. K., & Greenhaus, J. Organizational factors in job behavior. Unpublished manuscript, Baruch College, City University of New York, Department of Psychology, 1973.

Gerard, H. B. Some effects of status, role clarity and group goal clarity upon the individual's relations to group process. *Journal of Personality*, 1957, *25*, 475–488.

Ghiselli, E. A. *Explorations in managerial talent*. Pacific Palisades, Calif.: Goodyear Publishing Co., 1971.

Gibb, C. A. The principles and traits of leadership. *Journal of Abnormal and Social Psychology*, 1947, *42*, 267–284.

Gibb, C. A. Leadership. In G. Lindzey, & E. Aronson (Eds.), *The handbook of social psychology*. Vol. 4. Reading, Mass.: Addison-Wesley, 1969.

Glanzer, M., & Glaser, R. Techniques for the study of team structure and behavior. *Psychological Bulletin*, 1959, *56*, 317–332.

Glass, D., & Singer, J. *Urban stress*. New York: Academic Press, 1972.

Glass, G. V., & Maguire, T. O. Abuses of factor scores. *American Educational Research Journal*, 1966, *3*, 297–304.

Goldberg, S. C. Influence and leadership as a function of group structure. *Journal of Abnormal and Social Psychology*, 1955, *51*, 119–122.

Graen, G., Alvares D., Orris, J. B., & Martella, J. A. The contingency model of leadership effectiveness: Antecedent and evidential results. *Psychological Bulletin*, 1970, *74*, 285-295.

Graen, G., Dansereau, F. Jr., & Minami, T. Dysfunctional leadership styles. *Organizational Behavior and Human Performance*, 1972, *7*, 216–236.

Graen, G., Orris, J. B., & Alvares, K. M. Contingency model of leadership effectiveness: Some experimental results. *Journal of Applied Psychology*, 1971, *55*, 196–201. (a)

Graen, G., Orris, J. B., & Alvares, K. M. Contingency model of leadership effectiveness: Some methodological issues. *Journal of Applied Psychology*, 1971, *55*, 205–210. (b)

Grant, D. L., Katkovsky, W., & Bray, D. W. Contributions of projective techniques to assessment of management potential. *Journal of Applied Psychology*, 1967. *51*, 226–232.

Greene, C. N. A longitudinal analysis of relationships among leader behavior and subordinate performance and satisfaction. In T. B. Green & D. F. Ray (Eds.), *Proceedings of the Thirty-Third Academy of Management Annual Meeting*. State Collge: Mississippi State University, in press.

Guetzkow, H. S. (Ed.) *Groups, leadership and men: Research in human relations*. Pittsburgh: Carnegie Press, 1951.

Guilford, J. P. *Psychometric methods*. New York: McGraw-Hill, 1954.

Gulowson, Jon. Norsk Hydro. Unpublished manuscript, Work Research Institutes, Oslo, Norway, 1972.

Guttman, L. A general non-metric technique for finding the smallest Euclidian space for a configuration of points. *Psychometrika*, 1968, *33*, 469–506.

Hackman, J. R. Toward understanding the role of tasks and behavioral research. *Acta Psychologica*, 1969, *31*, 97–121.

Hall, D. T., & Schneider, B. *Organizational climates and careers*. New York: Seminar Press, 1972.

Halpin, A. W. The leadership ideology of aircraft commanders. *Journal of Applied Psychology*, 1954, *38*, 329–335.

Halpin, A. W., & Winer, B. J. Studies in air crew composition: The leadership behavior of the airplane commander. (Tech. Rep. No. 3) Columbus: Ohio State University, Personnel Research Board, 1952.

Halpin, A. W., & Winer, B. J. A factorial study of the leader behavior descriptions. In R. M. Stogdill & A. E. Coons, (Eds.), *Leader behavior: Its description and measurement*. Bureau of Business Research, No. 88. Columbus: Ohio State University, 1957.

Haney, C., Banks, C., & Zimbardo, P. Interpersonal dynamics in a simulated prison. (Office of Naval Research Tech. Rep. No. Z-09) Palo Alto, Calif., Stanford University, Department of Psychology, 1972.

Hardy, R. C. Effects of leadership style on the performance of small classroom groups: A test of the contingency model. *Journal of Personality and Social Psychology*, 1971, *19*, 367–374.

Harman, H. H. *Modern factor analysis*. Chicago: University of Chicago Press, 1960.

Hawkins, C. A study of factors mediating a relationship between leader rating behavior and group productivity. Unpublished doctoral dissertation, University of Minnesota, 1962.

Hawley, D. E. A study of the relationship between the leader behavior and attitudes of elementary school principals. Unpublished master's thesis, University of Saskatchewan, 1969.

Hays, W. L. *Statistics for psychologists.* New York: Holt, 1963.

Haythorn, W., Couch, A., Haefner, D., Langhan, P., & Carter, L. The effects of varying combinations of authoritarian and equalitarian leaders and followers. *Journal of Abnormal and Social Psychology,* 1956, *53,* 210–219.

Hazelhurst, R. J., Bradbury, R. J., & Corlett, E. N. A comparison of the skills of machinists on numerically-controlled and conventional machines. *Occupational Psychology,* 1969, *43,* 169–182.

Heller, F. A., & Yukl, G. Participation, managerial decision-making, and situational variables. *Organizational Behavior and Human Performance,* 1969, *4,* 227–234.

Hemphill, J. K. *Leader behavior description.* Columbus: Ohio State University, Personnel Research Board, 1950.

Hemphill, J. K., & Coons, A. E. Development of the Leader Behavior Description Questionnaire. In R. M. Stogdill & A. E. Coons (Eds.), *Leader behavior: Its description and measurement.* Bureau of Business Research, No. 88. Columbus: Ohio State University, 1957.

Herbst, P. G. *Autonomous group functioning.* London: Tavistock Publications, 1962.

Hill, J. W., & Hunt, J. G. Managerial level, leadership, and employee need-satisfaction. In E. A. Fleishman & J. G. Hunt (Eds.), *Current developments in the study of leadership.* Carbondale: Southern Illinois University Press, 1973.

Hill, W. A. Leadership style: Rigid or flexible. *Organizational Behavior and Human Performance,* 1973, *9,* 35–47. (a)

Hill, W. A. Leadership style flexibility, satisfaction, and performance. In E. A. Fleishman & J. G. Hunt (Eds.), *Current developments in the study of leadership.* Carbondale: Southern Illinois University Press, 1973. (b)

Hoffman, L. R. Conditions for creative problem solving. *Journal of Psychology,* 1961, *52,* 429–444.

Hoffman, L. R. Group problem solving. In L. Berkowitz (Ed.), *Advances in experimental social psychology.* New York: Academic Press, 1965.

Hollander, E., & Julian, J. Contemporary trends in the analysis of leadership processes. *Psychological Bulletin,* 1969, *71,* 387–397.

House, R. J. T-group education and leadership effectiveness: A review of the empirical literature and a critical evaluation. *Personnel Psychology,* 1967, *20,* 1–32.

House, R. J. Leader initiating structure and subordinate performance, satisfaction, and motivation: A review and a theoretical interpretation. Unpublished manuscript, University of Toronto, Faculty of Management Studies, 1973. (a)

House, R. J. A path-goal theory of leader effectiveness. In E. A. Fleishman & J. G. Hunt (Eds.), *Current developments in the study of leadership.* Carbondale: Southern Illinois University Press, 1973. (Originally published in *Administrative Science Quarterly*, 1971, *16*, 321–338.) (b)

House, R. J., Filley, A. C., & Kerr, S. Relation of leader consideration and initiating structure to R & D subordinates' satisfaction. *Administrative Science Quarterly*, 1971, *16*, 19–30.

House, R. J., & Wahba, M. A. Expectancy theory as a predictor of job performance, satisfaction and motivation: An integrative model and a review of the literature. Paper presented at the meeting of the American Psychological Association, Hawaii, August 1972. Working Paper 72–21, University of Toronto, Faculty of Management Studies, 1972.

Hunt, J. G. Fiedler's leadership contingency model: An empirical test in three organizations. *Organizational Behavior and Human Performance*, 1967, *2*, 290–308.

Hunt, J. G. Leadership style effects at two managerial levels in a simulated organization. *Administrative Science Quarterly*, 1971, *16*, 476–485.

Hunt, J. G. Another look at human relations training.*Training and Development Journal*, 1968, *22:2*, 2–10.

Hunt, J. G., Osborn, R. N., & Larson, L. L. Leadership effectiveness in mental institutions. (National Institute of Mental Health, Final Tech. Rep.) Carbondale, Southern Illinois University, Department of Administrative Sciences, 1973.

Jacobs, T. O. *Leadership and exchange in formal organizations*. Alexandria, Va.: Human Resources Research Organization, 1970.

Jun, J. S., & Storm, W. B. (Eds.) *Tomorrow's organizations*. Glenview, Ill.: Scott Foresman, 1973.

Kahn, R. L. The prediction of productivity. *Journal of Social Issues*, 1956, *12*, 41–49.

Kahn, R. L., & Katz, D. Leadership practices in relation to productivity and morale. In D. Cartwright & A. Zander (Eds.) *Group dynamics*. Evanston, Ill.: Row, Peterson, 1960.

Kaiser, H. F. The varimax criterion for analytic rotation in factor analysis. *Psychometrika*, 1958, *23*, 187–200.

Kast, F. E., & Rosenzweig, J. E. General systems theory: Applications for organization and management. *Academy of Management Journal*, 1972, *15*, 447–465.

Katz, D., & Kahn, R. L. *The social psychology of organizations*. New York: Wiley, 1966.

Kelly, F. J., Beggs, D. L., McNeil, K. A., Eichelberger, A., & Lyon, J. *Research design in the behavioral sciences: Multiple regression approach*. Carbondale: Southern Illinois University Press, 1969.

Kerr, S., & Harlan, A. Predicting the effects of leadership training and experience from the contingency model: Some remaining problems. *Journal of Applied Psychology*, 1973. *57*, 114–117.

Kerr, S., & Schriesheim, C. A. Consideration, initiating structure, and organizational criteria—an extension and update of Korman's 1966 review. Unpublished manuscript, Ohio State University, 1973.

Kerr, S., Schriescheim, C. A., Murphy, C. J., & Stogdill, R. M. Toward a contingency theory of leadership based upon the consideration and initating structure literature. *Organizational Behavior and Human Performance*, 1974, in press.

Ketchum, L. D. Diffusion in the General Foods corporation. Paper presented at the International Conference on the Quality of Working Life, Arden House, Harriman, New York, September 1972.

Korman, A. K. The prediction of managerial performance: A review. *Personnel Psychology*, 1968, *21*, 295–322.

Korman, A. K. Consideration, initiating structure, and organizational criteria: A review. *Personnel Psychology*, 1966, *19*, 349–363.

Korman, A. K. Organizational achievement, aggression and creativity: Some suggestions toward an integrated theory. *Organizational Behavior and Human Preference*, 1971, *6*, 593–613.

Korman, A. K. Application of management theory: A review of the empirical literature and a new direction. In V. F. Mitchell, R. T. Barth, & F. H. Mitchell (Eds.), *Proceedings of the Thirty-Second Meeting of the Academy of Management*. Vancouver: University of British Columbia, 1973. (a)

Korman, A. K. On the development of contingency theories of leadership: Some methodological considerations and a possible alternative. *Journal of Applied Psychology*, 1973, *58*, 384–387. (b)

Korman, A. K. *The psychology of motivation*. Englewood Cliffs, N.J.: Prentice-Hall, 1974, in press.

Korman, A. K., Greenhaus, J. G., & Gavin, J. F. Organizational perceptions, tenure, and job attitudes. Unpublished manuscript, Baruch College, City University of New York, Department of Psychology, 1973.

Kuhn, T. S. *The structure of scientific revolutions*. Chicago: University of Chicago Press, 1962.

Landsberger, H. A. The horizontal dimension in bureaucracy. *Administrative Science Quarterly*, 1961, *6*, 299–333.

Lawler, E. E. *Pay and organizatioanl effectiveness: A psychological view*. New York: McGraw-Hill, 1971.

Leavitt, H. J. Some effects of certain communication patterns on group performance. *Journal of Abnormal and Social Psychology*, 1951, *46*, 38–50.

Lewin, K., Lippitt, R., & White, R. K. Patterns of aggressive behavior in experimentally created social climates. *Journal of Social Psychology*, 1939, *10*, 271–299.

Likert, R. *New patterns of management*. New York: McGraw-Hill, 1961.

Lingoes, J. C. An IBM-7090 program for Guttman-Lingoes smallest space analysis, I. *Behavioral Science*, 1965, *10*, 183–184.

Lippitt, R., & White, R. K. The "social climate" of children's groups. In R. G. Barker, J. S. Kounin, & H. F. Wright (Eds.), *Child behavior and development*. New York: McGraw-Hill, 1943.

Lubin, A. The interpretation of a significant interaction. *Educational and Psychological Measurement*, 1961, *21*, 807–817.

Maier, N. R. F. *Problem-solving discussions and conferences: Leadership methods and skills*. New York: McGraw-Hill, 1963.

Maier, N. R. F. Assets and liabilities in group problem solving: The need for integrative function. *Psychological Review*, 1967, *74*, 239–249.

Mann, F. C. Toward an understanding of the leadership role in formal organization. In R. Dubin, G. Homans, F. Mann, & D. Miller (Eds.), *Leadership and productivity*. San Francisco: Chandler, 1965.

Mann, R. D. A review of the relationships between personality and performance in small groups. *Psychological Bulletin*, 1959, *56*, 241–270.

McGrath, J. E., & Julian, J. W. Interaction process and task outcomes in experimentally created negotiation groups. *Journal of Psychological Studies*, 1963, *14*, 117–138.

McGregor, D. *The professional manager*. New York: McGraw-Hill, 1967.

McMahon, J. T. The contingency theory: Logic and method revisited. *Personnel Psychology*, 1972, *25*, 697–710.

McNamara, V. D. Leadership, staff, and school effectiveness. Unpublished doctoral dissertation, University of Alberta, 1968.

McWhinney, W. H. Open systems and traditional hierarchies. Paper presented at the International Conference on the Quality of Working Life, Arden House, Harriman, New York, September 1972.

Meheut, Y., & Siegel, J. P. A study of leader behavior and MBO success. Unpublished manuscript, University of Toronto, Faculty of Management Studies, 1973.

Melcher, A. *Organizational behavior: Toward a systems approach*. Englewood Cliffs, N.J.: Prentice-Hall, in press.

Meuwese, W., & Friedler, F. E. Leadership and group creativity under varying conditions of stress. (Office of Naval Research Tech. Rep. No. 22) Urbana, University of Illinois, Group Effectiveness Research Laboratory, 1965.

Miller, J. A. Leadership in open systems. Unpublished doctoral dissertation, University of Rochester, 1974.

Mischel, W. *Personality and assessment*. New York: Wiley, 1968.

Mitchell, T. R. Leader complexity, leadership style, and group performance. Unpublished doctoral dissertation, University of Illinois, 1969.

Mitchell, T. R. Cognitive complexity and leadership style. *Journal of Personality and Social Psychology*, 1970, *16*, 166–173. (a)

Mitchell, T. R. The construct validity of three dimensions of leadership research. *Journal of Social Psychology*, 1970, *80*, 89–94. (b)

Mitchell, T. R., Biglan, A., Oncken, G. R. & Fiedler, F. E. The contingency model: Criticism and suggestions. *Academy of Management Journal*, 1970, *13*, 253–267.

Moment, D., & Zaleznik, A. *Role development and interpersonal competence*. Cambridge, Mass.: Harvard University Press, 1963.

Mott, P. E. *The characteristics of effective organizations*. New York: Harper & Row, 1972.

Mulder, M. Communication structure, decision structure and group performance. *Sociometry*, 1960, *23*, 1–14.

Mulder, M., Ritsema, V. E., & de Jong, R. D. An organization in crisis and non-crisis situations. *Human Relations*, 1971, *24*, 19–41.

Mulder, M., & Stemerding, A. Threat, attraction to group and need for strong leadership. *Human Relations*, 1963, *16*, 317–334.

Myers, A. E. Team competition, success, and the adjustment of group members. *Journal of Abnormal and Social Psychology*, 1962, *65*, 325–332.

Nealey, S. M., & Blood, M. R. Leadership performance of nursing supervisors at two organizational levels. *Journal of Applied Psychology*, 1968, *52*, 91–114.

Nealey, S. M., & Owen, F. W. A multitrait-multimethod analysis of predictors and criteria of nursing performance. *Organizational Behavior and Human Performance*, 1970, *5*, 348–365.

Oaklander, H., & Fleishman, E. A. Patterns of leadership related to organizational stress in hospital settings. *Administrative Science Quarterly*, 1964, *8*, 520–532.

O'Brien, G. E., Biglan, A., & Penna, J. Measurement of the distribution of potential influence and participation in groups and organizations. *Journal of Applied Psychology*, 1972, *56*, 11–18.

Oeser, O. A., & O'Brien, G. E. A mathematical model for structural role theory, III: The analysis of group tasks. *Human Relations*, 1967, *20*, 83–97.

Olmstead, J. A. Christensen, H. E., & Lackey, L. L. *Components of organizational competence: Test of a conceptual framework*. (Department of the Army, Tech. Rep. No. 73-19) Alexandria, Va., Human Resources Research Organization, 1973.

Osborn, R. N., Hunt, J. G., & Pope, R. Lateral leadership, satisfaction, and performance. In T. B. Greene & D. F. Ray (Eds.), *Proceedings of the Thirty-Third Academy of Management Annual Meeting*. State College: Mississippi State University, in press.

Parsons, T. *Structure and process in modern societies*. New York: Free Press of Glencoe, 1960.

Pelz, D. C., & Andrews, F. M. *Scientists in organizations: Productive climates for research and development*. New York: Wiley, 1966.

Pepinsky, H. B. & Pepinsky, P. N. Organizations, management strategy, and team productivity. In L. Petrullo & B. M. Bass (Eds.), *Leadership and interpersonal behavior*. New York: Holt, 1961.

Perrow, C. A. framework for the comparative analysis of organizations. *American Sociological Review*, 1967, *32*, 194–208.

Porter, L. W., & Lawler, E. E. *Managerial attitudes and performance*. Homewood, Ill.: Irwin-Dorsey Press, 1968.

Posthuma, A. B. Normative data on the least preferred co-worker scale (LPC) and the group atmosphere questionnaire (GA). (Office of Naval Research Tech. Rep. No. 70-8) Seattle, University of Washington, Organizational Research Group, 1970.

Prestat, C. A case of autonomous groups. Unpublished manuscript, Conservatoire Nation des Arts et Metiers, Institute of the Sociology of Work, Paris, France, 1972.

Prien, E. P., & Ronan, W. W. Job analysis: A review of research findings. *Personnel Psychology*, 1971, *24*, 371–396.

Pryor, M. W., & Distefano, M. K., Jr. Perceptions of leadership behavior, job satisfaction, and internal-external control across three nursing levels. *Nursing Research*, 1971, *20*, 534–536.

Pugh, D. S., Hickson, D. F., Hinnings, C. R., & Turner, C. Dimensions of organization structure. *Administrative Science Quarterly*, 1968, *13*, 65–105.

Reaser, J. M. The relationship between official and leader behaviors and the performance and satisfaction of mental health employees. Unpublished doctoral dissertation, Southern Illinois University at Carbondale, 1972.

Rice, A. K. *Productivity and social organization, the Ahmedabad experiment*. London: Tavistock Publications, 1958.

Rice, R. W., & Chemers, M. M. Behavioral correlates of leader LPC and leadership effectiveness. Paper presented at the meeting of the Western Psychological Association, Anaheim, California, April 1973. (a)

Rice, R. W., & Chemers, M. M. Predicting the emergence of leaders using Fiedler's contingency model. *Journal of Applied Psychology*, 1973, *57*, 281–287. (b)

Riesman, D. *The lonely crowd*. New Haven, Conn.: Yale University Press, 1950.

Rizzo, J. R., House, R. J., & Lirtzman, S. E. Role conflict and ambiguity in complex organizations. *Administrative Science Quarterly*, 1970, *15*, 150–153.

Rokeach, M. *The open and closed mind*. New York: Basic Books, 1960.

Ronan, W. W., & Prien, E. P. An analysis of organizational behavior and organizational performance. *Organizational Behavior and Human Performance*, 1973, *9*, 78–99.

Rossel, R. C. Required labor commitment, organizational adaptation and leadership orientation. *Administrative Science Quarterly*, 1971, *16*, 316–320.

Rotter, J. B. Generalized expectancies for internal versus external control of reinforcement. *Psychological Monographs*, 1966, *80* (Whole No. 609), 1–28.

Rush, C. H., Jr. Leader behaviour and group characteristics. In R. M. Stogdill and A. E. Coons (Eds.), *Leader behavior: Its description and measurement*. Bureau of Business Research, No. 88. Columbus: Ohio State University, 1957.

Sales, S. Supervisory style and productivity: Review and theory. *Personnel Psychology*, 1966, *19*, 275–286.

Sales, S. Authoritarianism: But, as for me, give me liberty, or give me maybe, a great big, strong, powerful leader I can honor, admire, respect and obey. *Psychology Today*, 1972, *8*(4), 94–143.

Sample, J. A., & Wilson, T. R. Leader behavior, group productivity, and rating of least preferred co-worker. *Journal of Personality and Social Psychology*, 1965, *1*, 266–270.

Sanford, F. H. Research on military leadership. In J. C. Flanagan (Ed.), *Psychology in the world emergency*. Pittsburgh: University of Pittsburgh Press, 1952.

Saxberg, B., & Slocum, J. The management of scientific manpower. *Management Science*, 1968, *14*, B-473–489.

Schein, E. H. *Organizational psychology*. (2nd ed.) Englewood Cliffs, N.J.: Prentice-Hall, 1972.

Schmid, J., & Leiman, J. The development of hierarchical factor solutions. *Psychometrika*, 1957, *22*, 53–61.

Schriesheim, C., & Kerr, S. Psychometric properties of the Ohio State Leadership Scales. Unpublished manuscript, Ohio State University, College of Administrative Science, 1973.

Scott, W. A. Conceptualizing and measuring structural properties of cognition. In O. J. Harvey (Ed.), *Motivation and social interaction: Cognitive determinants*. New York: Ronald Press, 1963.

Scott, W. E., Jr. Activation theory and task design. *Organizational Behavior and Human Performance*, 1966, *1*, 3–30.

Shackleton, V. J., Bass, B. M., & Allison, S. *PAXIT—A program comparing the effectiveness of five leadership styles*. Scottsville, N.Y.: Transnational Programs Corporation, 1973.

Shartle, C. L., & Stogdill, R. M. *Studies in naval leadership*. Columbus: Ohio State University Research Foundation, 1952.

Shaw, M. E. Scaling group tasks: A method for dimensional analysis. (Office of Naval Research Tech. Rep. No. 1) Gainesville: University of Florida, Department of Psychology, 1963.

Shiflett, S. C. The contingency model: Some implications of its statistical and methodological properties. U. S. Army Medical Research Laboratory Report No. 966 (Interim Report). Fort Knox, Kentucky, 1972.

Sparks, C. P. Personnel development series: Humble Oil & Refining Co. Mimeographed. Houston, Texas: Humble Co., 1966.

Standard Oil Company, (New Jersey). Early identification of management potential. Social Science Research Division, Employee Relations Department, 1961.

Steinzor, B. The spatial factor in face to face discussion groups. *Journal of Abnormal and Social Psychology*, 1950, *45*, 552–555.

Stinson, J. E., & Tracy, L. The stability and interpretation of the LPC score. In V. F. Mitchell, R. T. Barth, & F. H. Mitchell (Eds.), *Proceedings of the Thirty-Second Meeting of the Academy of Management*. Vancouver: University of British Columbia, 1973.

Stogdill, R. M. Personal factors associated with leadership: A survey of the literature. *Journal of Psychology*, 1948, *25*, 35–71.

Stogdill, R. M. *Manual for Leader Behavior Description Questionnaire–Form XII*. Columbus: Ohio State University, Bureau of Business Research, 1963.

Stogdill, R. M., & Coons, A. E. (Eds.) *Leader behavior: Its description and measurement*. Bureau of Business Research, No. 88. Columbus: Ohio State University, 1957.

Stogdill, R. M., & Koehler, K. *Measures of leadership structure and organization change*. Columbus: Ohio State University Research Foundation, 1952.

Stoner, J. A. F. A comparison of individual and group decisions involving risk. Unpublished master's thesis, Massachusetts Institute of Technology, Sloan School of Management, 1961.

Strauss, C. Professionalism and occupational associations. *Industrial Relations*, 1963, *2*, 7–31.

Susman, G. E. The impact of automation on work group autonomy and task specialization. *Human Relations*, 1970, *23*, 567–577.

Suttell, B. J., & Spector, P. Research on the specific leader behavior patterns most effective in influencing group performance. (Office of Naval Research Ann. Tech. Rep.) Washington, D.C., American Institutes for Research, 1955.

Swain, R. L. Catalytic colleagues in a government R & D organization. Unpublished master's thesis, Massachusetts Institute of Technology, Sloan School of Management, 1971.

Tannenbaum, A. S. (Ed.), *Control in organizations*. New York: McGraw-Hill, 1968.

Taylor, J. C. Measuring sophistication of production technology: Background, development, and results. (Office of Naval Research Tech. Rep.) Ann Arbor, University of Michigan, Center for Research on the Utilization of Scientific Knowledge, Institute for Social Research, 1970.

Taylor, J. C. An empirical examination of a four-factor theory of leadership using smallest space analysis. *Organizational Behavior and Human Performance*, 1971, *6*, 249–266. (a)

Taylor, J. C. Some effects of technology in organizational change. *Human Relations*, 1971, *24*, 105–123. (b)

Taylor, J. C. *Technology and planned organizational change*. Ann Arbor: Institute for Social Research, 1971. (c)

Taylor, J. C., & Bowers, D. G. *Survey of organizations: A machine-scored standardized questionnaire instrument*. Ann Arbor: Institute for Social Research, 1972.

Thompson, J. *Organizations in action*. New York: McGraw-Hill, 1967.

Tosi, H., Aldeg, R., & Storey, R. On the measurement of the environment: An assessment of the Lawrence-Lorsch Environmental Uncertainty Questionnaire. *Administrative Science Quarterly*, 1973, *18*, 27–36.

Touraine, A. An historical theory in the evolution of industrial skills. In C. R. Walker (Ed.), *Modern technology and civilization*. New York: McGraw-Hill, 1962.

Triandis, H. C. Notes on the design of organizations. In J. D. Thompson (Ed.), *Approaches to organizational design*. Pittsburgh: University of Pittsburgh Press, 1966.

Trist, E. L., Higgin, G. W., Murray, H., & Pollock, A. B. *Organizational choice*. London: Tavistock Publications, 1963.

Turner, A. N., & Lawrence, P. R. *Industrial jobs and the worker*. Cambridge, Mass.: Harvard University Press, 1965.

Valenzi, E. R., Miller, J. M., Eldridge, L., Irons, P., Solomon, R., & Klaus, R. Individual differences, task, structure and external environment and leader behavior: A summary. (Office of Naval Research, Tech. Rep. No. 49) Rochester, N.Y., University of Rochester, Management Research Center, 1972.

Vroom, V. H. *Work and motivation*. New York: Wiley, 1964.

Vroom, V. H. A comparison of static and dynamic correlational methods in the study of organizations. *Organizational Behavior and Human Performance*, 1966, *1*, 55–70.

Walker, C. R. *Toward the automatic factory*. New Haven: Yale University Press, 1957.

Wedderburn, D. & Crompton, R. *Workers' attitudes and technology*. Cambridge: Cambridge University Press, 1972.

Weick, K. E. *The social psychology of organizing*. Reading, Mass.: Addison-Wesley, 1969.

Weiss, H., & Sherman, J. Internal-external control as a predictor of task efforts and satisfaction subsequent to failure. *Journal of Applied Psychology*, 1973, *57*, 132–136.

Wherry, R. The past and future of criterion evaluation. *Personnel Psychology*, 1957, *10*, 1–5.

Woodward, J. *Management and technology*. London: Her Majesty's Stationery Office, 1958.

Woodward, J. *Industrial organization: Theory and practice*. London: Oxford University Press, 1965.

Woodward, J. Technology, material control, and organizational behavior. In A. Negandhi (Ed.), *Modern Organizational Theory*. Kent, Ohio: Kent State University Press, 1970.

Yuchtman, E., & Seashore, S. E. A system resource approach to organizational effectiveness. *American Sociological Review*, 1967, *32*, 891–903.

Yunker, G. W. A comparison of two measures of leader behavior at the first level of management. Unpublished master's thesis, Southern Illinois University at Carbondale, 1972. (a)

Yunker, G. W. A field test of Fiedler's contingency model of leadership and a proposed revised model. Unpublished doctoral dissertation, Southern Illinois University at Carbondale, 1972. (b)

Zand, D. E. Trust and managerial problem solving. *Administrative Science Quarterly*, 1972, *17*, 229–239.

Zavala, A. Determining the hierarchical structure of a multidimensional body of information. *Perceptual and Motor Skills*, 1971, *32*, 735–746.

Name Index

Subject Index

petence, 172, 173, 179–80; increase in, 173; and effectiveness, 173, 179–80; mentioned, 165

Probe: definition of, 162; and inputs 162; interlocking, 162; elements, 162, 165; complexity, 165; manuscript, 165; weight, 165; effectiveness score, 166; process score, 166; mentioned, 162–67 passim

Problems, 44, 45, 164

Processes: and influence, xviii; decision making, 89; variables, 156; and effectiveness, 158, 159, 172, 176, 180; and pressure, 158, 180; mission related, 159; and competence, 160, 184; performance 164–71 passim, 175–81 passim; quality, 164, 174; and frequencies, 167; scores of, 167; intercorrelations among, 171; contributions of, 180; relationships among, 180; and coordination, integration, 181; and experimental conditions, 186; analysis, 187; feedback, 188; mentioned, 168–88 passim. *See also* Organization

Productivity, 79, 95, 96, 105–15 passim, 130. *See also* Effectiveness; Performance

Psychological states of individuals: and motivation, 30; and satisfaction, 30; and influence, 30–32; and environment, 59; and structure, 59; and technology, 59; mentioned, 32, 58, 60. *See also* Effort; Expectancy; Motivation Satisfaction

Reality testing: described, 160; as competence component, 161; and relation to organizational process, 161; and adaptability, 168; and effectiveness, 170; importance of, 172; and pressure, 174; mentioned, 168–70 passim

Rochester, University of, 150

Role: ambiguity, 9, 23–40 passim, 57; conflict, 32; clarity, clarification, clarifying behavior, 38–57 passim, 60; demands, 45; colleague, 75–82 passim; playing, 76, 161; relationships, 185; mentioned, 158

Satisfaction: as dependent variable, xvi; and management styles (leader behavior), xvii, 54, 124, 146, 149; with supervision, 12, 140–49 passim; extrinsic, intrinsic, 30, 45–52 passim; with job, 30, 38, 145–49 passim, 186; and motivation, performance, 31; with co-workers, 49, 51, 52; items measuring, 135; as output, 145; and effectiveness, 146; mentioned, 12, 30–38 passim, 42, 57–59 passim, 93, 124, 135

Simulation (simulated organization): description of, 161; organization levels in, 161; and communication, 164; inputs, 165; scores, 166; effectiveness, 169; value of, 188; mentioned, 160–67 passim, 185

Situation: variables, 31, 32, 58, 94–98 passim, 135; conflicts, 93; factors, 94, 117, 123; demands, 116–23 passim, 144, 174; and differentiation, 118; determinants, 124, 192; traits, 140; analyses, 144; mentioned, 34, 35, 64, 94–98 passim, 107–14 passim, 122–29 passim, 157–61 passim, 192, 193

Situational favorability: in contingency model, 96; description of, 96; evaluation of, 96; as potential influence, 99; variables used to specify, 99; and ordering of data, 102; dimensions, 102, 106–18 passim, 122, 126, 197; eight cells of, 104; specification of, 106, 107; and training, experience, 108–10 passim, 126; assignments, 111; evaluation of, 113; measure of, 114; 125; and group task, 117; and relation of LPC and behavior, 117; favorable for leader, 118; and situation complexity, 118; and leader-situation fits, 125; components, 126; score, 126; change, 127; and leader intelligence, 129; mentioned, 100–110 passim, 126, 179

Skill mix theory dimensions: administrative, 37; technical, 37, 84; human relations, 74; mentioned, 75

Stabilizing: action, 167; necessity of, 167; vs. coping actions, 167; and integration, 170

Stress, 159, 160, 179, 183

Structure: and processes, 59; organization, 87; relations, 133; tight vs. loose, 133, 134; tightness, 143; and function, 160; variables, 188. *See also* Organization; Task structure

Subordinate: personality, xvii; psychological states of, 29; motivation, 29, 35; satisfaction, 29–39 passim; expectancy, 29, 39; characteristics, 32; role perceptions, 36; task variables, 37; expectancies, 37, 38; performance, 38, 39, 126; authoritarianism, 39; influence, 67; competence, 124; experience, 124; knowledge, 124; needs, 124; and power, 132, 134; relation with boss, 151; mentioned, 12, 140. *See also* Management

Superordinate, 184, 187

Supervisor: role, behavior, 4, 5, 37, 83; and technology, 6–9 passim; and environment, 8; leadership, 12, 18–27 passim, 68–76 passim; support, 16, 20, 21; work facilitation, 16, 21; definition of, 66; closeness of, 66, 69; and influence, 67, 69, 85; general, 69; dimensions, practices, approaches, functions, 69, 73–75 passim, 82–85 passim, 131, 147, 154, 156; and time pressure, 71, 73, 83; acceptance, 71, 73, 84; competence, 71, 73, 84; appropriateness of, 71, 73, 84; technical, 73, 74, 75; consultation, 75; decision making, 75; and colleague roles, 76, 81; and administrative functions, 78; and compe-